Improving Oral Communication

Jeanne Handschuh
Alma Simounet de Geigel
University of Puerto Rico

REGENTS/PRENTICE HALL, Englewood Cliffs, NJ 07632

Library of Congress Cataloging in Publication Data

Handschuh, Jeanne, (date)
    Improving oral communication.

    1. English language—Text-books for foreign
speakers.   2. Oral communication.   3. English language—
Composition and exercises.   4. English language—
Pronunciation.   I. Simounet de Geigel, Alma, 1941-
II. Title.
PE1128.H26 1985   428.3'4   84-11777
ISBN 0-13-452756-9

Editorial/production supervision and
    interior design: Sylvia Moore and Barbara Kittle
Cover design: Lundgren Graphics LTD.
Manufacturing buyer: Harry P. Baisley

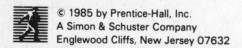

Printed in the United States of America

20   19   18   17   16   15   14   13   12   11

ISBN 0-13-452756-9

Prentice-Hall International (UK) Limited, *London*
Prentice-Hall of Australia Pty. Limited, *Sydney*
Prentice-Hall Canada Inc., *Toronto*
Prentice-Hall Hispanoamericana, S.A., *Mexico*
Prentice-Hall of India Private Limited, *New Delhi*
Prentice-Hall of Japan, Inc., *Tokyo*
Simon & Schuster Asia Pte. Ltd., *Singapore*
Editora Prentice-Hall do Brasil, Ltda., *Rio de Janeiro*

We dedicate this book to our husbands,
Bob and Wilfredo, for their continuing
support and patience, to our students,
from whom we are constantly learning,
and to Eugenio.

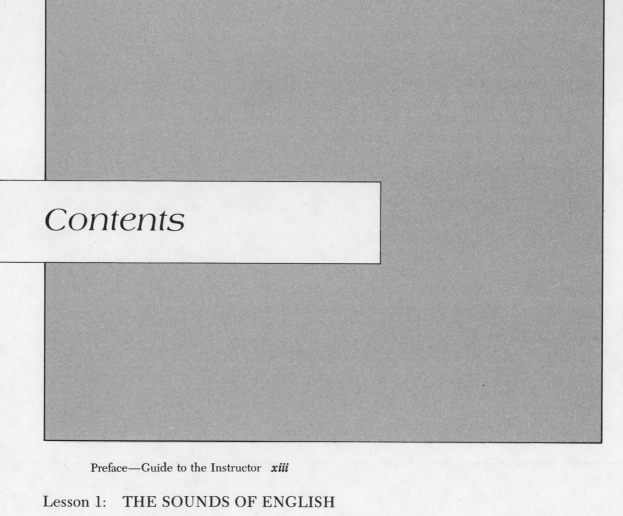

Contents

Lesson 25:   THE CONSONANTS: THE LIQUID SOUND [l]
218

Lesson 26:   THE CONSONANTS: THE NASAL SOUNDS [m], [n], and [ŋ]
225

Lesson 27:   FINAL REVIEW LESSON
234

Preface— Guide to the Instructor

Improving Oral Communication is a pronunciation, oral-communication manual for the intermediate-level student of English as a second language. The book is intended for students who can read and write English fairly well but who wish to improve their pronunciation and ability to communicate orally with other speakers of English. Starting with the first lesson, the emphasis is on speaking with another person through the use of question-and-answer exercises and dialogues, the subject matter of which can spark further classroom discussion.

In the dialogues, we have kept the sentences short because in conversation people do speak in short, grammatically uncomplicated sentences most of the time. But we have another purpose in keeping sentences short: the student can easily look at the question or the response, read it once or twice, and then look at the person he or she is addressing as though in actual conversation. We have deliberately labeled the speakers A or B so that the dialogues can be used by either male or female students, depending on the makeup of the class. Also, by not identifying the speakers or specifying the situation we give the instructor the opportunity to ask, "Who do you think the speakers are?" or "What is happening?" or "Where does this dialogue take place?" or "What is the relationship between the speakers?" and so on. In this way an instructor can determine whether or not a student really understands what he or she is saying. It has been our experience that often a student can give a grammatically correct response without having the slightest idea of what it means, especially if he has memorized it.

With the exception of the vowels [eʸ] and [oʷ] we have used the International Phonetic Alphabet (the IPA) to describe the various sounds of American English because this particular phonetic alphabet is the one used by most foreign-language dictionaries. The pronunciations given are those listed as most frequently used in Kenyon and Knott, *Pronouncing Dictionary of American English*, *Webster's New World Dictionary*, or the new *Longman's Dictionary of American English*.

Except for the dialogues in the "Appropriateness" sections, all dialogues from Lesson 5 on consist mainly of words containing the sounds being studied in a particular lesson. It is these specially constructed dialogues and "mini-dialogues" which we believe are an innovative feature of this text.

Improving Oral Communication (hereafter referred to as *IOC*) consists of twenty-seven lessons. Lessons 5–14 teach the vowel sounds, and Lessons 15–27 the consonant sounds. Lessons 1–4—dealing respectively with the sounds of English, word stress, sentence stress, and intonation—contain information vital to the successful use of the rest of the textbook; therefore, the various types of exercises have been carefully constructed to allow students constant practice in these necessary elements of oral communication.

The lessons in *IOC* do not have to be taken up successively, nor do all the lessons have to be covered in order for the material to be effective. Although the textbook contains sufficient material for a one-year course in pronunciation (vowels during the first semester, consonants during the second), an instructor can choose material according to the amount of time allotted for a particular course. Moreover, instructors should take into account the pronunciation difficulties of their own students and select the lessons that deal with those problems.

Beginning with Lesson 5, each lesson describes a sound or a pair of sounds and the production of each. The lesson contrasts two sounds with each other and with other related sounds, gives spelling hints, and lists frequently used words containing the sounds being studied.

The words listed in the last-mentioned section have been carefully chosen from the 4000 most frequently used. In Lessons 5–14, these words are arranged according to spelling and/or the number of syllables. In Lessons 15–27, the words listed contain the consonants being studied, and, at the same time, systematically review the vowel sounds. We have made a conscious effort to use as many of these words as possible in the various exercises and dialogues throughout the book so that students will learn to use the words in context.

There are a variety of listening and production exercises and at least one written exercise in every lesson. However, instructors should not feel that they must use all of the material presented. Some exercises may seem either too elementary or too involved for a particular class. Some will work well in one classroom situation but not in another. We have taken care to make all the exercises meaningful to the students. (Incidentally, except for the listening exercises, there are almost no drills which call for repetition because we have found that this type of exercise encourages "parroting.")

Another innovative and valuable feature of each lesson is the section called "Appropriateness" in which, through sample dialogues, explanation, and practice situations, the student learns language appropriate to various social situations such as making introductions, asking permission, expressing gratitude, and so on. No other pronunciation manual to date combines the teaching of pronunciation with the use of English in social contexts. In fact, the Appropriateness section can serve as a starting point for further class discussion as students talk about what is appropriate in similar situations in their own cultural backgrounds. (Instructors should be aware of the important features of nonverbal communication in the American culture, such as gestures, space, facial expression, and eye contact, which occur simultaneously with the language functions described in the various Appropriateness sections.)

An important section of Lessons 15–26 is the one labeled "Important Hints," which takes up such topics as aspiration or the lack of it and consonant clusters, and explains other idiosyncracies of the different consonant sounds.

Following are further suggestions we hope will be useful to instructors using *IOC* as a textbook.

1. The listening exercises can be used as quizzes or just for practice. A good technique is to assign one student to write the exercise on the board as the instructor dictates it, while the other students (with their chairs turned so that they cannot see the blackboard) write the exercise at their seats. When the exercise has been completed, the students turn their chairs back to the original position and compare their answers with those of the board. The instructor and the students correct any errors which appear on the board.

2. Students should be made to realize that learning the spelling rules (and the exceptions) given for each sound will help them to recognize and to pronounce correctly various combinations of letters. The instructor should make sure that the students understand the difference between a letter and a phonetic symbol. He or she should also call the students' attention to the silent letters (marked with a slash) as in *deɓt*.

3. In the substitution exercises, each student should be encouraged to look at the list of words to be used in the question or answer only long enough to choose the words he or she wishes to use. The student should then look at the person to whom he or she is speaking. It is helpful to have the students as a group repeat the question several times before beginning the exercise so that they can retain it in their memory and not have to look at the book and **read** it rather than **speak** it. This procedure can be used in all of the oral exercises which consist of questions and answers.

4. The oral reading exercises must be carefully monitored by the instructor, with close attention given to the use of correct stress, rhythm, and intonation. Students should be reminded to use their dictionaries and to ask questions about particular sentences if they do not understand them. Often when students read a sentence poorly it is because they have not looked up unfamiliar words and so haven't the slightest idea what the sentence means. Many of the sentences can provide a basis for further class discussion.

5. In assigning the written exercises, the instructor should remind the students to review the spelling hints. Students should not rely solely on their ears to tell them which symbol represents the sound of a particular group of letters. The exercises can either be assigned as homework and gone over later in class or used as quiz material. However, it must be remembered that *IOC* is not meant to be a phonetics text. Rather, the students are asked to use the phonetic symbols as a tool in learning the correct English pronunciation.

6. The homework activities listed at the end of each lesson are not planned according to the content of a particular lesson, and the instructor should feel free to choose among them, selecting whichever ones best suit the needs of a particular class.

7. To be most effective, the various Appropriateness sections should be taken up in the sequence in which they are presented in the text. If assigned to be studied as homework and then discussed in class, less class time will be consumed by this very important section of each lesson.

There are many people to whom we owe our gratitude for their help in making this textbook a reality. Therefore, we would like to extend our sincere thanks and appreciation to the following: our dean, Dr. José Ramón De la Torre; our chairman, Dr. John Larkin; the dean of academic affairs, Dr. Jaime Rosado Alberio; the assistant dean, Professor Doris Franqui; our colleagues and students at the University of Puerto Rico, Norma Maurosa who typed the first draft, Nancy Simounet for drawing some of the illustrations, David Rivera for his continuous support, and professors Joan Fayer and Emily Krasinski for their constructive criticism.

In addition, we owe special gratitude to Dr. Carmen Judith Nine Curt for commenting on and criticizing various aspects of the material and for encouraging us to continue with the project when the going got rough. Finally, a special word of thanks and appreciation to our editors at Prentice-Hall, Robin Baliszewski, Sylvia Moore, and Barbara Kittle for their expertise, advice, and understanding.

The Sounds of English

The Phonetic Alphabet

Students learning English as a second language often have trouble understanding English spoken by native speakers. They also have difficulty making themselves understood. Indeed, spoken English does have certain distinct features that require a great deal of practice in listening and speaking in order for a nonnative speaker to master the language. The first of these features we will take up is the sound system.

The English sound system is made up of 27 consonant sounds and 12 vowel sounds plus 3 diphthongs. Since English has more sounds than there are letters in the alphabet—21 consonants and 5 vowels—we need a special alphabet to represent the larger number of sounds. This alphabet, called the International Phonetic Alphabet (IPA), makes use of some of the letters of the English alphabet with which you are already familiar as well as a few new symbols to represent additional sounds. It is important for you to recognize the symbols of the IPA because the alphabet is used in most foreign language dictionaries.

Listed here is the phonetic alphabet. First, let us look at the consonant sounds represented by familiar symbols. Next to each symbol are words in which the letter or letters corresponding to that particular consonant sound are in boldface. Your instructor will pronounce each consonant sound and the word containing that sound. Listen carefully and then repeat the words as your instructor indicates.

[b] **b**all, jo**b**	[l] **l**and, tai**l**	[v] **v**oice, fi**v**e
[d] **d**ance, lan**d**	[ḷ] bott**le**	[w] **w**ant
[f] **f**ine, lea**f**	[p] **p**ark, ste**p**	[z] **z**oo, boy**s**
[g] **g**o, ba**g**	[r] **r**ed, hea**r**	[m] **m**y, fro**m**
[h] **h**at	[s] **s**ee, **c**ease, pa**ss**	[m̩] cust**om**
[k] **c**ap, **k**eep, pi**ck**	[t] **t**ime, ha**t**	[n] **n**o, su**n**
		[n̩] cott**on**

Notice below the special symbols used to represent those consonant sounds for which there is no corresponding letter in the English alphabet.

[ŋ] sing, think	[ʃ] show, fish	[tʃ] church
[θ] thing, tooth	[j] yes, million	[dʒ] judge, gem
[ð] this, bathe	[ʒ] television, beige	

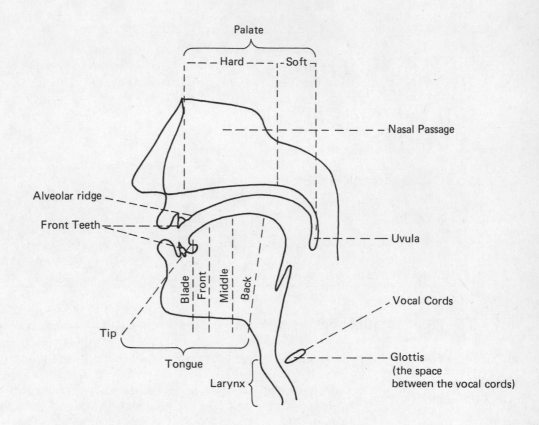

The Speech Organs

Now let us look at the vowel sounds that are represented by familiar symbols:

[i] feet   [eʸ]* make   [u] move   [oʷ]* no   [ɑ] lot

*The IPA uses the symbols [e] and [o] for these two sounds. However, since the production of [eʸ] and [oʷ] is similar to that of a diphthong, we have added a small [y] and [w] respectively to represent the diphthongization of the sounds. This we hope will facilitate their recognition and production by ESL students.

The following new symbols stand for the seven additional vowel sounds:

[ɪ] sit		[ʊ] foot	[ə] ago, cup**
[ɛ] bed	[æ] man	[ɔ] soft	[ɚ] bird, sister**

**The IPA has two symbols for each of these sounds: [ʌ] in a stressed position as in cup [kʌp] and [ə] in an unstressed position as in ago [əgo] or soda [sódə]. Likewise [ɝ] is used in a stressed position as in bird [bɝd] and [ɚ] in an unstressed position as in sister [sistɚ]. Also English foreign language dictionaries use these symbols to distinguish the stressed vowels from the unstressed vowels. However, for purposes of simplification we have used the symbols [ə] and [ɚ] to represent the respective sounds in both stressed and unstressed syllables.

English also has three diphthongs. A diphthong is made by gliding from the position of one vowel to that of another within the same syllable.

[aɪ] my   [aʊ] how   [ɔɪ] boy

In looking at these words and symbols for sounds, you should have noticed two important features of English: 1. The same letter may have more than one sound (**thing, this; lot, no, soft**). 2. The same sound may have different spellings (**cap, keep; judge, gem**). Therefore, familiarize yourself with the symbols, especially the ones that represent the sounds that differentiate one word from another in meaning such as the vowels in **sit** and **sat**. Mastering these sounds will help you to acquire a better accent, which will improve your ability to communicate. Learning and using all the symbols is not meant to be an end in itself, but rather a means by which you will be able to recognize the various sounds of English and produce them more accurately.

Voiced and Voiceless Sounds

There are many ways of classifying the sounds of English. One way is to speak of them as voiced and voiceless. You can tell to which group a sound belongs by putting your hand lightly around your throat and pronouncing a particular sound aloud. If you feel any vibration of the vocal cords in your throat, we say that sound is **voiced**. If you feel no vibration, the sound you are producing is **voiceless**. Take for example the sound [i] as in *feet*. Put your hand around your throat, take a big breath, and hold the sound [i] as long as you can. Do you feel the vibration? [i] is a voiced sound. In fact, **all vowels are voiced sounds**. Now, with your hand in the same position make the sound [s] (like a snake). You don't feel any vibration, do you? [s] **is a voiceless consonant**. Now make the sound [z] (like a mosquito). You should feel some vibration because [z] **is the voiced partner of** [s].

Another way to tell whether a sound is voiceless or voiced is to pronounce the sound with your hands over your ears. If the sound you are pronouncing is voiced, you will be able to hear the vibration. If the sound is voiceless, you will hear nothing except the rush of air as it passes through the parts of your speech mechanism.

Here is a list of the voiced and voiceless consonants in English as they are represented by their phonetic symbols.

Voiceless	*Voiced*	*Voiced*
[p] pop	[b] Bob	[m̥] custom
[t] tot	[d] did	[n] noon
[k] kick, cake	[g] gag	[ṇ] button
[f] fifty, knife	[v] vivid, leave	[ŋ] sing
[θ] thin, month	[ð] this, bathe	[l] leg
[s] sister, cent, walks	[z] zoo, quiz	[ḷ] little
[ʃ] ship, dish	[ʒ] vision, beige	[r] rear
[tʃ] church	[dʒ] judge	[w] want
[h] hat	[m] mom	[j] year, million

When a voiced consonant is in final position, the vowel immediately before it is lengthened. Listen as your instructor reads the following words: *back*, *bag*. Notice that although the vowel sound [æ] is the same in both words, the vowel is lengthened in *bag* because it is followed by the voiced sound [g].

listening exercise

In the exercise below, your instructor will read each sentence twice, the first time with the first word in the parentheses, and then with the second word. Circle the word that ends in a voiced consonant sound. Listening carefully to the length of the vowel will help you to tell the difference between the voiced and voiceless sounds. Remember that the vowel is lengthened before a voiced sound.

1. Please get me a (cab, cap).
2. He (hit, hid) my car.
3. That has already been (set, said).
4. Watch my (bag, back).
5. Farmer Jones bought a (pick, pig).
6. Can you hear the (buzz, bus)?
7. What's the (price, prize)?
8. I got a new (batch, badge).
9. She stared at the (ice, eyes).
10. He (wrote, rode) all day long.
11. She hasn't made the (bed, bet) yet.
12. That's a hard (seat, seed).

The Vowel Sounds

The diagram below is the vowel chart. The first group of vowels is called the **front vowels** because in order to produce them, the speaker moves the tongue toward the front of the mouth. The second group is known as the **central vowels.** They are produced in the middle of the mouth. Finally, the last group is called the **back vowels**, because to produce them, the speaker moves the tongue toward the back of the mouth.

Vowel Chart

	Front	Central	Back	
1. beat	[i]		[u]	9. boot
2. bit	[ɪ]	7. [ɚ] burn	[ʊ]	10. book
3. bait	[eʸ]		[oʷ]	
4. bet	[ɛ]	8. [ə] but		11. boat
5. bat	[æ]		[ɔ]	12. ball
6. pot		[ɑ]		

listening exercise

1. Listen carefully to your instructor pronounce the key words in the same order in which they appear on the chart. Pay close attention to the movement of the lips and jaws. Then repeat the sounds as your instructor indicates.
2. Your instructor will repeat the words, but this time out of order. Try to identify the word read by referring to the number next to each word.

Appropriateness: Saying Hello, Goodbye, and Making Introductions

In order to improve your ability to communicate orally in English, you must not only develop your listening and speaking ability, but you must also learn to understand and use the expressions and gestures appropriate to a particular English-language setting. For this reason, we have included a section of communication functions at the end of each lesson. While you may already be familiar with many of the expressions mentioned in the various "Appropriateness" lessons throughout the book, you may not know exactly how, when, and where to use them, or with whom. Listen to your instructor read the following dialogues. Notice the various expressions used, and then discuss with your instructor who the speakers might be and what their relationship is. In a few cases, you may also be able to suggest when and where a particular dialogue takes place. Follow these same instructions in reading and discussing the dialogues in the appropriate sections throughout the book.

Saying Hello

1. **Phil:** Hi, Chris. How are you?
   Chris: Just fine. And you?
   Phil: Mm, so-so.

2. **Janet:** Hello. How are you?
   Sue: Oh, pretty well, thanks. And you?
   Janet: I'm fine, thanks.
   Sue: It's good to see you again.
   Janet: Same here.

3. **Bob:** Hello. How's everything?
   Jack: Fine, thanks. How about you?
   Bob: Just fine. So what's new?
   Jack: Oh, nothing much.

4. **Susan:** Good morning, Mr. Parks. How are you?
   Mr. Parks: Oh, hello Susan. I'm fine, thank you. And how are you today?
   Susan: I have a bad cold. I feel miserable.
   Mr. Parks: Oh, that's too bad. I hope you'll feel better soon.
   Susan: Thank you, Mr. Parks. I hope so, too.

Saying Goodbye

1. **Jim:** Well, I have an appointment now, I'll have to go.
   Sam: Mm, I'm in a hurry too.
   Jim: Good to see you. Goodbye. (They shake hands)
   Sam: Goodbye. Take care of yourself.

2. **Al:** I guess I'd better go now.
   Betty: Me too. I'll be seeing you.
   Al: So long.
   Betty: Bye, bye. See you later.

3. **John:** It's getting late. Please excuse me, but I must leave right away.
   Burt: I'm sorry you have to leave so soon.
   John: I am too. I hope we can get together again.
   Burt: Yes, I hope so. I'll be looking forward to it.

Making Introductions

1. **Mark:** Hi, Gloria. How is it going?
   Gloria: OK, I guess.
   Mark: Gloria, this is a friend of mine, Joe.
   Gloria: Hi, Joe.
   Joe: Hi, Gloria. Glad to meet you.

2.
    Fred: Good afternoon, Mrs. Green. I'd like you to meet my girlfriend, Sally.

 Mrs. Green: Hello, Sally. I'm glad to meet you.

    Sally: It's a pleasure to meet you too, Mrs. Green. I've heard so much about you.

 Mrs. Green: Oh, thank you. That's very kind of you.

3. **Professor Jackson:** Good morning, Tom. How are you today?

     Tom: Fine, thank you, sir. May I present my mother, Mrs. Frank Wilson.

 Professor Jackson: Oh, how do you do, Mrs. Wilson. It's a pleasure to meet you. You have a fine young son there.

   Mrs. Wilson: Thank you, Professor Jackson. We're very proud of Tom.

practice

1. With a classmate, take turns imagining that each of you is one of the people on the following list. Practice saying hello and goodbye to each other in an appropriate manner, using the dialogues you have just read as models.
    a. a close friend
    b. your instructor
    c. your doctor
    d. a small child
    e. a business friend of your father's or mother's
    f. your superior or your boss
    g. the receptionist in your dentist's office
    h. an elderly neighbor
    i. someone you do not know very well but whom you see occasionally
    j. the dean of your college

2. Student A will introduce the person on his left (Student B) to the person who sits on his right. Student B will then do the same with the person on his left, and so on around the class.

3. Form groups of three, and following your instructor's directions, prepare a short dialogue using the expressions you have learned—saying hello, making an introduction, and saying goodbye. Present your dialogue to the class.

Word Stress

In Lesson 1 we gave you a general view of the sounds of English. We also pointed out how important correct pronunciation is to meaningful communication. But in order to speak English well, you also need to master other important aspects of the spoken language. These other aspects are stress, rhythm, and intonation.

Every time you dance, sing, or clap your hands you emphasize or stress particular beats or sounds. In speech, **stress** may be defined as the degree of intensity or loudness placed on a sound; that is, the amount of force one puts on a syllable or word to give it importance. **Stress** may also be referred to as **accent**. In some languages accents are actually written over particular vowels to indicate where the intensity of the voice falls. Written English does not have stress or accent marks, nor are there any rigid rules of accentuation. Yet, stress is such an important feature of spoken English that it determines not only the rhythmic flow of words, but also the quality of the vowels. Correct word and sentence stress in spoken English can mean the difference between good communication and no communication at all. Therefore, whenever you learn the meaning of a word, you must also learn its pronunciation.*

The English language has three types of stress: **primary** (´), **secondary** (`), and **zero**.** The expression **primary stress** or **accent** describes the strong emphasis a speaker puts on the most important syllable of a particular word. **Secondary** stress refers to a less strong emphasis on the next most important syllable. **Zero** stress refers to any syllable that receives **no stress**. (A syllable with **zero** stress will, from now on, be referred to as an **unstressed syllable**.) An unstressed syllable, therefore, receives no intensity or loudness at all. The frequent occurrence of unstressed syllables is one

---

*Although accent marks do not normally appear in written English, they are used in this textbook to help you pronounce the words with correct stress. If all the words in a list have the primary stress on the same syllable, only the first word will have the accent mark. However, if words in the list have the primary stress on a different syllable, those words will also have accent marks. In all cases the accent mark is placed above the stressed vowel.

**Some textbooks mention a fourth type of stress: tertiary. However, for purposes of simplification, and also because failure by a speaker to use or to hear tertiary stress does not in any way interfere with his or her ability to communicate, we have chosen to speak of only three types of stress.

of the fundamental characteristics of spoken English, and the one that most distinguishes English from other languages. A stressed syllable may contain any one of the vowel sounds shown on the vowel chart in Lesson 1, but any vowel except the diphthongs [aʊ] and [ɔɪ] can be reduced to [ə] or [ɪ]. Therefore, since in English there are many more unstressed syllables than there are stressed syllables, the two sounds [ə] and [ɪ] are the most frequently used vowel sounds.***

*** *In some dialects [ə] is used almost exclusively in unstressed syllables.*

Pronounce these words after listening to your instructor. Remember that in a **stressed syllable, the vowel sound is longer and louder** than it is in an unstressed syllable. Sometimes a medial syllable is so unstressed that it may be eliminated, as in the words *conference* [kánfrəns] and *interesting* [íntrəstɪŋ].

Stressed	*Unstressed*	*Stressed*	*Unstressed*
réason [i]	resént [ɪ]	confér [ɚ]	cónference [ə]
fish [ɪ]	sélfish [ɪ]	tune [u]	fórtune [ə]
face [eʸ]	súrface [ɪ] or [ə]	pecúliar [ju]	partícular [jə]
less [ɛ]	cáreless [ɪ]	full [ʊ]	cáreful [ə]
land [æ]	ísland [ə]	sócial [oʷ]	socíety [ə]
óbject (n) [ɑ]	objéct (v) [ə]	áuthor [ɔ]	authórity [ə]
some [ə]	hándsome [ə]	dígest [ɑɪ]	digést* [ɪ] or [ə]

*This word is also pronounced [dɑɪdʒést].

Although English has no infallible rules for determining which syllable or syllables should be stressed, any good dictionary will indicate which are the stressed syllables. Also, there are some general observations that can be made as to the location of stress in words.

NOTE: To determine the number of syllables in a word, simply count the number of vowel sounds.

    examples: *bath* One vowel sound,   *bathroom* Two vowel sounds,
               one syllable   two syllables

    beautiful Although this word contains *five vowels,* there are only *three vowel sounds,* and therefore only three syllables.

General Observations Concerning Word Stress

two-syllable words

Most words of two syllables have one stressed syllable (primary stress) and one unstressed syllable. As your instructor pronounces these words, notice the strong, clear vowel in the stressed syllable and the weak vowel [ɪ] or [ə] in the unstressed syllable.

fámous	fóreign	prómise	enoúgh	supplý	befóre
recent	engine	vocal	elect	police	pretend

However, in some two-syllable words there is no vowel reduction in the syllable that does not receive primary stress.

décade	víbrate	álly
digest(n)	concrete	hotél
dictate	compound(n)	outsíde (also óutsíde)
locate	concert	

Many two-syllable words may be used as either nouns or verbs. **These nouns usually have the stress on the first syllable, while the verbs usually have the stress on the second syllable.** (In a sentence, you can tell whether a word is used as a noun by looking for markers of nouns such as articles, possessives, demonstratives, numbers, prepositions, and adjectives). See the mini-dialogues on pages 14-15.

Nouns	Verbs	Nouns	Verbs
récord	recórd	óbject	objéct
present	present	rebel	rebel
permit	permit	desert	desert
project	project	conduct [ə]*	conduct
conflict	conflict	contrast [æ]*	contrast
subject	subject	contract [æ]*	contract
increase [i]*	increase	contest [ɛ]*	contest
insult [ə]*	insult	survey [eʸ]*	survey
protest [ɛ]*	protest	suspect [ɛ]*	suspect
		digest [ɛ]*	digest
		progress [ɛ]*	progress

In these words, there is no vowel reduction in the second syllable.

EXCEPTIONS: In the list of words below, both nouns and verbs have the same stress pattern.

Nouns	Verbs	Nouns	Verbs
exchánge	exchánge	cómfort	cómfort
express	express	comment [ɛ]*	comment
command	command	contact [æ]*	contact
control	control	promise	promise
campaign [æ]	campaign	program	program
delay	delay		
remark	remark		
surprise	surprise		
support	support		

In these words, there is no vowel reduction in the second syllable.

Reflexive pronouns receive primary stress on the *self* syllable.

mysélf	himsélf	itsélf	yoursélves
yourself	herself	ourselves	themselves

three-syllable words

Many words of three syllables have one stressed syllable and two unstressed syllables. Here again, the vowels in the unstressed syllables are reduced to [ə] or [ɪ].

ánimal	Cátholic	góvernment	fáctory***	expénsive	devélop
politics	Protestant	industry	accurate	attention	insurance
interest*	theater	faculty**	fortunate	committee	delicious
popular	hospital	president	delicate	cathedral	decision
everyone	probably	senator	moderate (adj.)	determine	professor

Also pronounced [íntrɪst].
**Also pronounced [fǽkəlti].*
***Also pronounced [fǽktrɪ].*

Some words of three syllables have the primary stress on the final syllable.

represént	enginéer	discontént	cigarétte*
interfere	pioneer	gasoline*	
guarantee	volunteer	magazine*	

These words may also have the primary stress on the first syllable.

Many three-syllable words have a primary accent on the first syllable and a strong secondary accent on the third syllable. This is especially true of verbs ending in *ate*, *ise*, and *ize*.

ádvocàte	índicàte	ádvertìse	crít-icìze	énvelòpe
celebrate	operate	exercise	organize	telephone
decorate	regulate	analyze	recognize	microphone
educate	delegate(v)	civilize	realize	telegram
hesitate	moderate(v)	dramatize		diagram
				photograph

polysyllabic words

A great many words of four or five syllables (polysyllabic) have the primary accent on the second syllable. This is especially true of words ending in *ate* or *ous*.

coóperate	demócracy	oríginal
appreciate	emergency	invisible
communicate	mysterious	responsible
investigate	industrious	intelligent
participate	arithmetic(n)	immediate*

Important Exceptions

árchitecture	télevision
agriculture	accuracy
legislature	laboratory
literature	indepéndence
temperature	manufácture

*Immediate *is an adjective and therefore the* ate *ending is pronounced* [ɪt] *or* [ət].

Usually when a suffix is added to a word, the location of the primary accent remains the same.

contáin	contáiner	contáining
condúct (v)	condúctor	condúcting
interfére	interférence	interféring
célebrate	célebrated	célebrating

compáre	compárison
cómfort	cómfortable
devélop	devélopment
appárent	appárently

exception: ádvertise   advertísement

However, if the suffix is *ic, ical, ial, al, tion,* or *ity,* **the syllable before the suffix receives the primary stress.** See the exercises on pages 13-14.

scíence	scientífic	psychólogy	psychológical
démocrat	democrátic	pólitics	polítical
ecónomy	económic	ecónomy	económical
phótograph	photográphic	philósophy	philosóphical
áccident	accidéntal	cólony	colónial
devélopment	developméntal	cómmerce	commércial
ínstrument	instruméntal	fínance	fináncial
góvernment	governméntal	índustry	indústrial

coóperate*	coóperative	cooperátion	aváilable	availabílity
législate*	législative	legislátion	cápable	capabílity
represént*	represéntative	representátion	próbable	probabílity
éducate*	éducator	educátion	respónsible	responsibílity
			invísible	invisibílity
			cáptive	captívity
			húman	humánity
			pérsonal	personálity
			oríginal	originálity
			hóspital	hospitálity

Notice that in these words, the position of the primary stress remains the same with the addition of the suffixes tive and tor, but the addition of tion necessitates a shift in the position of the primary stress.

compound nouns

Nouns consisting of more than one word usually have a primary stress on the first element and a secondary stress on the second. These two stresses fall on the syllable that would normally be stressed. Notice that some of these compound nouns are written as one word while others are written as two words. The only way you can be sure how an unfamiliar word is written is to check it in the dictionary.

pópcòrn	nótebòok	tóothpàste	téenàger
daylight	airport	bus stop	tennis court
baseball	flashlight	taxicab	traffic light
drugstore	chalkboard	newspaper	basketball
bathroom	bookcase	sun glasses	record player
		grandfather	

exceptions: àfternóon   wéekénd   ícecréam (also íce crèam and ìce créam)

Compound **proper nouns** normally have a **primary** accent on the **second** element and a secondary stress on the first.

Àsh Wédnesday	Lòng Ísland	Gèorge Wáshington
Gòod Fríday	Nèw Jérsey	Àbraham Líncoln
Eàster Súnday	Unìted Státes	Ròosevelt Ávenue
Hàllowéen	Atlàntic Ócean	Fòrest Róad
Thànksgíving	New Yórk	Thìrd Ávenue
	New Yòrk Cíty	Beàch Hotél
	Sòviet Únion	Làke Míchigan
	Unìted Nátions	

> **NOTE:** With *street* the primary stress falls on the first element: Fórest Strèet, Thírd Strèet, Fifty-Sécond Strèet, Jéfferson Strèet

However, in compound proper nouns ending in the word *day*, this accent pattern is reversed. Look at the following examples.

Thanksgíving Dày	Eléction Dày
Lábor Dày	St. Válentine's Dày
Móther's Dày	Indepéndence Dày

exceptions: Chrìstmas Éve   Chrìstmas Dáy   Nèw Yèar's Éve   Nèw Yèar's Dáy

> **NOTE:**   In adjective-noun combinations, the primary stress is almost always on the noun.
>
> *Example:*   a beautiful dréss
> a democratic socíety
> a mysterious stránger

For exercises using compound nouns, see mini-dialogues on page 15.

two-word verbs

Combinations of verbs plus prepositions or adverbs have a *secondary* stress on the **first** element and a **primary** stress on the **second** element. These verbs are usually referred to as **two-word verbs**.

Some of these verbs are "inseparable." That is; the first element may not be separated from the second. However, others are called "separable" which means that the first element may be separated from the second by a noun. If the noun is replaced by a pronoun, the pronoun always comes between the two elements.

examples: Please **get ón** the bus.   **Take óff** your jacket.
(inseparable)   (separable)

Take your jacket **óff**.
Take it **óff**.

There are many verbs which consist of three elements. In that case, the primary stress falls on the second element. -*get óut of*

Inseparable		*Separable*
get ín	get óut of	wake úp
get on	keep up with	make up
get up	take care of	look up
get down	run out of (exhaust the	put on
get alóng	supply)	take off (remove)
get awáy	get along with	turn on
stand up	get through with	turn off
sit down		point out
lie down		pick up
come in		take out
take off (leave the ground)		put away

Some of these verb-preposition, verb-adverb combinations may also function as nouns. In that case, the **primary** accent is on the **first** element.

tákeoff   mákeup   gétaway   hóldup

There are some frequently used, separable verb-preposition combinations in which the stress is on the first element.

cáll for	lóok for	thínk about
listen to	laugh at	write about
look at	talk about	worry about
ask for		

For exercises using two-word verbs, see the mini-dialogues on page 15.

Listening Exercise

Each of these pairs of words has the same number of syllables. Some have the same stress pattern. Others do not. Listen as your instructor pronounces each pair. If the words have the same stress pattern, write **S** on the line. If the words have different stress patterns, write **D**. Each pair will be read twice.

1. ____ locate
   hotel

2. ____ recent
   desert

3. ____ get off
   hand in

4. ____ comfort
   control

5. ____ Mother's Day
   Christmas Eve

6. ____ legislature
   manufacture

7. ____ exercise
   realize

8. ____ cooperative
   administrative

9. ____ comfortable
   vegetable

10. ____ famous
    record (v)

11. ____ develop
    committee

12. ____ emergency
    apparently

13. ____ tennis court
    basketball

14. ____ politics
    attention

15. ____ enough
    concert

16. ____ represent
    engineer

17. ____ television
    advertisement

18. ____ Forty-Second
    Street
    United Nations

19. ____ promise
    police

20. ____ Catholic
    Protestant

21. ____ representative
    nationality

22. ____ conversation
    architecture

23. ____ themselves
    progress (v)

24. ____ give away
    turn around

25. ____ industry
    government

Oral Practice

mini-dialogues

These dialogues contain words that illustrate various word-stress patterns. Be sure you pronounce the words correctly. (Your instructor may ask you to memorize some of the dialogues.)

1. **A:** Jim isn't being very **cooperative**, and Bill refuses to **cooperate** with us at all.
   B: What did you expect? Neither of them knows the meaning of the word **cooperation**.

A: Then why did they volunteer to work on the committee?

B: Don't ask me. Perhaps they have political ambitions and they thought being on a committee would be good public relations.

2. A: Is your grandmother a **Democrat** or a Republican?

B: She isn't a registered member of either party but she voted for the **Democratic** candidate in the last election.

3. A: Which do you prefer—**instrumental** music or vocal music?

B: I like to listen to all kinds of music.

A: Oh, that's right. You're a music major. What **instrument** do you play?

B: I play the piano.

4. A: Your brother certainly takes beautiful **photographs**. Has he ever studied **photography**?

B: I don't think he's taken any courses since high school, but he's always buying magazines to keep up with the latest **photographic** techniques.

5. A: I wonder if that **politician** will keep any of his campaign promises.

B: Who knows. Some **political** parties will promise anything to get their candidate elected.

oral reading

Practice reading these sentences applying the rules for word-stress you have learned in this lesson. Be sure to reduce the vowels in the unstressed syllables.

1. Jim stayed at a famous hotel near the United Nations Building in New York City.

2. Economic conditions were very bad during the decade of the thirties.

3. Both Catholic and Protestant churches participated in the recent conference held in the cathedral.

4. The language laboratory offers foreign students an opportunity to practice English.

5. My grandfather, Senator Wilson, sent us some interesting photographs of South America.

6. Joan majored in political science, but she says she's more interested in theater than in politics.

7. A committee of government officials is investigating the possibility of developing this desert land as an industrial park.

8. John is completing his studies in agricultural engineering at the local college of agriculture.

mini-dialogues: two-syllable words as nouns and verbs

As you read these dialogues make sure that you use the correct stress in pronouncing the two-syllable words used as nouns and verbs.

1. A: Do you have that rock group's latest **record**?

B: No, but I **recorded** their TV program.

2. A: Did you remember to **project** your voice when you gave your oral report today?

B: Yes, I did. In fact, my professor commented on how well I spoke about my **project**.

3. A: Don't forget to **contact** your travel agent about your accommodations in West Germany.

B: I won't forget. He's my best **contact** for hotel reservations.

4. **A:** How can I **control** the temperature in the language laboratory? It's very cold in there.

   B: Just turn the knob on the temperature **control**. It's located on the rear wall to the right of the door.

5. **A:** The police won't **permit** you to park here. You'll get a parking ticket.

   B: Don't worry. I have a special press photographer's **permit**.

mini-dialogues: compound nouns

Read these dialogues in a natural manner, paying careful attention to the various types of compound nouns. Remember that **in adjective-noun combinations, the noun receives the stronger stress.** Also, notice the use of the two-word verb in Dialogue 4.

1. **A:** Where are you going for **Thanksgiving**?

   B: I think I'll be going to my **grandparents'** home in **New York**, and maybe I'll visit some other relatives in **New Jersey**.

2. **A:** Do you remember when Lent began last year?

   B: **Ash Wednesday** was on March 4, and **Easter Sunday** was on April 19.

3. **A:** Are you going to do anything special for the **Labor Day weekend**?

   B: I'm going to visit my parents; I haven't seen them since **Mother's Day**.

4. **A:** Driver, I think I'm on the wrong bus. Does this bus go to the **airport**?

   B: No, sir, it doesn't. Get off at the next **bus stop**. You can get a **taxicab** by the **traffic light** on the corner.

5. **A:** I'm hungry. Let's get a big bag of **popcorn**.

   B: **Popcorn** makes me thirsty. How about a **hot dog** and a chocolate **milkshake** instead?

mini-dialogues: two-word verbs

As you read these dialogues be sure to use the correct stress pattern on the two-word verbs. Pay particular attention to the way in which the separable two-word verbs are used.

1. **A:** How are you **getting along with** your new roommate?

   B: Jill is a very responsible and dependable person. And she has a wonderful personality. We're getting along just fine.

2. **A:** When do you expect to **get through with** your work?

   B: If I don't have any interruptions, I'll finish it this afternoon.

3. **A:** Hi, Jane. Please **come in** and **sit down**. Betty **will be down** in a minute.

   B: Please tell her to **hurry up** or the plane will **take off** without us.

4. **A:** What time did you **get up** this morning?

   B: Well, I **woke up** at six-thirty, but I didn't **get up** until seven-fifteen. I **stayed up** until very late last night watching a movie on television.

5. **A:** Maria, before you **turn on** the TV set, please **turn off** the light in the kitchen.

   B: I'm not going to watch TV tonight. Billy is **picking** me **up** in half an hour. We're **taking** his sister **out** to dinner. It's her birthday.

Homework

1. Choose two rooms: bedroom, living room, bathroom, kitchen, etc., and make a list of all the compound nouns in that room; for instance, table lamp, bathtub, etc. After you have made a list, practice pronouncing the nouns, putting the stress on the first element.

2. Make a list of compound nouns associated with your favorite sport: baseball bat, tennis ball, jogging shoes, etc. Practice pronouncing the nouns, putting the stress on the first element.

Appropriateness: Introducing Yourself and Opening a Conversation

dialogue

Tony: Biology 3250, Section 2?
Rowshan: Right.
Tony: Boy! What a day to start classes! Is this seat taken?
Rowshan: No, it isn't.
Tony: Cigarette?
Rowshan: No, thanks. I don't smoke.
Tony: Do you mind if I smoke?
Rowshan: No, not at all. Go right ahead.
Tony: Do you know who's teaching this section?
Rowshan: I've no idea.
Tony: Are you new here?
Rowshan: I'm a transfer student. I hardly know anyone.
Tony: You don't? Are you free after this class?
Rowshan: Yes, I am. Why do you ask?
Tony: Well, I thought I might give you a short tour of the campus and introduce you to some of my friends.
Rowshan: Oh, that sounds great!
Tony: Then it's a deal. By the way, my name's Tony.
Rowshan: Hi, Tony. I'm Rowshan. Oh, here comes the instructor now.

useful expressions

Starting a conversation with a person you already know, of course, presents no problem. But making conversation with a stranger requires the use of particular expressions. You may begin by introducing yourself informally.

"Hello, I'm John." or "My name is John Harris."

Or, depending on the situation, you may want to be more formal:

"I would like to introduce myself. My name is John Harris." or "May I introduce myself? I'm John Harris."

If you want to open a conversation with someone without an initial introduction, you might use one of the following expressions:

"Hot, isn't it?"
"What a beautiful day!"

"Have you been waiting long?"
"Could you tell me the time, please?"
"Do you mind if I smoke?"
"Excuse me. Is this seat taken?"
"Are you new here?"
"You're new here, aren't you?"
"You look familiar; haven't we met before?"

practice

1. Pretend that you and the person on your left are strangers who meet at a party, in a classroom, or some other place. Introduce yourself and begin a conversation. End your conversation in an appropriate manner. Practice first, and then, according to your instructor's directions, present the dialogue to the class.

2. Count off 1, 2, 1, 2, etc. Students who have #1 will introduce themselves to students who have #2 and continue a short conversation.

3. #2 students will now introduce themselves to the #1 student on their left and continue with a short conversation.

Sentence Stress, Rhythm and Blending

Definitions

sentence stress and rhythm

In Lesson 2 we made some general observations regarding the location of stress in isolated words. But since speech is made up of words strung together, we must also look at these words in groups, in phrases, or in sentences in order to observe what happens to the stress pattern. **Sentence stress** refers to the word or words in a sentence that receive a strong accent. In most sentences you will find a series of both stressed and unstressed words. This alternation of different kinds of stress in a sentence is called **rhythm**. In "normal" rhythm there is a tendency to stress certain classes of words and to unstress others. In addition to this, when the sentence stress falls on a word of two or more syllables, it almost always falls on the same syllable that receives the primary stress when the word is in isolation. The other syllables also keep their original stress. Look at the following examples.

Hélĕn   píctuře   Hèlĕn sàw thĕ píctuře.
                                                    We sàw Hélĕn.

In every English sentence there is at least one strongly stressed word or syllable that stands out. This word or syllable usually comes near the end of the sentence. Certain other words in the sentence receive a lesser degree of stress, and still others receive no stress at all. In the following sentence, notice how the strongest stress falls on the last word.

She arrived at tén.

The most strongly stressed word or syllable may occur earlier in the sentence, as in the examples on the following page.

I want tén of them.
He ópened it.

In longer sentences there may be more than one strongly stressed syllable or word.

He answered the phóne although he didn't wánt to.

Notice in the following sentences that the compound noun and the two-word verb retain their original stress patterns.

He's a cóllege stùdent.
Plèase pùt it awáy.

Which word or syllable gets the strongest stress depends largely on what the native speaker wants to emphasize. However, there are several guidelines that will help you to know which word or words to stress.

Words are usually classified in two categories: **content words** and **function words**. Content words are those which have meaning in themselves, and function words are those which have little or no meaning except to show a grammatical relationship with other words in the sentence. **Content words are usually stressed, and function words are usually unstressed.**

content words

1. Nouns: names for persons (*Karim, John, Pedro, secretary, nurse*) or names of abstract ideas (*love, beauty*) or things (*ball, pencil*)
2. Verbs: show an action (*walk, do, write*) or state of being (*look, feel*)
3. Adjectives: show a special quality about a noun (*red péncil, new dréss*)
4. Adverbs: modify a verb, an adjective, or another adverb (*walks slówly; very slów; rather heavily*)
5. Demonstratives: point out or contrast (*this, that, these, those*)
6. Possessive Pronouns: show possession or ownership (*mine, ours, hers*)
7. Negatives: show negation, denial, or refusal (*no, not, none, never*)
8. Intensive or reflexive pronouns: a combination of **self** and one of the personal pronouns or the impersonal **one** (*mysélf, onesélf*)
9. Interrogatives: introduce an information question (*who, what, why*)
10. Numerals and expressions of quantity: (*two, much*)

function words

1. Personal Pronouns: *it, he, us,* etc.
2. Auxiliary Verbs: *has, must, may, can, should,* etc.

> **NOTE:**   1.   Remember that *have, has,* and *had* are not always auxiliaries. Sometimes they function as main verbs, and, if so, they are stressed.
>
> I *have* a book.   She *has* a dog.   She *had* the car yesterday.
>
> 2.   Auxiliary verbs are usually stressed when they occur at the end of a sentence or in a tag (echo) question.
>
> I'll go if I cán.   You couldn't do it, coúld you?

3. Possessive Adjectives: *my, your, our,* etc.
4. Relative Pronouns: *that, which, who, whom, whose*

He's the man *that* I met.   I saw *Hamlet, which* is my favorite play.

5. Conjunctions: *in, but, and,* etc.
6. Prepositions: *in, on, of,* etc.
7. Articles: *a, an, the*
8. All forms of the verb *be* (except *been* and *being*)
9. The pronoun *one*

The native speaker of English may emphasize any word in order to express a particular idea. He or she may put emphasis on a word which would normally be unstressed.

1. **A:** That's my sweater
    B: Oh no, it isn't. It's **my** sweater.
2. **A:** Would you like me to write the létter?
    B: No. I want **him** to write it.

In our previous discussion of word stress, we mentioned that the vowels of unstressed syllables are usually pronounced [ə] or [ɪ]. This same rule applies to the vowels of the one-syllable function words *a, an, the, of, to, that* in phrases, clauses, or sentences. For example, the popular American dish, ham and eggs, is advertised many times as "ham'n eggs" because in spoken English, the word *and* is obscured or weakened to [ən] or even [n̩].

Listen to your instructor read the following dialogue. Notice how short and unstressed the one-syllable words are.

A: Can you tell me how to get to Willow Park?
B: Go straight ahead. At the end of the next block you'll see a sign that says "Willow Park."

Listen as your instructor reads the following three sentences.

1. We mèt Ánn.
2. We mèt Ànn in the párk.
3. We mèt Ànn in the pàrk with the chíldren.

The first sentence is obviously shorter than the second, and the second shorter than the third. Yet, if you listened carefully you noticed that it took your instructor about the same amount of time to read each one. Why? Listen to the sentences again and see if you can tell what your instructor does. Did you notice that a native speaker of English tends to stretch out or prolong the stressed words or syllables?

  mét   Ánn   párk   chíldren

A native speaker also compresses the unstressed syllable with the previous or following stressed syllable or word.

  we mét   in the párk   with the chíldren

It is the pattern of stressed and unstressed words and/or syllables that gives English its own particular rhythm.

pausing and blending

Two other important aspects which you have to master in order to achieve good rhythm in spoken English are **pausing** and **blending**.

Pausing

A **pause** may be defined as a break, a stop, or a rest. In spoken English, this is precisely what a speaker does when he or she divides a sentence into two or more parts depending on the length of the sentence. A speaker makes these breaks or pauses to clarify meaning, to emphasize a feeling or an idea, or just to take a breath. Although English does not have a set of rules for pausing, here are some suggestions to help you know when to pause.

Do not make a pause between the following elements:

1. adjectives and noun they modify (new dress)
2. articles and noun they modify (a coat)
3. auxiliary verb and main verb (was going to buy)
4. preposition and its object (on Saturday)
5. adverbs and verb, adjective, or adverb they modify (definitely going, really good, very quickly)
6. subject, verb, and object (Mary told me)

Listen as your instructor reads this sentence. Notice the places where he or she pauses.

Mary told me that she was definitely going to buy a new coat on Saturday, but evidently she changed her mind.

Blending

Once you have arranged your words into groups or thoughts, you must be very careful to join or blend the words within these groups so that they do not stand out as separate words. That is, you must move smoothly from one word to the next without making any sudden stops. One way to do this is by **blending** or joining the final consonant of one word with the initial vowel of the following word as these examples show:

post office   get off   walk up

Allen Street and Evans Avenue

(Remember that **and** becomes [ənd], [ən], or [n].)

In the dialogue below pauses and blending have been marked. Listen as your instructor reads the dialogue. Then practice reading the dialogue aloud.

A: Where can I get a bus to the post office?
B: Which post office are you talking about?
A: The one at the corner of Allen Street an(d) Evans Avenue.
B: Take a number Eleven bus and get off at Evans Avenue. Walk up Evans Avenue to Allen Street. It's about two blocks.
A: Thanks a lot.

There are some voiceless sounds in English that are produced by exploding air. We say they are **aspirated**. Listen to the following words.

people [p]   **t**ea [t]   **c**offee [k]

Did you hear the small explosions of air at the beginning of each word? Now say the words: *people, tea, coffee*

Whenever these aspirated sounds follow one another, the air is held back a little and is then released. Listen to the following examples and then repeat them after your instructor. Notice how the two sounds are blended.

1.   **Stop P**eter before it's too late.
2.   Don't **take** the car.
3.   I drin**k C**oke.

The voiced partners of these sounds are [b], [d], and [g]. When they follow one another, the voicing of the sound is also held back a little and is then released. Listen to the following examples.

1.   **Bob b**lew the whistle as hard as he could.
2.   It's a ba**d d**ay.
3.   His father owns a bi**g g**as station.

As you can see, blending prevents the abrupt staccatolike rhythm that is characteristic of the speech of beginning students of English. Therefore, if you work toward achieving a smooth flow of words, the rhythm of your speech will improve dramatically.

Oral Practice

unstressing pronouns

This is an exercise to help you practice unstressing pronouns. One student will ask the question and another will answer, substituting the correct pronoun for the noun or pronoun in the question. The sentence stresses have been marked for you. Notice that the rhythm of all the items in each group of sentences is the same.

example: Did you tell Jéan?   Yes, I told her.

Remember to look at the person to whom you are speaking. Do not read from the book. **Be sure to use the correct pronoun in your answer.**

1.   Did you see Jáne?   Yes, I went to the beách with her.*
         Bill   store
         Tim   play
         Sue   dance
         Joe   show

2.   Did you meet the bóys?   Yes, we went to the párk with them.
         girls   pool
         men   club
         teams   game
         scouts   fair

3.   Did you read the nótice?   Yes, I réad ____ .
         meet the children   met
         feed the chickens   fed
         see the program   saw
         fry the bacon   fried

The [h] in the words he, him, and her is lost except when they are used as the first word in a sentence or in contrast.

This exercise will give you practice in unstressing the pronoun *one*.

1. Which dress does she wánt?   _____ wants the réd one.

pen	he
car	he
hat	she
blouse	she

   _____ blue
   _____ black
   _____ white
   _____ pink

2. Which suit do you like bést?   I like (thís, thát) one.

house	they
shirt	you
boat	they
cap	you

   ____ _____ .
   ____ _____ .
   ____ _____ .
   ____ _____ .

blending

This is an exercise to practice **blending**. Ask the student next to you the question choosing one of the items listed. Listen to your classmates so that you do not choose an item which someone else has chosen (unless all the items have already been used).

Do you like ham and eggs?*   Yes, I _____ _____ .

    ham and cheese   No, I don't _____ .

    rice and beans

    bread and butter

    chicken and rice

    bacon and eggs

    cheese and fruit

    lettuce and tomatoes

    pork and beans

    peas and carrots

    coffee and toast

Can you think of any other combinations?

Remember that and becomes [ŋ] in these combinations.

oral reading

Listen to your instructor read the following sentences. Identify the words that are stressed. Then read the sentences yourself using correct stressing, unstressing, pausing, and blending. Do not forget to compress unstressed words and syllables.

1. We made the same mistakes on the test.
2. I called her at home, but she was at school.
3. The salad needed only a few drops of oil and vinegar.
4. He was going to buy the blue suit, but he decided to buy the brown one instead.
5. Keep her from moving so I can take her picture.
6. Please don't drink Coke now; you'll ruin your appetite.
7. I'd love to have rice and beans, but she's serving ham and cheese sandwiches.
8. Tell Lilly not to worry about her roommate.
9. We bought only a melon and some apples.

10. Nothing happened to Ted during the storm because he was inside all the time.
11. Take it or leave it; the choice is up to you.
12. That's a nice scarf you have on.
13. We must thank Cathy for the wonderful lunch.
14. Susan needs some money; she wants to buy a new dress, but she can't afford it.
15. The Christmas season is such a lovely time of the year.

Oral Communication

telling time

Some of the most frequently used expressions in any language are those used in asking for or giving the time. Often, asking for the time is a way of starting a conversation. Study the drawings and learn the vocabulary related to telling time.

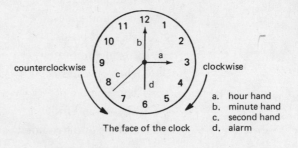

counterclockwise · clockwise

The face of the clock

a. hour hand
b. minute hand
c. second hand
d. alarm

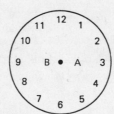

Minutes on side B of the clock face are expressed by the words *of, to, till* or *before* the hour. *Past* and *after* are also used, as in "forty-five minutes after one."

Minutes on side A of the clock face are expressed with the words *after* or *past* the hour.

The following clocks show you the many different ways of expressing time in English. It's not necessary for you to learn to use all of them, but you should be able to recognize them when they are used by another speaker.

I

a. four o'clock
b. four sharp
c. exactly four

II

a. four-ten
b. ten (minutes) past four
c. ten (minutes) after four

III

a. four-fifteen
b. fifteen minutes past four
c. fifteen minutes after four
d. (a) quarter past four
e. (a) quarter after four

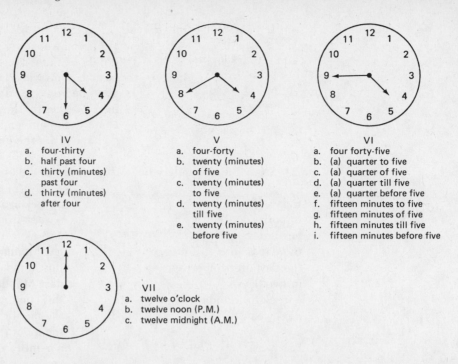

IV
a. four-thirty
b. half past four
c. thirty (minutes) past four
d. thirty (minutes) after four

V
a. four-forty
b. twenty (minutes) of five
c. twenty (minutes) to five
d. twenty (minutes) till five
e. twenty (minutes) before five

VI
a. four forty-five
b. (a) quarter to five
c. (a) quarter of five
d. (a) quarter till five
e. (a) quarter before five
f. fifteen minutes to five
g. fifteen minutes of five
h. fifteen minutes till five
i. fifteen minutes before five

VII
a. twelve o'clock
b. twelve noon (P.M.)
c. twelve midnight (A.M.)

listening exercise

1. Your instructor will dictate different times. Write them down in numbers. Your instructor will then ask a student to go to the board and draw the hands in the correct position on the clock.

2. Use as many phrases as you can to express the time shown on each of the clocks below.

A.   B.   C.

D.   E.   F.

oral practice

1. Ask the student next to you one of these questions. He or she will answer in a complete sentence and ask the next student a question. Your instructor may require everyone to ask and answer the same questions.

a.   (At) What time do you _____ ?   b.   I _____ at _____ .

get up on weekdays?
get up on Saturdays and Sundays?
go to bed on weekdays?
go to bed on Saturdays and Sundays?
have breakfast?   lunch?   dinner?
come to the university?
go home from the university?

2.   Study the vocabulary below to be used in the exercise that follows.

today   a week ago yesterday
tomorrow   a week from tomorrow
yesterday   a week from Sunday
the day before yesterday   last Monday
the day after tomorrow   this Monday
in two days   next Monday
a week from today   this coming Monday
next week   the month after next
a week ago   the month before last
last week   a month from now

S	M	T	W	TH	F	S
		1	2	3	4	5
6	7	8	9	10	11	12
13	14	15	16	17	18	19
20	21	22	23	24	25	26
27	28	29	30	31		

3. Referring to the calendar above, ask the student next to you a question. He or she will answer and then ask the next student a question.

a. If today is the _____ , what is the date tomorrow?
the day after tomorrow?

was the date yesterday?
the day before yesterday?

b. If today is the 17th, how would you refer to the following?

1. the 18th?   4. the 15th?   7. the 14th?
2. the 16th?   5. the 23rd?   8. the 24th?
3. the 19th?   6. the 21st?   9. the 27th?
                                           10. the 9th?

c.   What was the date a week ago today?
last Saturday?
two weeks ago?
a week ago yesterday?

d.   What will the date be a week from today?
next Thursday?
a week from now?
two weeks from tomorrow?
this coming Monday?

4. What was last month?
   the month before last?
   two months ago?

5. What is next month?
   the month after next?
   two months from now?

6. What is the opposite of tomorrow?
   next week?
   a year ago?
   a week from now?
   the day after next?

Homework

Interview the student next to you about his or her daily activities during the week and on weekends. Report your findings to the class according to your instructor's directions.

Appropriateness: Asking for the Time

dialogue

Bob: I wonder why the concert hasn't begun yet.
Ann: I think it's still early, but I'm not sure. Why don't you ask the man sitting next to you?
Bob: Good idea. Excuse me, sir. Do you have the time, please?
Man: I'm very sorry. I don't have a watch.
Ann: Let me ask the lady next to me. Excuse me, madam. I wonder if you could tell me the time.
Lady: Let me see. It's about eight o'clock.
Ann: Thank you very much. Oh, look! They're dimming the lights. The concert is going to start now.

useful expressions

There are various ways of asking the time in English. The expression you use depends on the situation you are in. If you know the person to whom you are speaking, you may be direct and ask:

"What time is it, Sally?"

If you have just met the person or do not know him or her at all, you should be very polite. You might say:

"Do you have the time, please?"
"Do you happen to know the time?"
"Excuse me, sir. Could you please tell me the time?"
"I hope you don't mind my asking, but I'd like to know the time." (Very formal)
"I wonder if you could be so kind as to tell me the time." (Extremely formal)

If someone asks you any of these questions, what would you say before you give them the time? You could say:

"Certainly . . . "
"Just a moment I'll see . . . "
"Of course . . . "
"Why sure (or surely) . . . "
"Let me see . . . "

If you cannot give the time, you might say:

"I'm very sorry. I don't have a watch."
"Sorry, I don't have the time."
"I'm not sure."
"I'm sorry. My watch has stopped."
"I'm sorry. I don't have the slightest idea."
"Yes, but I think my watch is fast (slow)."
"Yes, but my watch is ten minutes fast (slow)."

practice

1.   Complete these short dialogues orally using the expressions presented on pages 27–28. Do not write the expressions. Speak them.

A: Excuse me . . .
B: Yes, . . .
A: Thank you.

A: Do you happen to know the time?
B: I'm sorry . . .
A: Thanks anyway.

2.   According to your instructor's directions, work with another student. Student A will be one of these people, and Student B will ask for the time using an appropriate expression. Repeat the exercise, changing roles.

a. a waiter
b. a friend
c. a professor
d. a salesperson
e. a stranger

f. a secretary or receptionist
g. a police officer
h. a young teenager
i. an elderly stranger

3.   Think of other situations in which you have to ask someone for the time. Use some of the expressions listed on page 27. Work out dialogues with other students according to your instructor's directions.

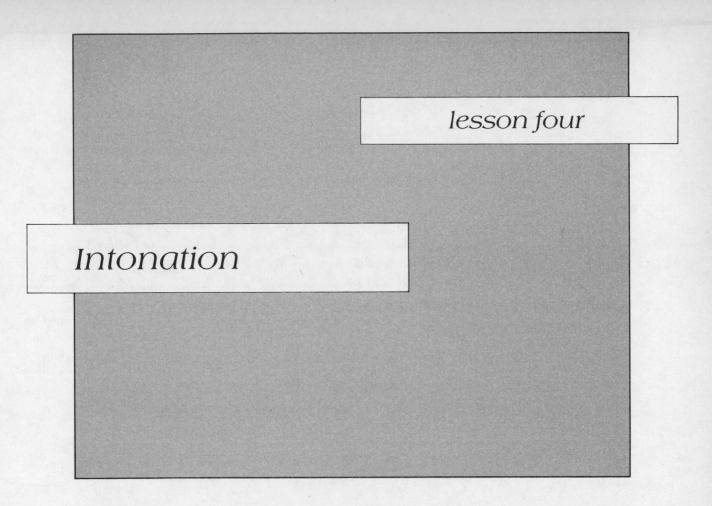

lesson four

Intonation

Definition

Intonation, the rising and falling of the voice when a person is speaking, is another important element of spoken English. It is sometimes called the melody or the tune of speech. A speaker can change the meaning of an utterance just by using a different intonation pattern. For example, "She's here" spoken with a falling voice at the end makes a statement. But "She's here?" said with a rising voice asks a question. The arrow shows the rising or falling of the voice.

Statement: She's here.

Question: She's here?

In this rising and falling of the voice, there are four levels (or pitches) that the speaker may use. **Pitch**, then, is the relative highness or lowness of the voice. Here are the four generally recognized pitches:

4   Very high
3   High
2   Mid
1   Low

Very high pitch is used only in expressions of great surprise, disbelief, or fear. **Low pitch** signals the end of a sentence. Normal conversation moves between **mid** and **high pitch**. We can use curved lines to show the movement of the voice. The voice does not jump suddenly or abruptly from one pitch to another; it makes a gradual change upward or downward.

29

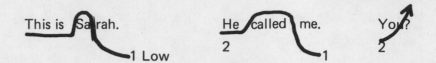

Notice in "You?" how the voice glides up from one pitch to the other within the same syllable.

rising-falling intonation

The rising-falling pattern looks like this: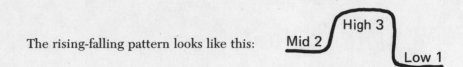

The voice begins on a mid pitch and rises to a high note which usually coincides with the last sentence stress and/or the last stressed syllable. Then the voice begins a gradual downward glide to the end of the sentence, with each syllable being on a slightly lower pitch than the preceding one. In English, this type of intonation pattern is generally used at the end of:

1. **Simple statements** (normal declarative sentences)

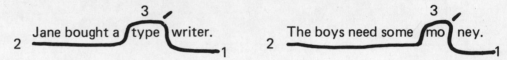

2. **Commands and requests**

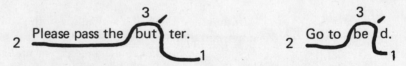

3. **Questions with interrogative words**: which, why, how, when, what, where, who

4. **Echo (tag) questions**: sentences in which the speaker is really making a statement of fact and expects a "yes" answer from the person to whom he or she is speaking.

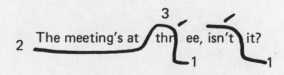

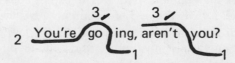

rising intonation

The rising pattern looks like this:

The voice glides upwards starting with the last strong stress (or sentence stress) and remains at this high level until the end of the sentence. Sustaining this high pitch (sometimes very high) communicates a feeling of incompleteness or suspense. In English rising intonation is used at the end of the following:

1. **Questions without interrogative words** (Yes-No questions)

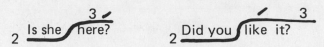

2. **Questions expressing disbelief or surprise**

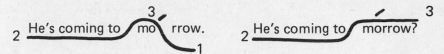

3. **Special question repetition:** the listener is not sure what he or she heard.

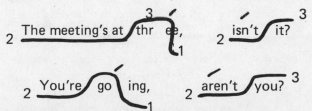

4. **Echo (tag) questions:** sentences in which the speaker is really asking a question.

Notice in these two examples that the voice rises in the final pronouns *it* and *you* even though the strong stress falls on the auxiliaries *isn't* and *aren't*.

5. **Direct address:** Addressing another person by the first name, surname, or title calls for a rising intonation pattern.

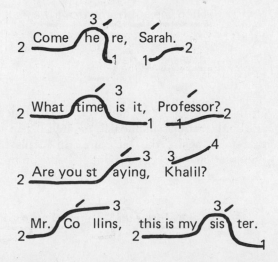

nonfinal intonation

Enumeration

When the native speaker enumerates a series of items in a sentence, he or she uses rising intonation for each item except the last one; then the speaker uses falling intonation.

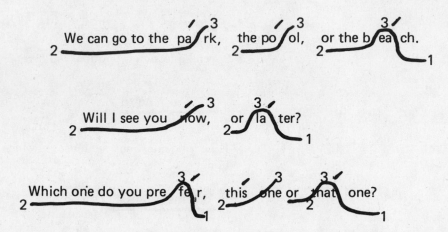

Statements and Questions of Choice

Offering a choice in a statement or question calls for rising intonation for all the alternatives except the last one. In that one, the speaker uses rising-falling intonation.

Long Sentences

When the speaker utters a rather long statement, he or she may divide it into two parts, each part having one strong stress. Notice in the example below that the sentence begins with a subordinate clause. The intonation line does not fall to pitch 1, thereby creating a sense of expectation or suspense and signaling the listener, "Wait; there's more; I haven't finished."

In the example below, however, the sentence begins with an independent clause and so the intonation line falls to pitch 1. The subordinate clause appears at the end; therefore, again, the intonation line falls to pitch 1. Notice the difference in punctuation—there is no comma between the two clauses.

Contrast and Comparison

So far we have discussed the rules of intonation under normal circumstances. Quite frequently, however, the native speaker finds it necessary to break these rules (as we mentioned previously in the section on sentence stress). The speaker may want to emphasize a particular word or idea because he or she did not understand a word or misunderstood it, wants to contrast that word or idea with one mentioned before, or wants to give the item special importance. Whatever the reason, the speaker will use a contrastive intonation pattern in order to give prominence to the word or idea to be emphasized.

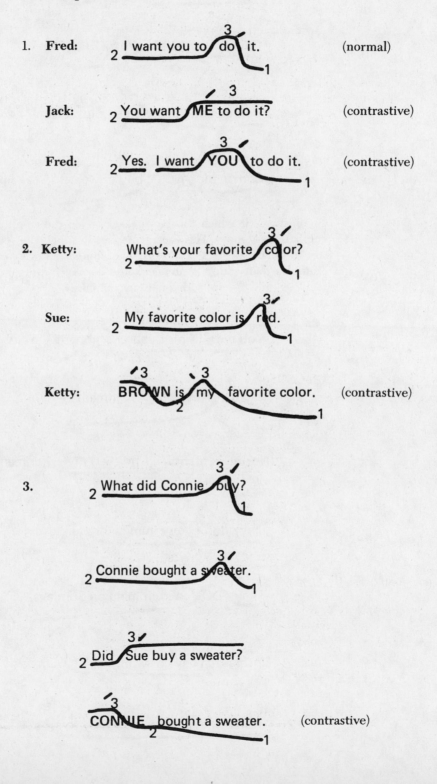

1. **Fred:** I want you to do it. (normal)

    Jack: You want ME to do it? (contrastive)

    Fred: Yes. I want YOU to do it. (contrastive)

2. **Ketty:** What's your favorite color?

    Sue: My favorite color is red.

    Ketty: BROWN is my favorite color. (contrastive)

3. What did Connie buy?

    Connie bought a sweater.

    Did Sue buy a sweater?

    CONNIE bought a sweater. (contrastive)

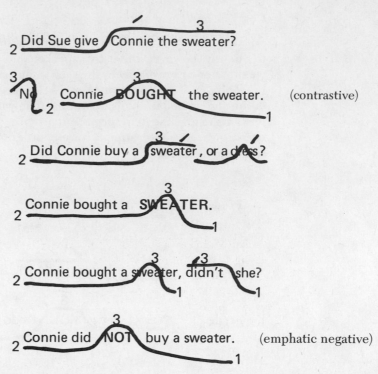

Did Sue give Connie the sweater?

No, Connie BOUGHT the sweater. (contrastive)

Did Connie buy a sweater, or a dress?

Connie bought a SWEATER.

Connie bought a sweater, didn't she?

Connie did NOT buy a sweater. (emphatic negative)

One instance in which a native speaker breaks the rules of intonation is in the use of emphatic sentences. These are sentences in which the speaker must stress the auxiliary (normally unstressed) in order to emphasize the verb. Notice in the following examples that while a sentence would normally contain no auxiliary, the auxiliaries *do*, *does*, and *did* are added here for emphasis.

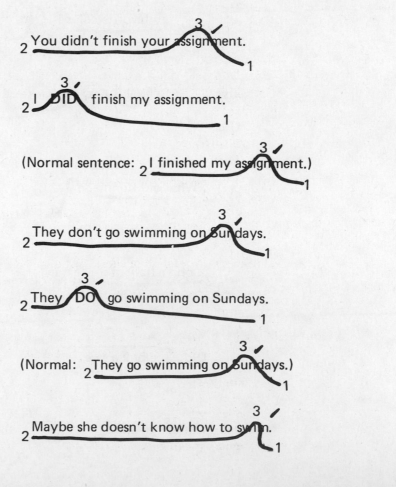

You didn't finish your assignment.

I DID finish my assignment.

(Normal sentence: I finished my assignment.)

They don't go swimming on Sundays.

They DO go swimming on Sundays.

(Normal: They go swimming on Sundays.)

Maybe she doesn't know how to swim.

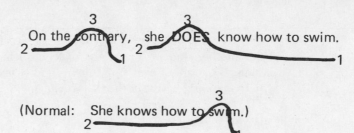

On the contrary, she DOES know how to swim.

(Normal: She knows how to swim.)

Oral Practice

1. Study these dialogues. Some of the sentences would normally be spoken with **rising-falling** intonation. Others would be spoken with **rising** intonation. Decide which pattern should be used for each sentence and read the sentence aloud. Then read the dialogues with another student.

1. **A:** Hassan, what time did you get up this morning?
   B: I didn't get up until ten o'clock.

2. **A:** What did you say? I didn't hear you.
   B: I said, "Please turn down the radio; it's too loud."
   A: OK, OK. You don't have to shout. I'll turn it down.

3. **A:** Did you find out what that man wanted?
   B: What did you think he wanted? Money!

4. **A:** Bill's leaving the university.
   B: He's leaving the university? In the middle of the year?
   A: He says he just got a very good job.
   B: If Bill says it's a good job, it must be excellent.

5. **A:** The plane's leaving at 5:50.
   B: 5:50? Are you sure? I thought they said 4:50.
   A: It **is** leaving at 5:50. I just called the airline.

6. **A:** It's so hot! Let's go for a swim.
   B: Great! I'd love to.
   A: Shall we go to the swimming pool or to the beach?
   B: Let's go to the beach. I went to the pool yesterday.

7. **A:** You took your car this morning, didn't you?
   B: Of course. Why do you ask?
   A: I thought you said you were going to take the bus.
   B: I did, but I changed my mind.

2. Make up a question of choice using one of the following sets of alternatives. Address your question to the person sitting on your left. He or she will answer and then ask the next student a question using a different set of alternatives from the list. Make up your own set of choices if you wish.

examples: Carmen, which do you prefer, swimming or jogging?
          Joe, do you speak Italian or Spanish?

1. coffee, tea
2. cherry pie, apple pie
3. a novel, a short story
4. watch TV, read a book
5. jogging, walking

6. basketball, volleyball
7. England, Scotland
8. German, French
9. the movies, the theater
10. rock, salsa

mini-dialogues

With another student, read these dialogues using correct blending, stress, and intonation. Be aware of compound nouns and two-word verbs. Your instructor may ask you to memorize some of the dialogues.

1. **A:** What time is it?
   B: I'm sorry. I don't have a watch. Why don't you ask Helen?
   A: I can't. She just went out.

2. **A:** Where do we get off the bus?
   B: We get off at the next corner by the gas station.

3. **A:** Who's going to blow up the balloons for your birthday party?
   B: I'm going to blow them up myself.

4. **A:** Where can I lie down for a few minutes?
   B: You can lie down on the sofa in the living room.
   A: Thank you.

5. **A:** When does the plane take off?
   B: It's going to take off in a few minutes. If you don't hurry up, we'll miss the plane.

6. **A:** When did Jack come in?
   B: He came in a while ago. I heard him turn on the television set.

7. **A:** When can I make up the comprehension test I missed?
   B: You can make it up on Friday in the laboratory.
   A: Thank you very much.

8. **A:** Is this elevator going up?
   B: No, it's going down. Why didn't you look at the light panel?
   A: I did. But the lights aren't working.

Homework

Prepare a list of items you can buy in the following stores: drugstore, supermarket, dress shop, men's store, and department store. Think of as many compound nouns as you can. At the next class meeting,

Student A will ask (for example): "What are you going to buy at the drugstore?"
Student B will answer (for example): "I'm going to buy mouthwash, toothpaste, and shaving cream."

Make long lists of items so that you don't repeat anything another student has already mentioned.

Appropriateness: Offering, Accepting, Refusing

dialogues: informal and formal situations

1. **A:** Would you like to try some typical native food?
   B: I'd love to. It looks delicious.

2. **A:** Would you like some grapefruit juice or some tomato juice?
   B: Tomato juice, please.

3. **A:** Would you like some of the sugar cookies I've just baked?
   B: How can I refuse! I know I shouldn't eat them, but they look so good!

4. **A:** Would you like a cocktail before dinner?
   B: No, thank you, but I'd like a glass of water.
   A: Certainly.

5. **A:** Would you like some more fruit punch?
   B: No thanks. I've had plenty already.

6. **A:** How about some more beef stew?
   B: No thanks. I'm so full I couldn't eat another mouthful. It certainly is delicious.
   A: I'm glad you like it. It's one of my favorite recipes.

7. **A:** Would you like to try some shrimp salad?
   B: I'm sorry. I'm allergic to seafood.
   A: Oh, I'm sorry. I didn't know that. I have some roast chicken in the refrigerator, and I think there's a little ham, too. Which would you prefer?
   B: The cold chicken would be fine, thanks.

8. **A:** Would you like to try some Chicken à la King?
   B: I've never tasted that. What's in it besides chicken?
   A: It's chicken and mushrooms and mixed vegetables in a cream sauce. It's usually served over a biscuit.
   B: It sounds good, but I'd rather not. I'm on a diet. I'll just have a tossed salad.

9. **A:** Would you like something to eat? A sandwich perhaps?
   B: No, thanks. I've just eaten. But I would like a cup of coffee if it's not too much trouble.
   A: Not at all. I just made a fresh pot. What do you take? Cream or sugar?
   B: I drink it black, thank you.

10. **A:** Would you care for a drink?
    B: No, thank you. I don't drink.
    A: Well, may I bring you a soft drink?
    B: Just a glass of water, thank you.

useful expressions

The preceding dialogues demonstrate several ways of offering something to someone. The expression, "Would you like . . . ?" is a very useful one. You may use it with a close friend, with an acquaintance, with someone you've just met, or with someone you don't know at all. Here are some other expressions. The first three are used in informal situations; the fourth is for more formal situations.

"How about something to eat (drink) . . . ?"

"Can I get you some (a) . . . ?"

"How about some more . . . ?"

"Would you care for some . . . ?" or "Would you care to try some . . . ?"

If you decide to accept what is being offered, you may answer with one of the following expressions. Some are informal; some are formal. Can you tell which ones you would use in a formal situation? In an informal situation?

"That sounds great! I'm starved."

"I'd love one. I'm very thirsty."

"Yes, thank you. I'd like . . . "

"I'd like to try some . . . "

"I'd like some more . . ., thank you."

If you decide to refuse an offer, you may answer with one of these expressions. Can you tell which ones are appropriate for informal situations? For formal situations? Several would be appropriate for either.

> "No thanks. I'm not hungry right now."
> "No thanks. I've already eaten."
> "No thanks. I've just had something."
> "Not right now, thanks."
> "I'm sorry. I'm allergic to . . . "
> "I'd rather not, thank you."
> "I'd love to, but I really can't."
> "No thank you. I've had plenty."
> "Not right now, thank you. Perhaps later."
> "No thanks. I'm not feeling well, and I don't feel like eating anything."

If you would prefer something other than what is being offered, you may request it by saying

> "No, thank you, but I'd like something hot if it's not too much trouble." (You've been offered a cold drink.)
> "No, thank you. It really looks delicious, but could I try some . . . instead?" (You have been offered a particular food.)
> "Thanks, but I'd prefer . . . "

"I'd like . . . .", "Could I have . . . ?", and "May I have . . . ?" are basic expressions which can be used to order something in a restaurant or to request something. They are polite and may be used in either an informal or a formal situation.

practice

1. A offers B a cold drink. B has just spent several hours in an air-conditioned room, and so B asks for something hot instead. A responds accordingly.

2. A offers B a cocktail. B refuses, saying that he or she doesn't drink. A offers something else and B responds accordingly.

3. A offers B a dish which B has never tasted. A explains what the dish is made of and B decides to try it.

4. A offers B something; B says he or she is allergic to that food. A offers something else and B accepts with an appropriate response.

5. A offers B a dish; B says he or she is on a diet. A offers a substitute and B accepts with an appropriate response.

Think of other situations and practice them with other students according to your instructor's directions. Use some of the expressions listed on pages 37–38.

The High Front Vowels [i] and [ɪ]

The Sound [i]

description of the sound

[i] is a tense, high front vowel. It is called a front vowel because to produce the sound, you raise the front of the tongue as high as you can. There should be only a very narrow space between the top surface of your tongue and the hard palate. The tip of your tongue should rest lightly against the back of your lower front teeth. Lower your jaw slightly so that your teeth are barely parted. Spread your lips apart and pull them back toward the corners of your mouth. [i] is called a tense vowel because the muscles of the tongue and of the lips, as well as the muscles at the corners of the mouth and just under the chin, are tense. [i] is a long sound. You can hold it as long as you have breath. The vowel chart and the diagram show the tongue position used to produce the sound [i].

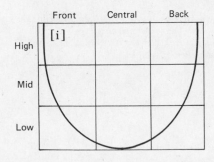

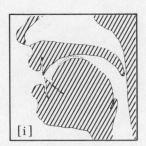

Pronounce these words after your instructor.

39   see   bee   pea   tea   key

Vowels are always lengthened before voiced consonants. Listen as your instructor pronounces the following words. Notice that the vowel is longer before the voiced consonants [d], [g], [z], [v], and [ð].

Voiceless	*Voiced*		*Voiceless*	*Voiced*
feet	feed		leaf	leave
leak	league		teeth	teethe
peace	peas			

spelling hints

Because [i] is a long vowel sound **it is usually found in strongly stressed syllables**. [i] appears initially as in *eat*, medially as in *reason*, and finally as in *tree*. [i] is represented in writing by:

> *e:* féver, sécret
> me, we, he, she, be (in stressed position only)
> *ea:* leave, meat
> *ee:* tree, seem, guarantée
> *ei:* éither, recéive
> *e* + consonant + *e:* éven, compléte (final **e** is almost always silent)
> *i:* políce, maríne
> *ie:* beliéve, chief

Some troublesome words containing the sound [i] are

éven*	éach	three	éither	these
evil	leave	seem	neither	scene
equal	meat	feed	leisure	compéte
fever	cheat	seen	recéive	compléte
secret	breathe	seéing	receipt	
frequent	reason	degrée		
being	teacher	guarantee**		
evening	diséase			
immédiately				
cathédral				

políce	field	people (unusual spelling)
marine	priest	
machine	niece	
magazíne***	piece	
gasolíne***	chief	
	beliéve	

*Accent marks do not normally appear in written English. They are used here only to help you pronounce the words with the correct stress.
**A slash through a letter means that the letter is silent.
***Often pronounced mágazine, gásoline.

The Sound [ɪ]

description of the sound

[ɪ] is also a high front vowel, but to make this sound, place your tongue slightly lower than for the [i] sound. Relax your lips and part them slightly. [ɪ] is called a lax vowel. It is very short in duration. The vowel chart and the diagram show the tongue position used to produce the sound [ɪ].

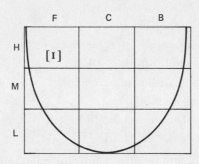

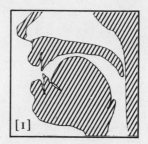

Pronounce these words after listening to your instructor.

is   his   it   pin   fit

Remember that vowels are lengthened before voiced consonants. Pronounce these words after listening to your instructor. Lengthen the vowel in the second word of each pair.

Voiceless	*Voiced*		*Voiceless*	*Voiced*
rip	rib		pick	pig
kit	kid		hiss	his

listening exercises and oral practice: distinguishing [i] from [ɪ]

1. In the following exercise, your instructor will read one word from each pair of words in each group. Circle the words that you hear. Your instructor will then pronounce each pair of words. Listen carefully and then practice reading the following sentences aloud, making a clear distinction between the boldfaced words.

[i]	[ɪ]	[i]	[ɪ]	[i]	[ɪ]
ease	is	feel	fill	he's	his
seat	sit	feet	fit	he'll	hill
heat	hit	sheep	ship	we'll	will
leave	live	sleep	slip	heels	hills
cheap	chip	teen	tin	field	filled

1. Don't **sit** in that **seat**.
2. **He'll** climb the **hill**.
3. **We'll** go if yóu **will**.
4. **He's** eating **his** dinner.
5. He thinks potato **chips** are **cheap**.
6. The **field** is **filled** with people.
7. I **feel** we can **fill** the position.
8. The **ship** is taking the **sheep** to market.
9. It's difficult to climb **hills** in high **heels**.
10. These shoes don't **fit** his **feet**.

2. Your instructor will read these sentences using one of the words in parentheses. Circle the word that you hear. Each sentence will be read twice.

1. Isn't she going to (leave, live)?
2. First you must (heat, hit) it.
3. Those (heels, hills) are quite high.
4. Don't (sleep, slip) on the floor.
5. They sold the (sheep, ship) right away.
6. I want you to (feel, fill) this dish.
7. The word (we'll, will) is often confused with the word (we'll, will).
8. Take (this, these) with you.
9. We need to get more (beads, bids).
10. I asked him to take the (lead, lid).

spelling hints

[ɪ] is used in both stressed and unstressed syllables. It appears initially as in *is*, medially as in *this*, and finally as in *party*.

1. In stressed syllables the sound [ɪ] is represented in writing by:

  i: if, pin, fill
  u: busy, business
  y: system, myth
  o: women
  e: pretty
  ea: ear, near (before *r* in the same syllable)

> **NOTE:**   Before the letter *r*, especially within the same syllable, the sound [ɪ] is usually heard instead of [i]
> **examples:** here   interfére   enginéer   sérious
>
> Also, although the letters **ee** are usually pronounced [i] as in *see, bee, meet, need*, in the word *been*, the **ee** is always pronounced [ɪ]—[bɪn].

Some Troublesome Words Containing the Sound [ɪ]

big	scíssors	sígnature	búsy	sýstem	théater
give	liquid	industry	business	myth	appéar
live	liquor	Christmas	build	mystery	míschief
kiss	little	interesting	pretty	year	physícian
milk	signal	women	English	fear	biscuit

2. In unstressed syllables the sound [ɪ] is represented in writing by:

  be: belíeve, beneath, behave, behind, before, beside, between [bɪ]
  de: decéive, deceit, decrease, degree, defeat, decide, decision [dɪ]
  pre: presént (v), prevent, pretend, prepare [prɪ]
  re: recéive, receipt, remain, retain, repeat, retire, revision [rɪ]
  et: pócket, ticket, picket [ɪt]
  ect: súbject, object, project [ɪkt]
  ace: préface, surface, necklace [ɪs]
  ess: háppiness, actress, waitress, careless, business, witness [ɪs]
  y: in final position: cíty, easy, lady, pretty, (also [i])
  ate: in adjectives and nouns: clímate, chocolate, private, senate, delicate, separate, graduate, moderate, fortunate, accurate [ɪt]

> *ain:* cáptain [ɪn]
>
> *ex:* as unstressed syllable before a consonant is pronounced [ɪks] explaín, **expect**
>
> as unstressed syllable before a vowel is pronounced [ɪgz] exhíbit, **examine** (See lesson 17.)
>
> *age, iage, ege:* as final unstressed syllable in the following words is pronounced [ɪdʒ]

páckage	víllage	mórtgage	cóurage	márriage
manage	image	bandage	encóurage	mileage
damage	message	garbage	discóurage	college
baggage	average		advántage	knowledge

> **NOTE:** Some native speakers of English use the sound [ə] in almost all unstressed syllables.

Oral Practice

These very simple exercises will allow you to concentrate on blending and on producing a clear contrast between the sounds [i] and [ɪ]. Be sure to blend the final consonant of a word with the initial vowel of the word which follows it.

1. We'll eat it.*   We'll freeze it.   We'll repeat it.*

heat it	keep it	complete it
read it	sweep it	receive it
need it	seal it	increase it

2. When the word *please* is the first word in a sentence, there is no pause after the word. However, when *please* is the last word in a sentence, it is preceded in writing by a comma. The use of this comma indicates that when the sentence is spoken, there should be a slight pause before the word *please*.

Please eat it.*   Eat it,* please.

heat it	teach it		Heat it	Teach it
keep it	sweep it		Keep it	Sweep it
clean it	feel it		Clean it	Feel it
leave it	freeze it		Leave it	Freeze it

See Lesson 16 for explanation of intervocalic [t].

The S Endings

The pronunciation of the *s* or *es* or *'s* endings for the third person singular in the present tense form of the verb, the plurals of most nouns, possessive forms, or contractions follows a regular system.

1. The *s* ending is **voiceless** [s] when preceded by **all of the voiceless consonants except** [s], [ʃ], and [tʃ].

[p]	[t]	[k]	[f]	[θ]
keeps	sits	kicks	chiefs	Ruth's
Rip's	it's	picnics	laughs	months
			graphs	

2. The *s* ending is **voiced** when preceded by the **vowels and all the voiced consonants except** [z] [ʒ] and [dʒ].

sees	cities	pays	says	Sam's	goes
[siz]	[sɪtɪz] or [sɪtiz]	[peʸz]	[sɛz]	[sæmz]	[goʷz]

laws	boys	eyes	cows	gives	hills	builds
[lɔz]	[bɔɪz]	[aɪz]	[kaʊz]	[gɪvz]	[hɪlz]	[bɪldz]

bathes	swims	skins	sings	years	jobs	bags
[beʸðz]	[swɪmz]	[skɪnz]	[sɪŋz]	[jɪrz]	[dʒabz]	[bægz]

3. The *s* ending **must add an extra syllable** [ɪz] or [əz] **when preceded by** [s], [ʃ],
[tʃ], [z], [ʒ], or [dʒ].

[s]	[z]	[ʃ]	[ʒ]	[tʃ]	[dʒ]
kisses*	quizzes	wishes	garages	peaches	bridges
pieces*	pleases	dishes	corsages	riches	wages

Final ce and ss are always pronounced [s].

Study these rules and apply them as you do all the oral exercises in this text.

mini-dialogues

s endings and the sounds [i] and [ɪ]

Observe the rules of blending and use the correct intonation patterns. Try to look at
the person with whom you are having the dialogue.

1. **A:** When does Ann get up?
    B: She gets up at six-fifteen on weekdays.

2. **A:** What subject does Alice teach?
    B: She teaches English and arithmetic.

3. **A:** How's your political science class? Is it as difficult as it was last semester?
    B: It seems a little easier. I've passed all the quizzes so far.

4. **A:** Where's Tippy? Bob wants to give him a bath.
    B: He was around a few minutes ago. He always manages to disappear when it's
    bath time.

5. **A:** When can we see Tim?
    B: As soon as he finishes his work.

Oral Practice

interrogative words

Some of these questions require rising-falling intonation and others need rising
intonation. (Refer to Lesson 4 to refresh your memory.) All of the questions have

verbs with the sounds [i] and [ɪ]. They are all frequently used verbs, so if you don't remember the meaning of any of them, look them up in the dictionary. Remember to use the correct *s* ending on the third-person singular present tense and to observe the rules of blending. Student A will ask the first question of Student B. Student A will ask Student C the second question, and so on. Use complete sentences.

NOTE TO THE INSTRUCTOR: You may want to have everyone in the class ask and respond to questions 1, 4, 5, 6, 7, 8. This exercise can also be used to practice the *s* form.

example: Student A: Which newspaper do you read?
   B: I read *The Star*.
   A: Which newspaper does (B) read?
   C: He reads *The Star*.

---

1. Which newspaper do you read?
2. What does every student of English need?
3. At what temperature does water freeze?
4. Who cleans your room?
5. What do you usually drink with your lunch?
6. What subject interests you most?
7. Who sits next to you on your right?
8. Where do you usually study?

oral reading

In these exercises and in all the other oral reading sections in this book you should practice everything you have learned about word stress, sentence stress, intonation, rhythm, blending, and phrasing. Be careful to pronounce the *s* endings correctly.

The sentences in this group contain many of the troublesome words listed in this lesson.

1. This engineer says we'll get better gasoline mileage if we drive at a moderate speed.
2. The chief of police didn't hear the people screaming.
3. Neither of the women's colleges competed in the recent swimming meet.
4. Breathe deeply before you begin to swim.
5. The captain didn't see the other ship's signal in time to avoid a collision.
6. There's an interesting foreign language film at the movie theater this weekend.
7. Does one need a knowledge of English to become a member of this scientific expedition?
8. Which of your nieces received a scholarship to complete her college education?
9. The laboratory technician says neither of these liquids contains any liquor.
10. If you expect to take advantage of the guarantee on this machine, keep your receipt.

Each of the sentences below contains at least one word with the sound [ɪ] in an unstressed syllable. Before you read the sentences aloud, underline all the words — including the function words — that contain the *unstressed* [ɪ] sound.*

1. This waitress seems to be very careless with the dishes.
2. Please leave a message for me at the college. I'll pick it up this evening.

3.   You didn't put enough postage on the package.
4.   Have you read the preface in your English book?
5.   I took advantage of a recent sale and bought a pretty necklace.
6.   My sister can't keep a secret. Neither can I.
7.   Steven reads a weekly news magazine, but Peter prefers the comics.
8.   To my kid sister, happiness is a delicious chocolate milkshake.
9.   Put the ticket in your pocket so no one can steal it.
10.   What does Tillie mean when she says she has an average marriage?

Written Exercises

practice with the front vowel [i] and stressed and unstressed [ɪ]

Write the correct symbol [i] or [ɪ] for the sound of the boldface vowel on the line. In words which have two lines, two sounds are asked for. Be sure to review the spelling hints on pages 40, 42–43.

1. ___ basket	13. ___ receive ___	25. ___ quickly
2. ___ relief ___	14. ___ message	26. ___ climate
3. ___ necklace	15. ___ committee ___	27. ___ pretend
4. ___ ticket ___	16. ___ decide	28. ___ senate
5. ___ clinic ___	17. ___ idea	29. ___ even
6. ___ meaning	18. ___ surface	30. ___ receipt ___
7. ___ women ___	19. ___ machine	31. ___ deliver ___
8. ___ marine	20. ___ minute ___	32. ___ delicate
9. ___ defeat ___	21. ___ chocolate	33. ___ business
10. ___ increase ___	22. ___ being	34. ___ engineer ___
11. ___ college	23. ___ busy	35. ___ region
12. ___ pretty	24. ___ present (v)	36. ___ project (n)

practice with *s* endings

Write the correct symbol [s], [z], or [ɪz] for the sound of the final *s*, in the third person singular, possessive, or plural forms. See rules on pages 43–44.

1. ___ lips	17. ___ quizzes	33. ___ eats
2. ___ lives	18. ___ he's	34. ___ receipts
3. ___ sits	19. ___ bridges	35. ___ men's
4. ___ keys	20. ___ it's	36. ___ breathes
5. ___ picks	21. ___ Bill's	37. ___ teaches
6. ___ pays	22. ___ believes	38. ___ wishes
7. ___ hills	23. ___ misses	39. ___ builds
8. ___ chiefs	24. ___ sees	40. ___ villages
9. ___ Dick's	25. ___ mountains	41. ___ equals
10. ___ kisses	26. ___ Rip's	42. ___ necklaces
11. ___ Pat's	27. ___ leaves	43. ___ here's
12. ___ fishes	28. ___ needs	44. ___ women's
13. ___ fixes	29. ___ advises	45. ___ clinics
14. ___ laughs	30. ___ businesses	46. ___ witnesses
15. ___ pieces	31. ___ loves	47. ___ Jim's
16. ___ peaches	32. ___ children's	48. ___ images

Homework

Go home and ask six of your neighbors, friends, or relatives the following question:

"Who are the three most famous people in the world today?"

Take notes as to who says what and then report the information you get at the next class meeting. You may also add your own opinion, of course.

Appropriateness: Asking About and Describing One's Health

dialogue: at the supermarket

Sal: Oh! Hi, Bob.
Bob: Hello, Sal. Are you all right?
Sal: I don't know . . . I . . .
Bob: What's wrong? You don't look very well.
Sal: I feel a bit dizzy and I have an awful headache.
Bob: Why don't you go home right now?
Sal: I have to finish shopping.
Bob: But it'll be worse if you stay here!
Sal: I think I'll be all right. I'm beginning to feel better now.
Bob: Well, I'll be here for some time if you need any help. Please look for me.
Sal: Thanks, Bob. I really appreciate your concern.

useful expressions

In Lesson 1 we discussed the appropriate way of greeting people formally and informally. In most cases there was a brief exchange such as:
A: Hello! How are you?
B: Fine. And you?
A: Very well. Thank you.

But if you meet a friend or notice a person who looks ill, then it is appropriate to use any of the following expressions:

"Is there anything wrong?"
"You don't look very well. Do you need help?"
"Are you feeling all right?"
"What's wrong? Are you sick?"
"What's the matter?"

Depending on how you feel, there are different expressions you may use to describe your health. By the way, you may also use these expressions to describe your condition to a doctor.

"I'm not feeling well."
"I feel a bit dizzy." (weak, strange)
"I have a bit of a headache." (a terrible headache)
"My ____ is hurting somewhat." (back, neck)
"I've got a sore throat."
"I have a stuffed-up nose." or "I have a runny nose."

"I've got these awful pains in my _____ ." (side, leg)

"I ache all over. Every joint in my body aches."

"I have a terrible toothache." (backache, earache, stomachache)

If you feel very sick you might use the following:

"I can't _____ ." (walk, open my mouth)

"I can hardly _____ ." (breathe, walk, speak)

"This pain is killing me!"

"I feel awful." (terrible)

"I think I'm going to die."

"I have a terrible pain in my _____ ." (arm, knee)

If someone complains about poor health you might say:

"I'm sorry to hear that."

"I hope you'll feel better soon."

"I hope you'll get well quickly."

"I hope it isn't anything serious."

practice

According to your instructor's directions, prepare a dialogue about one of these situations (or about any other similar situation), and present it to the class. **Remember that you must present it orally**.

1. Get together with a friend. One of you is calling to invite the other to a party. That person has to refuse the invitation because he or she feels sick.

2. Imagine that your friend is very ill and can hardly talk. You take him or her to see the doctor and you must explain the symptoms. Please refer to Figure 5-1 on page 49.

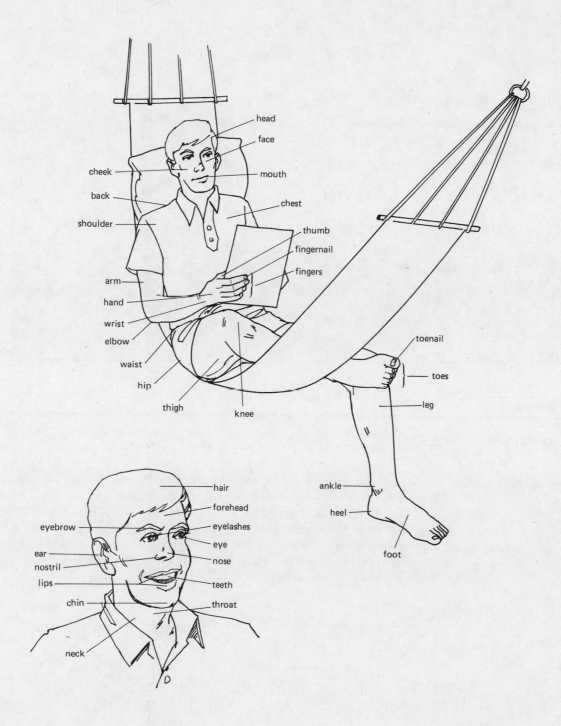

head
face
cheek
mouth
back
chest
shoulder
thumb
fingernail
fingers
arm
hand
wrist
elbow
waist
toenail
hip
toes
thigh
knee
leg

hair
forehead
eyebrow
eyelashes
eye
ear
nose
nostril
lips
teeth
chin
throat
neck
ankle
heel
foot

The Mid-Front Vowels [eʸ] and [ɛ]

The Sound [eʸ]

description of the sound

[eʸ] is a tense, mid-front vowel. To produce the sound, push the blade of the tongue forward and raise it halfway between the hard palate and the bottom of the mouth. The tip of the tongue may touch the bottom of the front teeth. Pull the lips back and make them fairly tense. As you produce the sound [eʸ] move the tongue upward and forward toward the position used to produce the sound [ɪ]. This gliding movement produces a sound which resembles a diphthong. The vowel chart and the diagram show the tongue position used to produce the sound [eʸ].

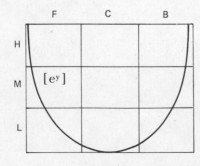

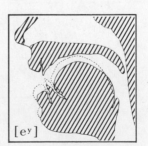

Pronounce these words after listening to your instructor. Make sure you make the gliding effect by moving the tongue toward the front of the mouth.

50   day   say   pay   late

The sound [eʸ] is lengthened before a voiced consonant. Practice reading these pairs of words.

Voiceless	*Voiced*
face	phase
safe	save
fate	fade

listening exercises and oral practice: distinguishing [i], [ɪ], and [eʸ]

Your instructor will read one word from each of the columns below. Circle the words that you hear. Next, he or she will pronounce all the words in each column. Listen, and then pronounce the words making a clear distinction between the three sounds.

a	*b*	*c*	*d*	*e*	*f*	*g*
sheep	peel	heat	feel	beat	lead	meal
ship	pill	hit	fill	bit	lid	mill
shape	pale	hate	fail	bait	laid	mail

Listen as your instructor reads one sentence in each of these groups. Circle the letter next to the sentence read. Then practice reading each sentence using correct stress, blending, and intonation.

1. a. Did you feel it?   b. Did you fill it?   c. Did you fail it?
2. a. They'll heat it.   b. They'll hit it.   c. They'll hate it.
3. a. It's the same sheep.   b. It's the same ship.   c. It's the same shape.

spelling hints

The sound [eʸ] appears initially as in *aim*, medially as in *behave*, and finally as in *today*.

[eʸ] is a long, tense sound which usually appears in strongly stressed syllables. [eʸ] is most often represented in writing by:

a: late, ache, nation, potato, patriot
ai: rain, mail
ay: pay, May
ea: steak, break

> **NOTE:** When a word ends in a silent e, the vowel in the strongly stressed syllable usually "says its name" as in *change* [tʃeʸndʒ]. When there are two vowels, the sound is usually that of the first vowel as in *raise* [reʸz].

Some Troublesome Words Containing the Sound [eʸ]

ache	áncient	pátient	raise	break
change	nation	decade	praise	steak
strange	native	beháve	straight	great
dánger	naval	occásion	afráid	weigh
radio	major	vacátion		obéy
famous	favorite			
fatal				

> **NOTE:** 1. The suffix -*day* may be pronounced either [dɪ] or [deʸ] in *yesterday*, and in the names of the days of the week: *Monday, Tuesday, Wednesday, Thursday, Friday, Saturday* and *Sunday*. In *birthday, holiday* and *today*, however, -*day* is pronounced [deʸ].
>
> 2. In verbs the ending -*ate* is pronounced [eʸt].
>
> séparate   éducate   régulate   óperate
> celebrate   indicate   graduate   appreciate

The Sound [ɛ]

description of the sound

[ɛ] is a lax, mid-front vowel. As in producing the vowel [eʸ], raise the tongue and push it forward in the mouth, slightly lower than for [eʸ]; however, there is no gliding effect. Relax the lips and keep them in a normal position. [ɛ] is a short, lax sound, while [eʸ] is a long, tense sound. The vowel chart and the diagram show the tongue position used to produce the sound [ɛ].

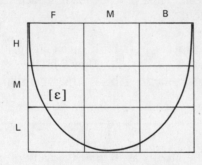
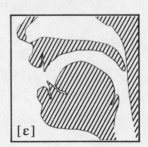

Pronounce these words after listening to your instructor. Make sure you raise the tongue and relax the lips.

said   let   bell   hair   friend   bread

The vowel [ɛ] is lengthened before voiced consonants.

Voiceless	*Voiced*		*Voiceless*	*Voiced*
bet	bed		debt	dead
set	said		peck	peg

listening exercises and oral practice: distinguishing [i], [ɪ], [eʸ], and [ɛ]

1. Your instructor will read some of the words from each of the following four sections. Circle the words that you hear. After each section, your instructor will pronounce all of the pairs or groups of words in that section and then ask you to pronounce them.

Distinguishing [eʸ] *from* [ɛ]

[eʸ]	[ɛ]	[eʸ]	[ɛ]	[eʸ]	[ɛ]
bait	bet	pain	pen	waste	west
wait	wet	main	men	lace	less
late	let	age	edge	saint	cent
date	debt	mate	met	gate	get

Distinguishing [ɪ] *from* [ɛ]

[ɪ]	[ɛ]	[ɪ]	[ɛ]	[ɪ]	[ɛ]
bid	bed	kin	Ken	pit	pet
din	den	lid	led	Syd	said
fill	fell	miss	mess	sit	set
Jill	gel	rid	red	tin	ten

Distinguishing [ɪr] *from* [ɛr]

[ɪr]	[ɛr]	[ɪr]	[ɛr]	[ɪr]	[ɛr]
ear	air	hear	hair	we're	wear
beer	bear	fear	fair	tear	tear

Distinguishing [i], [ɪ], [eʸ], *and* [ɛ]. *Read in vertical columns.*

lead [i]	read	heel	feel	beat	meet
lid [ɪ]	rid	hill	fill	bit	mitt
laid [eʸ]	raid	hail	fail	bait	mate
led [ɛ]	red	hell	fell	bet	met

2. Practice reading these sentences after listening to your instructor. Make a clear distinction between the boldface words.

1. You'd better **wait** or you'll get **wet**.
2. The **men** came in the **main** gate.
3. On what **date** did he pay the **debt**?
4. **Will** the child get **well**?
5. She broke into **tears** when she saw the **tears** in her dress.
6. **We're** going to **wear** our old clothes.
7. The circus **bear** drank **beer**.
8. You can get your **hair** cut **here**.
9. He was trying to **fill** the tank when he **fell** in.
10. The doctor blew **air** into Tim's left **ear**.

spelling hints

[ɛ] appears initially as in *any* and *else* and medially as in *again* and *success*. It never appears finally.

The sound [ɛ] usually occurs in stressed syllables. It is most often represented in writing by:

e: set, help, nephew

ea: bread, head, weapon

ai: said, again

a: any, various

> **NOTE:** Before [r], especially in the same syllable, the letters which would normally be pronounced [eʸ] are pronounced [ε] by most native speakers.
>
> | aim [eʸ] | fail [eʸ] | stale [eʸ] | race [eʸ] | steak [eʸ] |
> |----------|-----------|------------|-----------|------------|
> | air [ε] | fair [ε] | stare [ε] | rare [ε] | bear [ε] |

Some Troublesome Words with the Sound [ε]

prepáre	deaf	héavy	thréaten	várious*
bear	meant	jealous	breakfast	parents*
pear	sweat	leather	says	character*
wear	breath	measure	said	marriage*
tear	read (past)	pleasure	agáin	carry*
debt	thread	pleasant		

These words are often pronounced [æ].

> **NOTE:** The ending -ary is pronounced [εrɪ].
>
líbrary	sécretary	mílitary	Fébruary
primary	necessary	ordinary	vocábulary
sécondary	dictionary	January	extraórdinary

Oral Practice

substitution exercises

---

1. Ask the student sitting beside you the question. That student will answer using one of the words on the list and then ask the next student the question. Remember to look at the person to whom you are speaking.

What's the matter? I have (a, an) earache
                              headache
                              toothache
                              backache
                              stomachache
                              neckache

2. Ask the student next to you this question, choosing one of the holidays on the list. You may also use any other holiday you can think of which ends in the word *day*. (Refer to Compound Nouns, pages 11–12.)

When do we celebrate Memórial Day?

                    Lábor Day?
                    Mother's Day?
                    Indepéndence Day?
                    Fáther's Day?
                    Washington's Birthday?

We celebrate _____ on _____ .

Ask the student next to you for the information requested in each item below. Be sure to answer in a complete statement.

example: A. What's your favorite _____ ?
B. My favorite _____ is _____ .

Your instructor may decide to have everyone in the class ask the same question of the person sitting next to him or her.

1. dessert?
2. color?
3. flavor of ice cream?
4. holiday? (besides Christmas)

5. national food?
6. sport?
7. popular singer? (use *who* instead of *what*)
8. actor? actress? (use *who* instead of *what*)

Pronunciation: Past Tense Ending of Regular Verbs

In written English, both the past tense and the past participle of regular verbs are formed by adding the suffix *ed*. The pronunciation of this ending varies according to the following conditions:

1. When the **base** form of the verb ends in [t] or [d], the *ed* suffix is pronounced [ɪd] or [əd]. Pronounce these words after listening to your instructor.

rest	rested	need	needed
want	wanted	decide	decided
graduate	graduated	record	recorded

2. When the base form of the verb ends in a **voiceless sound** other than [t], the *ed* suffix is pronounced [t]. Pronounce these words after listening to your instructor.

help	helped	watch	watched	laugh	laughed
walk	walked	miss	missed	photograph	photographed
wash	washed	place	placed		

3. When the base form of the verb ends in a **voiced sound** other than [d], the *ed* suffix is pronounced [d]. Remember that **all vowels are voiced sounds**. Pronounce these words after listening to your instructor.

rub	rubbed	bang	banged	breathe	breathed
beg	begged	heal	healed	change	changed
love	loved	fear	feared	learn	learned
use	used			claim	claimed

Vowels

free	freed	claw	clawed	study	studied
cry	cried	plow	plowed	review	reviewed
stay	stayed	show	showed	annoy	annoyed

> **NOTE:** In most words ending in *se*, the *s* is pronounced [z], and, therefore, the *ed* suffix is pronounced [d] as in *refused*. However, in words ending in a consonant + *ase, ease, erse,* or *urse,* the *s* is pronounced [s], and therefore, the *ed* suffix is pronounced [t].

Pronounce these words after listening to your instructor.

base	based	cease	ceased	decrease	decreased
chase	chased	lease	leased	increase	increased
erase	erased	crease	creased	release	released

converse	conversed	curse	cursed
disperse	dispersed	nurse	nursed
reverse	reversed		

exceptions:

| ease | eas**ed** | tease | teas**ed** | please | pleas**ed** |
| [z] | [d] | [z] | [d] | [z] | [d] |

| rinse | rins**ed** | promise | promis**ed** |
| [s] | [t] | [s] | [t] |

substitution exercise: past tense ending

This exercise is extremely simple to allow you to concentrate on pronouncing the *ed* suffix correctly. Remember to look at the person to whom you are speaking. Blend the final consonant with the vowel.

Student A: Did he *spill* it?   Student B: Yes, he spilled it.

print
want
touch
carry
bake
need
weigh
charge
replace
mix
use
study

sentences using the past tense of regular verbs

Practice reading these sentences, making sure to pronounce the past tense endings according to the rules you have just learned. Be sure to blend the final consonant of the ending with the initial vowel of the word that follows.

1. It **rained** all day yesterday.
2. Yesterday my neighbor's dog **chased** a cat up a tree; I **climbed** up and took it down.
3. Edward **erased** all of the blackboards for the professor.
4. Belén **opened** a beach umbrella and **relaxed** on the sand.
5. Mother **baked** a birthday cake for each of the children.
6. The students **talked** all afternoon about their trip to Mexico last summer.
7. His father was **educated** in England, but he **lived** in Paris most of his life.
8. I **stayed** up late last night and **watched** a movie on television.
9. Larry **washed** out a sweater in warm water.
10. Our flight was **delayed** an hour because of bad weather.

incomplete dialogues using past tense of regular verbs

In completing these dialogues, be sure to pronounce the past tense ending correctly and blend it with the initial vowel of the following word. In some cases this word has been given to you. Use the correct intonation in both the question and answer.

1. **A:** How long did you wait for me at the cafeteria this noon?
   B: I _____ about _____ .

2. **A:** Did the diplomats converse in English or French?
   B: They _____ in _____ .

3. **A:** To whom did Evelyn address the letter?
   B: She _____ it to _____ .

4. **A:** In what century did Edison invent the electric light?
   B: Edison _____ .

5. **A:** What did you collect when you were a child?
   B: When I was a child I _____ .

6. **A:** How much did the package weigh?
   B: It _____ about _____ pounds.

7. **A:** About how much money did you save last year?
   B: I _____ about _____ .

8. **A:** When did the police locate the stolen car?
   B: They _____ it _____ .

Oral Practice

questions

The following questions begin with interrogative words using irregular verbs containing the sounds [i], [ɪ], [eʸ], and [ɛ].

Practice reading these questions with rising-falling intonation. Be prepared to answer the questions orally in complete sentences. The verbs are all frequently used words. If you do not know the meaning or the past tense form of a verb, look it up in your dictionary. As usual, Student A will ask Student B a question and so on.

> **NOTE TO THE INSTRUCTOR:** In some instances, you may want to have everyone in the class ask the same question.

1. How many hours did you sleep last night?
2. How many books did you read last summer?
3. What time did you leave the university yesterday?
4. What did you eat for dinner yesterday?
5. On what date did you pay your rent last month?
6. How much money did you spend on books last semester?
7. Where did you first meet your best friend?
8. How did you feel when you left your family for the first time?

dialogues

As you read these dialogues with a classmate, pay particular attention to the pronunciation of the troublesome words. Use correct intonation and blending. Discuss with your instructor who the speakers might be.

1. **A:** Do you have a favorite radio station?
   B: No. I never listen to the radio any more; I only watch television.

2. **A:** Have you studied the vocabulary from yesterday's lesson?
   B: Yes, I have. I wasn't sure what some of the words meant so I went to the library and looked all of them up.

3. **A:** Yasmine's English has improved a lot lately, hasn't it? I'm jealous of her ability to carry on a conversation with native speakers.
   B: And you know, she's studied English for only six months, too. When she arrived in February, she could hardly speak a word.

4. **A:** Ummm. This pear is sweet and juicy. Fresh pears are my favorite fruit.
   B: I don't eat pears very often. They're quite high in calories. I prefer vegetables like celery or carrots when I want a snack.

5. **A:** Good afternoon, Miss. I have an appointment with the doctor at 3:30.
   B: But, sir, you're two hours early. It's only 1:15.
   A: Please, miss. I have to see the doctor right away. I have a terrible headache and I think I have a fever. Also, I can't hear anything with my left ear. Maybe I'm getting deaf.
   B: Please have a seat. There are several patients ahead of you.
   A: Oh, well, that's OK. I'll go down to the cafeteria and get something to eat. It's better than waiting here. I'll be back later.

Written Exercises

the sounds [i], [ɪ], [eʸ], and [ɛ]

This exercise contains many of the troublesome words studied in Lessons 5 and 6. On the line to the left of each word write the correct symbol [i], [ɪ], [eʸ], or [ɛ] for the sound of the boldface vowel. If a word contains two boldface sounds, write the symbol for the second sound on the line to the right of the word.

1. ＿＿ evening	14. ＿＿ magazine	27. ＿＿ wear
2. ＿＿ favorite	15. ＿＿ change	28. ＿＿ say
3. ＿＿ pleasant	16. ＿＿ preface ＿＿	29. ＿＿ says
4. ＿＿ message ＿＿	17. ＿＿ bear	30. ＿＿ jealous
5. ＿＿ meant	18. ＿＿ key	31. ＿＿ great
6. ＿＿ necklace ＿＿	19. ＿＿ ancient	32. ＿＿ radio
7. ＿＿ senate ＿＿	20. ＿＿ sweat	33. ＿＿ danger
8. ＿＿ been	21. ＿＿ said	34. ＿＿ native
9. ＿＿ famous	22. ＿＿ paid	35. ＿＿ nation
10. ＿＿ breathe	23. ＿＿ educate ＿＿	36. ＿＿ fear
11. ＿＿ breath	24. ＿＿ threaten	37. ＿＿ pear
12. ＿＿ steak	25. ＿＿ raise	38. ＿＿ naval
13. ＿＿ again	26. ＿＿ hear	39. ＿＿ weapon

past tense endings of regular verbs

Identify the correct past tense ending [t], [d], or [ɪd], and write the symbol on the line to the left of each verb.

1. ___ ended		11. ___ used		21. ___ spelled
2. ___ planted		12. ___ erased		22. ___ passed
3. ___ threatened		13. ___ appreciated		23. ___ chased
4. ___ depended		14. ___ protected		24. ___ cleaned
5. ___ packed		15. ___ disappeared		25. ___ continued
6. ___ carried		16. ___ tried		26. ___ realized
7. ___ regulated		17. ___ decided		27. ___ decided
8. ___ taxed		18. ___ laughed		28. ___ wished
9. ___ landed		19. ___ released		29. ___ stressed
10. ___ happened		20. ___ pronounced		30. ___ excused

Homework

Make up an original dialogue with a friend using some of the troublesome words and/or the verbs on pages 51, 55–56. Your dialogue should have at least six lines: (A, B, A, B, A, B). Be prepared to present it to the class.

Appropriateness: Family Relationships

An immediate family includes the parents, children, and (sometimes) grandparents. Here is a list of words to use in the following exercises:

parents	father-in-law
mother	daughter-in-law
father	son-in-law
children	only child
siblings	orphan
brother	stepchildren
sister	stepbrother
aunt	stepsister
uncle	stepmother
cousin	stepfather
niece	half sister
nephew	half brother
grandparents	aunt by marriage
grandfather, grandpa	uncle by marriage
grandmother, grandma	relatives
great-grandparents	close relatives
grandchild	distant relatives
grandchildren	godparents: godfather, godmother
great aunt	godchild
great uncle	foster parents
in-laws	foster children
brother-in-law	adopted son
sister-in-law	adopted daughter
mother-in-law	

Study these other words:

single	retired
married	disabled
divorced	unemployed
divorcé	dead
divorcée	on maternity leave
widow	on sick leave
widower	on vacation
separated	
bachelor (unmarried man)	
fiancé	
fiancée	

In the English-speaking setting, a person's family problems are not subjects for general conversation. If you know the person very well, you may ask about the well-being of the members of the family. But you should not ask very personal questions — about topics such as family relations, mental health, or financial problems — unless the other person volunteers information.

example: How's everyone? (appropriate)
Is it true that your husband lost his job? (inappropriate)

From the list of words on pages 59–60, find the one that fits each description below.

example: Your father's sister is your aunt.

1. your brother's or sister's son, daughter
2. your father's or your mother's mother, father
3. your grandparents' parents
4. your mother and father
5. your mother, father, sisters, and brothers
6. your sister's husband
7. your brother's wife
8. the parents of your wife
9. the mother of your husband
10. the father of your wife
11. the children of your father's first wife
12. your brothers and sisters
13. daughters and sons of your mother's first husband
14. a person who has no brothers and sisters
15. a person who has no close relatives
16. your mother's or your father's sister, brother
17. your mother's brother's children
18. your grandfather's or grandmother's brother, sister
19. your mother's sister's husband
20. your uncles, aunts, grandparents
21. your mother's husband (not your real father)
22. your father's wife (not your real mother)
23. a child you baptized
24. the couple who have brought you up

Prepare a three-minute talk about your family. Refer to pages 59–60 for the vocabulary. Be prepared to answer questions related to your presentation.

The Low Front Vowel [æ] and the Low Central Vowel [ɑ]

The Sound [æ]

description of the sound

[æ] is a low front vowel. To produce this sound, push the tongue forward and let it rest on the bottom of the mouth with the tip touching the base of the lower teeth. Arch the front of the tongue slightly. Open your mouth farther than for the [ɛ] and draw your lips back toward the corners of the mouth. The muscles at the corners of the mouth as well as those in the throat at the base of the tongue should be tense. [æ] is a long sound. (You can say it for as long as you can hold your breath.) [æ] is sometimes referred to as the "happy" sound because you can smile while you say it. Try it and see. Smile and say the word *happy*. The vowel chart and the diagram show the tongue position used to produce the sound [æ].

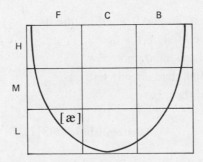

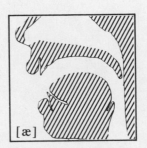

Pronounce the following words after listening to your instructor. Be sure to pull your lips back toward the corners of your mouth. Try to smile.

bat	fat	back	gas	match
cat	dad	bag	mash	laugh

Remember that all vowels are lengthened before voiced consonants. Pronounce these words after listening to your instructor.

Voiceless	*Voiced*			*Voiceless*	*Voiced*
cap	cab			half	have
cat	cad			lack	lag

listening exercises and oral practice

Distinguishing [ɛ] from [æ]

In the following exercises, your instructor will read one word from each pair of words in each group. Circle the words that you hear. Your instructor will then pronounce each pair of words. Listen carefully and then practice reading the sentences aloud, making a clear distinction between the boldface words.

[ɛ]	[æ]	[ɛ]	[æ]	[ɛ]	[æ]
bet	bat	bed	bad	men	man
pet	pat	dead	dad	pen	pan
met	mat	said	sad	hem	ham
set	sat	head	had	bend	band
left	laughed	guess	gas	send	sand

1. I'll **bet** Tom will **bat** in a home run.
2. He **sat** in front of the television **set**.
3. Sleeping in that **bed** is **bad** for my back.
4. Bill **said** he felt **sad** about leaving.
5. Ask them to **send** the **sand** today.
6. We **laughed** when he **left** the room.
7. She **set** the table and then **sat** down to rest.
8. My **pen** fell into a greasy **pan**.
9. While the **ham** cooked, I fixed the **hem** of my dress.
10. The **man** saw the **men** running away.

Your instructor will read the following sentences using one of the words in parentheses. Circle the word that you hear. Each sentence will be read twice.

1. Everyone (left, laughed) when I came in.
2. The (pen, pan) fell on the floor.
3. I'll fix the (hem, ham) tomorrow.
4. The (men, man) had already left.
5. That's a good (bet, bat).

Distinguishing [i], [ɪ], [eʸ], [ɛ], and [æ]

Your instructor will read the words from each column out of order. After each word, raise your hand and identify the word by its number. Then practice saying all the words after your instructor reads them again.

A	B	C	D
1. meat	1. beat	1. seat	1. peat
2. mitt	2. bit	2. sit	2. pit
3. mate	3. bait	3. sate	3. pate
4. met	4. bet	4. set	4. pet
5. mat	5. bat	5. sat	5. pat

spelling hints

[æ] appears initially as in *apple* and medially as in *banana*. It does not appear in a final position.

The letter *a* is usually pronounced [æ] when it appears as follows:

1. in a one-syllable word followed by one or more consonants except *w**, *r*, or *r* + another consonant.

   examples: am, cab, add, back

   exceptions: words ending in double *l* such as *all, ball, call*

   [ɔ] [ɔ] [ɔ]

2. in a stressed syllable followed by one or more consonants except *w*, *r*, or *r* + another consonant.

   examples: animal, answer, apple, damage, demand

   exceptions: father, wander, watch, water

   [ɑ]   [ɑ]   [ɑ]   [ɑ] *or* [ɔ]

> **NOTE:** The words *character, vary, various, parents,* and words in which *a* is followed by double *r* as in *carry, marry,* are also pronounced [æ] or [ɛ].

*This spelling will be taken up in lesson 12.

Some troublesome words containing the sound [æ]

man	ánswer	ánimal	hándkerchief	understánd
half	apple	national	exámine	afternoon
chance	balance	natural	exámple	láboratory
aunt**	parents	family	advántage	ágriculture
laugh	damage	character	mathemátics	

***Also [ɑnt]*

The Sound [ɑ]

description of the sound

[ɑ] is a lax low central vowel. To produce this sound, let the tip and front of the tongue lie flat in the mouth. Open your mouth wide, relax, and raise the back of the tongue slightly. The muscles of the tongue, mouth, and throat should all be relaxed. ([ɑ] is the sound you produce when the doctor wants to look at your throat and tells you to open your mouth wide and say "ah-h-h-h-h-h.") The vowel chart and the diagram show the tongue position used to produce the sound [ɑ].

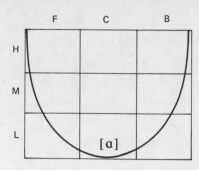

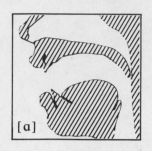

Pronounce the following words after listening to your instructor. Make sure your mouth is open wide and that the muscles are relaxed. Lengthen the vowel before the voiced sound.

Voiceless	*Voiced*		*Voiceless*	*Voiced*
cop	cob		cock	cog
cot	cod		lock	log

listening exercise and oral practice

Distinguishing [æ] from [ɑ]

In the following exercises, your instructor will read one word from each pair of words in each group. Circle the words that you hear. Your instructor will then pronounce each pair of words. Listen carefully and then practice reading the following sentences aloud, making a clear distinction between the boldface words.

[æ]	[ɑ]		[æ]	[ɑ]		[æ]	[ɑ]
hat	hot		sack	sock		packet	pocket
cat	cot		rack	rock		battle	bottle
map	mop		lack	lock		racket	rocket
cap	cop		black	block			
tap	top		stack	stock			

1. It's too **hot** to wear a **hat**.
2. When I asked for a **map**, she brought a **mop**.
3. We set the **rack** on a **rock**.
4. What a **racket** that **rocket** made when it went off.
5. Doesn't the door **lack** a **lock**?
6. That **black** car will **block** the gate.
7. He put the **packet** of pills in his **pocket**.
8. The **cop** took off his **cap**.
9. We found this **bottle** after the **battle**.
10. The **top** will come off easily if you **tap** it.

Your instructor will read the following sentences using one of the words in parentheses. Circle the word that you hear. Each sentence will be read twice.

1. This is a new (map, mop).
2. We put the (cat, cot) in the bedroom.
3. That red (sack, sock) is mine.

4. The (battle, bottle) was lost two weeks ago.
5. Set the box on that (rack, rock).

Distinguishing [i], [ɪ], [eʸ], [ɛ], [æ], and [ɑ]

Your instructor will read the words from each column out of order. After each word, raise your hand and identify the word by its number. Then practice saying all the words after your instructor reads them again.

A	B	C	D	E
1. seeks	1. seal	1. peel	1. peat	1. seat
2. six	2. sill	2. pill	2. pit	2. sit
3. sakes	3. sale	3. pail	3. pate	3. sate
4. sex	4. sell	4. pell	4. pet	4. set
5. sacks	5. Sal	5. pal	5. pat	5. sat
6. socks	6. Sol	6. Poll	6. pot	6. sot

spelling hints

In English the sound [ɑ] appears initially as in *opera*, medially as in *copy*, but it appears finally only in the word *Panama*.

Because [ɑ] is a long sound, **it appears only in strongly stressed syllables.** It is represented in writing by

a: in most stressed syllables followed by *r* or *r* + consonant
far, army, card, farther

o: as in odd, lock, mob, doll

> **NOTE:** Words in which *o* is followed by double *r* may be pronounced [ɑ] or [ɔ]: sorry, tomorrow

Some troublesome words containing the sound [ɑ]

calm	dóctor	knówledge	pólish	schólarship	astónish
palm*	collar	promise	occupy	probable	cooperate
bomb	dollar	conscious	operate	poverty	responsible
guard	commerce	model	opera	possible	apology
not	problem	modern	obvious	politics	biology
shot	honor	body	hospital	property	philosophy
heart	honest	object (n)	popular	architecture	psychology
hearty					conversátion
hearth					

*Occasionally pronounced with the l.

Oral Practice with the Sounds [ɛ], [æ], and [ɑ]

dialogues

Some of these dialogues contain words which contrast the sounds [æ] and [ɑ]. Others contain some of the troublesome words listed earlier in this lesson and review some of those from Lesson 6. Some also contain two-word verbs. Practice reading the dialogues using the correct pronunciation, intonation, and blending.

1. **A:** I heard your organization is trying to raise half a million dollars for the heart fund.
   B: Yes, in fact, the Chamber of Commerce has promised to help in the campaign.

2. **A:** How long has Anita been involved in national politics?
   B: Ever since she graduated with honors in political science.

3. **A:** Calm down! Don't be so upset! The police said you're not responsible for the accident. Here, take my handkerchief and wipe your face.
   B: But my car! I just had it washed and polished and now look at it. It'll probably cost over a hundred dollars to have it repaired. My father will be furious.
   A: Don't worry. Your father won't be angry; he'll be happy nobody was hurt. Come on, I'll drive you home.

4. **A:** I hear your friend won a large scholarship.
   B: Yes, he got $10,000 to study economics at a famous college.
   A: Is he going to Harvard by any chance?
   B: I can't remember the name of the college, but I know it's internationally famous.

5. **A:** Is your new compact car much more economical than that larger model you used to have?
   B: Oh, yes. I was astonished at how much less money I'm spending for gasoline. It operates like a dream, and it's so easy to park.
   A: You sound like an advertisement.
   B: That's true, but I really like the car; it's a pleasure to drive.

oral reading

The following sentences contain troublesome words with the sounds [æ] and [ɑ]. Practice reading these sentences aloud using the correct pronunciation, phrasing, and blending.

1. My nephew was just awarded a scholarship to the college of architecture.
2. Nancy spent five dollars for a fancy leather collar for her cat.
3. The real estate agent gave us the chance to occupy the apartment with a month's free rent.
4. Whenever Mary gives her dog a bath, she puts on her bathing suit.
5. The patient remained conscious and was cooperating with his doctors.
6. The doctor said John should be operated on as soon as possible.
7. My parents were obviously astonished when I explained the object of my visit.
8. My biology professor says there's some truth in the old proverb, "An apple a day keeps the doctor away."

substitution exercise

In the following exercise be sure to blend the past tense ending [t] with the vowel that follows.

Where did Carl stop? He stopped at the farm.

card shop
barber shop
hardware store
parking lot
doctor's office
department store
park
college
market
pharmacy
hospital
apartment

questions: irregular verbs containing the vowel sounds [æ] and [ɑ]

Practice reading these questions aloud using rising-falling intonation. Be able to answer the questions in complete sentences. Student A asks; Student B responds.

1. Where do you often have to stand in line?
2. Where do you usually hang your clothes?
3. What time did your last class begin yesterday?
4. How many glasses of water did you drink yesterday?
5. What did you forget to do yesterday? (last week?)
6. When you watch an English T.V. program, how much do you understand?
7. What kind of songs did you sing when you were a child?
8. What time did your alarm clock ring this morning?

| Written Exercise

practice with the vowels [eʸ], [ɛ], [æ], and [ɑ]

Write the correct symbol for the sound of the boldface vowel in each of these words. Where there are two lines, write the first symbol on the line to the left of the word and the second symbol on the line to the right. Only stressed syllables are involved in this exercise.

1. ___ pear	20. ___ chance	39. ___ sweat
2. ___ heart	21. ___ change	40. ___ persuade
3. ___ laugh	22. ___ danger	41. ___ examine
4. ___ guard	23. ___ nation	42. ___ breath
5. ___ guarantee	24. ___ national	43. ___ jealous
6. ___ weather	25. ___ family	44. ___ shot
7. ___ break	26. ___ advantage	45. ___ dollar
8. ___ language	27. ___ says	46. ___ answer
9. ___ example	28. ___ say	47. ___ analyze
10. ___ again	29. ___ bear	48. ___ calm
11. ___ secretary ___	30. ___ meant	49. ___ collar
12. ___ bathing	31. ___ apple	50. ___ heir
13. ___ bath	32. ___ banana	51. ___ far
14. ___ favorite	33. ___ native	52. ___ hair
15. ___ famous	34. ___ holiday ___	53. ___ wear
16. ___ April	35. ___ half	54. ___ understand
17. ___ fatal	36. ___ carry	55. ___ thank
18. ___ commerce	37. ___ nobody	56. ___ have
19. ___ patient	38. ___ great	57. ___ catalogue
		58. ___ cotton

Articles of Clothing

vocabulary

Study these words to use in the following exercises.

Outer Clothes for Men and Women	*Footwear*	*Hosiery*
dress	shoes	hose
blouse	slippers	socks
skirt	loafers	stockings
suit	oxfords	pantyhose
jumper	boots	sport socks
three-piece suit	riding boots	dress socks
vest	pumps	knee socks
evening gown	high heels	tennis socks
nightgown	low heels	athletic socks
cocktail dress	walking shoes	
pajamas	sandals	
bathrobe	thong sandals	
housecoat	workshoes	
lounging pajamas	moccasins	
T-shirt	tennis shoes	
long-sleeved blouse	sneakers	
long-sleeved shirt	platform shoes	
short-sleeved blouse	wedgies	
short-sleeved shirt	clogs	
sleeveless blouse		
sport shirt		
polo shirt		
dress shirt		
formal dress shirt		
pants		
slacks		
trousers		
jeans		
dungarees		
overalls		
jumpsuit		
shorts		
athletic shorts		
Bermuda shorts		
bathing suit		
swimsuit		
bathing trunks		
leisure suit		
jacket		
sport jacket		
poncho		
raincoat		
tuxedo		
dinner jacket		
pants suit		

Accessories	*Jewelry*	*Underwear for Men and Women*
belt	necklace	T-shirt
tie belt	chain	undershirt
string belt	pendant	athletic shirt
handbag	string of pearls	shorts
purse	beads	boxer shorts
shoulder bag	charms	jockey shorts
tote bag	bracelet	briefs
bookbag	bangle bracelet	brassiere (bra)
briefcase	ankle bracelet	panties
scarf	wristwatch	slip
kerchief	earrings	half slip
handkerchief	engagement ring	girdle
umbrella	wedding ring	panty girdle
bathing cap	class ring	
sunglasses	pinkie ring	
	birthstone	
	signet ring	

Add any other items of clothing that come up in class discussion.

Colors

blue: baby, navy, peacock, teal, royal, marine
red: maroon, wine, rust, Titian red
pink: shocking, rose, dusty, melon, coral, peach, strawberry
yellow: lemon, gold, daffodil
orange: red-orange, salmon-colored
white: off-white, beige, taupe, tan, khaki, cream
brown: tan, cinnamon
green: lime, Kelly, emerald, olive, hunter, forest, chartreuse, spring
purple: lavender, lilac, orchid, mauve
black: jet black, blue black
gray: slate, charcoal, silver

Common Adjectives Used to Describe Colors

pale, bright, light, medium, dark, deep, yellowish, reddish, etc.

Fabrics

cotton	synthetics	rayon
silk	polyester	acrylic
wool	nylon	Lycra
linen	Banlon	

Homework

questions for a class discussion of clothing

directions: Using the vocabulary listed on the previous pages as a guide, answer these questions. Remember: the noun *clothing* is singular, but the noun *clothes* as well as *pants, panties, shorts* and other synonyms for these nouns are plural and require a plural verb.

1. What articles of clothing are you wearing right now?
2. What color are your pants (jeans)?
3. Is the person on your left carrying a briefcase, a totebag, or a handbag?
4. What accessories are you wearing?
5. What is the professor wearing?
6. What jewelry is the person on your right wearing?
7. What colors is the person sitting opposite you wearing?
8. What colors do you prefer for everyday clothes?
9. What colors do you usually wear when you are dressed up?
10. What clothing do you wear when you are at home?
11. What do you usually wear when you go to the movies?
12. What sort of clothing do you usually wear to come to the university?
13. What do you wear when you go to a party?
14. (For women) Do you like to wear evening gowns? On what occasions would you wear them?
15. (For men) Do you like to wear a suit? A tuxedo? On what occasions would you wear it?
16. Do you jog? Play tennis? Basketball? Volleyball? What do you wear?
17. What article of clothing do you put on first when you get dressed in the morning?
18. What articles of clothing do you take off first when you get undressed at night?
19. Is there any particular article or kind of clothing that you dislike to wear?
20. (For women) Do you prefer to wear pants or dresses?

homework

Write a physical description of yourself in which you include the answers to the following questions, though not necessarily in the order listed. Do not give your name. When you come to class the instructor will collect your description and give it to someone else to read. The class will try to guess whom your description fits.

> **NOTE:** When you write your description at home, remember to write clearly so that whoever gets your description can read it easily.

1. How tall are you?
2. How much do you weigh?
3. Would you describe yourself as thin, heavy, plump, tall, short, or medium height?
4. What clothes are you wearing today? What colors?
5. What accessories are you wearing?
6. Do you wear glasses? What color are your eyes?
7. What color is your hair? Is it long, short, straight, curly, wavy?
8. Are you usually smiling or are you usually serious?
9. Are you a talkative person or are you usually quiet?
10. Do you usually sit near the window, the door, or the blackboard?

Appropriateness: Shopping for Clothes

dialogue

Miss Walters: May I help you?
Helen: Do you have any evening dresses?
Miss Walters: Yes, we do. Come this way, please . . . What size do you wear?
Helen: 9-10.
Miss Walters: All the 9-10s are in this rack over here.
Helen: Oh, that red-orange one is stunning and not too expensive. May I try it on?
Miss Walters: Why certainly.
Helen: Where's the dressing room?
Miss Walters: Behind the counter, to your left.
(A few minutes later.)
Miss Walters: How did it fit?
Helen: Very well! I'll take it.
Miss Walters: Cash or charge?
Helen: Do you accept personal checks?
Miss Walters: Yes, we do. Do you have a driver's license?
Helen: Here it is.
Miss Walters: Very well. Please pay the cashier.
Helen: Thank you very much.

useful expressions

Below you will find a number of expressions related to different questions you might have to ask when shopping for clothes.

Asking for an item

Where can I find . . .?
Do you sell . . .?
Do you have any . . .?
Would you show me what you have in . . .?
Could you help me with these . . . , please?
May I look at . . .?
Do you happen to know where I can find . . .?

You can also use the following expressions to ask for an item:

I'd like to see what you have in . . .
I'm looking for . . .
I'm interested in seeing some . . .

> **NOTE:**   If you are only looking at the items in the store and the salesperson asks "May I help you?" you should answer, "No, thank you. I'm just looking." Otherwise, preface the expressions above with "Yes, please."

Asking for information about an item

Is it machine-washable?
Will this material wear well?
Is it best to dry clean this?
What colors (sizes) does it come in? (the blouse, the tie)
Do you have it in . . .? (blue, green, polyester, cotton)

Trying on something

Where may I try it on?
Do you have a dressing room?
Where's the dressing room?
May I try it on?

Asking about prices

How much is this?
What do these _____ cost?
What's the price for those _____ ?
What're you asking for these _____ ?
What would the whole set cost?
Do you have something for less?
Is this _____ *for* sale?*
Is this _____ *on* sale?**

*It is there for people to buy.
**Selling at a lower price.*

> **NOTE:** If you decide not to buy an item after looking at it or trying it on, you may use
> these expressions:
>
> "Thank you, but that's not what I'm looking for."
> or
> "I think I'll wait. Thanks anyway."

At the cashier's desk

Do you accept credit cards? (personal checks)
Which credit cards do you accept?
Do you have change for a fifty (dollar bill)?
Will you please gift-wrap it?

practice

Get together with a classmate and take the roles of salesperson and customer. Imagine one of you is a customer shopping for a particular item from the list on pages 68–69. Ask the other person questions about the item: size, color, price, etc. If you are the salesperson, try to persuade the customer to buy the item.

Review: Lessons 1—7

Listening Exercises

word stress

Your instructor will read these words. Put a check (✔) in column 1, 2, 3, or 4 depending upon which syllable of the word receives the primary accent. Follow the example. Your instructor will read each word twice. Listen carefully.

Word	First Syllable	Second Syllable	Third Syllable	Fourth Syllable
1. decade	✔			
2. locate				
3. afternoon				
4. organize				
5. record (n)				
6. cooperation				
7. representation				
8. professor				
9. committee				
10. engine				
11. police				
12. foreign				
13. comfort				

Table continued

Word	First Syllable	Second Syllable	Third Syllable	Fourth Syllable
14. promise				
15. Catholic				
16. government				
17. interesting				
18. understand				
19. emergency				
20. politics				

vowel discrimination

Your instructor will read the following sentences twice using one of the words in the parentheses. Circle the word that you hear.

1. That's the (list, least) we need.
2. I want you to (feel, fill) this pot.
3. The students (laughed, left) when the professor arrived.
4. The old man (slipped, slept) on the steps last night.
5. The man lost his (ship, sheep) in the storm.
6. The (leather, lather) is very thick.
7. Did you fix the (hem, ham) for me?
8. The boys are making a (rocket, racket) in the back yard.
9. There's a hole in the (sock, sack).
10. Peter is (selling, sailing) his boat today.
11. Please set the box on the (rock, rack).
12. Jane put the (pin, pen) in her pocket.
13. I'm sure I put the (pen, pan) on the table.
14. The cook (tested, tasted) the fish.
15. I bought a new (map, mop) today.
16. It was too dark to see the (men, man).
17. I'll buy the (meat, mitt) tomorrow.
18. Please mail (this, these) for me.
19. There was a (battle, bottle) here last night.
20. Those (heels, hills) are very high.

Written Exercise

vowel sounds: front vowels [i], [ɪ], [eʸ], [ɛ], [æ], and [ɑ]

Remember that the same combination of letters may have more than one pronunciation. Also don't forget that in an unstressed syllable the vowel is reduced to [ɪ] or [ə]. Pronounce each word; then write the symbol for the sound of the boldface vowel.

1. ___ heart	11. ___ various (2 possibilities)	21. ___ fever
2. ___ wear	12. ___	22. ___ favorite
3. ___ year	13. ___ nature	23. ___ again
4. ___ steak	14. ___ natural	24. ___ secretary
5. ___ eat	15. ___ character (2 possibilities)	25. ___ secret ___
6. ___ leather	16. ___	26. ___ fatal
7. ___ said	17. ___ project (v)	27. ___ field
8. ___ paid	18. ___ object (n) ___	28. ___ filled
9. ___ captain ___	19. ___ women ___	29. ___ feel
10. ___ knowledge ___	20. ___ necklace ___	30. ___ fell

Dialogues Using the Front Vowels and [ɑ]

Read these dialogues with a classmate. Use correct intonation, stress, and blending. Your instructor may ask you to memorize one of them.

1. **Jack:** Hey, Bill, I hear you went on a hunting trip to Canada. How was it?
   Bill: Great! But that's the last time I'll ever go hunting. I had a bad experience with a bear.
   Jack: A bear! What happened? Did he chase you up a tree?
   Bill: No, not exactly. I stopped to put on my jacket because the weather turned cold. I got separated from my friend somehow. Suddenly there was this black bear about twenty yards away from me.
   Jack: What did you do? Shoot him?
   Bill: No, unfortunately I didn't have the right kind of weapon for that. I just lay down quietly. When he came close, I held my breath and pretended to be dead. He just sniffed at me and went away. I hardly dared even breathe for about ten minutes. I was too scared. Then I got out of there as fast as I could. No more hunting for me!

2. **A:** What's happened to your friend Joe? I haven't seen him since last April.
   B: He's in the Navy.
   A: The Navy's OK, I guess. It's supposed to be a good way to see the world, but it's not for me.
   B: I thought you were interested in sailing.
   A: I am, but I only like to watch sailboat races. I have such a weak stomach, I could get seasick in a bathtub.

Past Tense of Irregular Verbs Containing the Front Vowel Sounds

Practice reading these questions aloud using rising-falling intonation. Be prepared to answer the questions orally in complete sentences. If you don't know the meaning of a verb or its past tense form, remember to look it up in your dictionary. As usual, Student A will ask a question, Student B will answer, and so on. In some instances, your instructor may want to have everyone in the class answer the same question.

1. When did you do your English assignment for today?
2. What did you give your best friend for his or her birthday last year?
3. Where did you keep your favorite toys when you were a child?
4. How did you feel after you had finished all your exams last semester?
5. What time did you leave your home this morning? afternoon?
6. When did you last speak to someone on the telephone?
7. How much did you spend for food last week?
8. About how many pages did you read for your various assignments yesterday?
9. What did you say when you first saw your classmates today?
10. Where did you eat lunch yesterday?

The Central Vowel [ə]

The Sound [ə]

description of the sound

[ə] is an unrounded mid-central vowel. To produce this sound, let your tongue lie completely at rest, and part your lips only slightly. [ə] is a very short vowel and can be produced with very little effort. It is often referred to as the "schwa."

The IPA uses the symbol [ʌ] to represent this sound in stressed syllables, but for purposes of simplification, only the symbol [ə] will be used in this book. The vowel chart and the diagram show the tongue position used to produce the sound [ə].

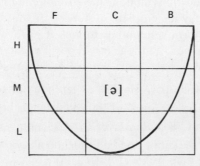

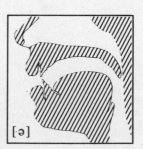

Pronounce these words after listening to your instructor. Relax. There is a complete lack of tension in this sound.

run   come   bus   son

Remember: the vowel is lengthened before a voiced consonant. Pronounce these words after listening to your instructor.

Voiceless	*Voiced*		*Voiceless*	*Voiced*
cup	cub		luck	lug
but	bud		bus	buzz

listening exercises and oral practice

Your instructor will read some of the words from the following sections. Circle the words you hear. Then pronounce all the words in each section after your instructor reads them again.

Distinguishing [ɛ] from [ə]

[ɛ]	[ə]		[ɛ]	[ə]
bet	but		hem	hum
bed	bud		ten	ton
deck	duck		many	money
beg	bug			
net	nut			

Distinguishing [ə] from [ɑ]

[ə]	[ɑ]		[ə]	[ɑ]		[ə]	[ɑ]
cup	cop		rub	rob		color	collar
shut	shot		putt	pot		rubber	robber
nut	not		hut	hot		wonder	wander
luck	lock		duck	dock			

Distinguishing [æ], [ɑ], and [ə]

Your instructor will read the words from each column out of order. After each word, raise your hand and identify the word by its number.

A	*B*	*C*	*D*	*E*	*F*	*G*	*H*
1. cap	1. cab	1. cat	1. cad	1. lack	1. bag	1. hat	1. gnat
2. cop	2. cob	2. cot	2. cod	2. lock	2. bog	2. hot	2. not
3. cup	3. cub	3. cut	3. cud	3. luck	3. bug	3. hut	3. nut

Your instructor will read the following sentences using one of the words in parentheses. Circle the word that you hear. Each sentence will be read twice. Then read the sentences aloud. Be sure you make a distinction between the words circled. Notice that each sentence must have two words circled.

1. There's a (duck, dock) on the (duck, dock).
2. What is the (color, collar) of your shirt (color, collar)?
3. Give the (cup, cop) a (cup, cop) of coffee.
4. It's (hot, hut) inside the (hot, hut).
5. Please try your (lock, luck) with this (lock, luck).
6. I (wander, wonder) where he'll (wander, wonder) next.
7. Please take that (cot, cat) off the (cot, cat).
8. The (robber, rubber) wore (robber, rubber) boots.

9. This fruit is (nut, not) a (nut, not).
10. When he heard the (shot, shut), he (shot, shut) the door.

spelling hints

The sound [ə] in stressed syllables may appear initially as in *onion* or medially as in *mother*. It does not appear finally.
[ə] is represented in writing by:

u plus one or more consonants as in: **sun**, m**ust**
o plus one or more consonants as in: **son**, m**onth**
ou plus one or more consonants as in: c**ountry**

Some troublesome words containing the sound [ə] in stressed syllables

cut	cústom	púnish	does	cólor	touch	blood*
club	funny	study	done	comfort	enóugh	flood*
lunch	hundred	subject	front	dozen	rough	
much	hungry	summer	love	money	tough	
must	husband	struck	month	nothing	cóusin	
shut	public	uncle	some	mother	country	
	punctual		one	other	trouble	
				brother	young	

The words blood and flood are the only words in which the letters oo are pronounced [ə].

the sound [ə] in unstressed syllables

Unstressed [ə] and unstressed [ɪ] are the most frequently used vowels in English, and they are often interchangeable. For example, you can say [bɪlív] or [bəlív] and [mínɪt] or [mínət]. Any vowel in an unstressed syllable may be reduced to either [ə] or [ɪ]. (See pages 7–8.)

1. The indefinite articles *a* and *an* are pronounced [ə] and [ən]. *A* [ə] precedes a word beginning with a consonant, and *an* [ən] precedes a word beginning with a vowel.

A man is coming. **An** old man is coming.

2. The definite article *the* is pronounced [ðə] before a word beginning with a consonant, and usually [ðɪ] before a word beginning with a vowel.

A man is coming down **the** street.
[ə]   [ðə]

An old man is coming down **the** other side of the street.
[ən]   [ðɪ]

3. The prepositions *of* and *to* are usually unstressed and therefore are pronounced [əv] and [tə]. (*To* is sometimes pronounced [tʊ] before a word beginning with a vowel.)

It's time **to** get out **of** bed.   I went **to** open the door.
   [tə]   [əv]   [tʊ]

4.   Both initial and final unstressed *a* are pronounced [ə].

agrée	amóng	sóda	umbrélla	América
attack	ago	sofa	vanilla	África
away	across	extra	banana	Aśia
accept	alive	papa	idea	Austrália
again	about	mama		Antárctica
above	another	comma		Chína

5.   Unstressed *col*, *com*, and *con* are pronounced [kəl], [kəm], and [kən].

colléct	compléte	contáin
collision	compare	connect
colonial	command	contínue
colossal	commíttee	condition

6.   Unstressed *sub*, *suc*, *sup*, and *sus* are pronounced [səb], [sək], [səp], and [səs].

subjéct (v)	subtráct	succéed	supplý	suspéct (v)
submit	subscribe	success	support	suspend
submerge	subscription	succession	suppose	sustain
subside			suppress	suspicious

7.   The unstressed endings *em*, *om*, *ome*, *en*, and *on* are pronounced [əm] and [ən]; this includes all of the past participles of irregular verbs ending in *en*, such as *given*. However, in those words in which *en*, *em*, *on*, or *om* are preceded by [t], [d], or [z], the final syllable may also be pronounced as a syllabic *n* [n̩] or syllabic *m* [m̩].

sýstem	cústom	háppen	séven	wéapon
problem	seldom	dozen	heaven	common
	symptom	sudden	eléven	person
	handsome	oven		lesson
	welcome			reason
				season

8.   The unstressed ending *ous* is pronounced [əs].

fámous	sérious	delícious	indústrious
nervous	curious	religious	mysterious
jealous	generous	ambitious	continuous
anxious	numerous	nutritious	repetítious
precious	dangerous	malicious	superstitious

9.   The unstressed endings *ment*, *ent*, and *ant* are pronounced [mənt] and [ənt].

móment	apártment	predícament	íncident
argument	department	acknowledgment	accident
management	excitement	assistant	president
government	development	attendant	resident
agréement	experiment	consistent	
		resistent	

10.   The unstressed endings *ance* and *ence* are pronounced [əns].

assístance	acquáintance	ínfluence	expérience
assurance	acceptance	confidence	coincidence
insurance	appliance	preference	incompetence
attendance	importance		

11.   As the second element of a compound noun, *man* is usually reduced to [mən].

fíreman	sálesman	géntleman	cháirman
postman	watchman	congressman	workman
			políceman

12.   The unstressed endings *al* and *el* and the unusual *il* are all pronounced [əl].

céntral	áctual	sócial	colónial
moral	annual	special	historical
plural	casual	matérial	political
final	manual	indústrial	electrical
	usual		

púpil	ángel	géneral	ánimal
evil	towel	natural	hospital
civil	vowel	cereal	typical
	quarrel	ordinal	radical
		cardinal	practical

13.   The unstressed endings *able* and *ible* are pronounced [əbḷ].

próbable	agréeable	póssible	incrédible
vegetable	reliable	terrible	responsible
syllable	dependable	horrible	
comfortable	respectable	sensible	

14.   The unstressed ending *ful* is pronounced [fəl].

hélpful	yóuthful	wásteful	succéssful
careful	colorful	faithful	delightful
grateful	wonderful	useful	

15.   The auxiliary verb *can* is pronounced [kən] except when it comes at the end of phrase or a sentence, or in a tag (echo) question. The negative *can't* is always pronounced [kænt].

He **can** act.   He **can't** act.   He **can't** act but she **cán**.
  [kən]   [kænt]   [kænt]   [kæn]

He **can't** act, **cán** he?
  [kænt]   [kæn]

Oral Practice

using *can* and *can't*

These very simple exercises will allow you to concentrate on the correct pronunciation of *can* and *can't*. Student A will ask the question and Student B will respond. Answer the questions according to the examples using words from the lists. Be sure to pronounce *can* [kən] and *can't* [kænt]. Practice blending.

1. Can he *hunt*?   Yes, he can hunt.
   [kən]   [kən]

        run
        jump
        come
        study
        conduct
        command
        succeed
        progress

2. Can she *run* it?   No, she can't run it.   *or*
   [kən]   [kænt]

        accept   Yes, she can run it.
        arrange   [ʃikən]
        brush
        touch
        submit
        support
        supply
        cut

3. Example: A: I can swim; can you?
              [kən]   [kən]

           B: No, I can't, but I can jog.
                [kænt]   [kən]

   A: I can _____. Can you?   B: No, I can't, but I can ____.
      [aıkən]   [kən]   [kænt]   [aıkən]

        sing   dance
        cook   sew
        play tennis   play volleyball
             dominoes   chess
             baseball   basketball
             soccer   hockey
             the piano   the violin
             flute   clarinet
             trumpet   trombóne
        speak French   speak German
             Italian   Portuguese
             Chinese   Japanése

reducing unstressed vowels

These very simple exercises will allow you to concentrate on reducing the vowels in the unstressed syllables.

1. What do you want? I _____ another cup of coffee.

> lump of butter
> bunch of bananas
> month's vacation
> lemon cupcake
> dozen oranges
> cup of nuts
> vanilla soda
> hundred dollars

2. Answer this question according to the example. Choose words from the list or any others you can think of that begin or end with an unstressed *a*.

example: Was hé from Índia. Nó, he wásn't. He was from Líbya.
[wəzi]

Was he from _____ ? No, he wasn't. He was from _____ .

Rússia	Zámbia	Chína	Kénya
Tunísia	Iceland	Arábia	Ugánda
Cánada	England	Indonésia	Gréenland
Gambia	Scotland	Ireland	New Zéaland
Burma	Holland	Finland	Póland

oral reading: [ə] in stressed and unstressed syllables

Read the sentences with correct rhythm and intonation. Reduce the vowels in the function words *of*, *a*, etc., and in all the unstressed syllables. Pay particular attention to the troublesome words.

1. In some cultures, superstitious people consider seven a lucky number.
2. I'd like some more of that delicious custard.
3. My mother has dozens of cousins in the country.
4. In just one month, my brother doubled the money he invested.
5. Some of the pupils had trouble understanding the professor.
6. I suspect that young couple in front of us is on their honeymoon.
7. On Sunday, it's our custom to eat brunch instead of breakfast and lunch.
8. Her husband got a substitute position as an instructor of political science.

mini-dialogues

These dialogues also contain many of the troublesome words containing the [ə] sound. Pay special attention to unstressing and blending.

1. **A:** Can you come over for a couple of hours?
   B: No, I can't. I promised Mother I'd cut the grass.
2. **A:** Can you come to lunch with us?
   B: I'd love to, but I have to rush right home.

3. **A:** Can you go to the movies with us tonight?
   B: No, I can't. I have to study my biology assignment.

4. **A:** I can't get accustomed to riding the public buses. They're so slow and uncomfortable.
   B: And they're so unreliable. I don't understand why the bus company doesn't run more extra buses during the rush hours.

5. **A:** Does your cousin have enough insurance?
   B: Yes, he just took out another hundred-thousand-dollar policy a month ago.

Homework

Tell the class about something funny that happened to you recently.

Written Exercise: Practice with Vowels [ɛ], [æ], [ɑ], and [ə]

Write the symbol representing the vowel sound of the boldface letter or letters.

1. ____ nothing	13. ____ not	25. ____ touch
2. ____ young	14. ____ nut	26. ____ blood
3. ____ progress (v) ____	15. ____ probable ____	27. ____ color
4. ____ study	16. ____ project (v)	28. ____ collar
5. ____ preface	17. ____ jealous ____	29. ____ banana ____
6. ____ country	18. ____ possible ____	30. ____ national ____
7. ____ local	19. ____ possess ____	31. ____ collect ____
8. ____ doesn't	20. ____ costume	32. ____ ambitious
9. ____ command ____	21. ____ custom	33. ____ oven
10. ____ cousin	22. ____ an onion ____	34. ____ committee
11. ____ object (v) ____	23. ____ apple	35. ____ animal ____
12. ____ object (n)	24. ____ the cover ____	36. ____ character

Appropriateness: Asking for a Favor and Requesting Permission

dialogues

Asking for a Favor

1. **A:** Can you lend me a dime, please. I have to make a phone call.
   B: I'm sorry. I don't have any change. You can get some at the service desk.
   A: Thanks anyway.

2. **A:** Can you lend me your dictionary a minute. I have to look up some words.
   B: I'm sorry. I can't let you have it right now. I'm using it myself.
   A: OK.

3. **A:** Can you lend me a couple of bucks? I have to get something at the drugstore.
   B: I'm sorry. I can't. I don't have any money.
   A: Thanks anyway.

4. **A:** Excuse me, Judy, could you lend me a cup of sugar? I forgot to get some at the supermarket this afternoon.
   B: Sure, come on in. Help yourself. I don't use much sugar anymore. I'm trying to reduce.
   A: Thanks. I really appreciate it.

Requesting Permission

5. **A:** Can I please hand in my assignment tomorrow, professor? I have to copy it over.
   B: Yes, you can put it in my box in the English office.
   A: Thank you, professor.

6. **A:** Do you mind if I smoke here?
   B: Yes, I do.
   A: OK, I'm sorry.

7. **A:** May I speak to you for a moment after class, professor?
   B: Of course you may. Come to my office. It's much quieter there.
   A: Thank you, professor.

8. **A:** May I borrow your textbook until tomorrow, professor?
   B: Of course you may. Here it is. Be sure to return it by seven o'clock tomorrow.
   A: Thank you very much. I'll bring it back early tomorrow morning.

9. **A:** May we reserve this room for a meeting, Dean Williams?
   B: I'm sorry; it's already been reserved by another group. You can use Room 106 if you wish.
   A: Thank you, sir.

10. **A:** May I have the scotch tape, please?
    B: Certainly. Here it is.
    A: Thanks.

11. **A:** May I park here, officer?
    B: No, you can't. This is a restricted zone for trucks. Didn't you see the sign?
    A: I'm sorry. I didn't see it.

12. **A:** Hi, Sue. Could I borrow your vacuum cleaner for a few minutes?
    B: I'm sorry. I'm using it right now. I'll call you when I'm through with it.
    A: OK. Thank you.

13. **A:** Can I use your car tonight, Sis? I have an important date.
    B: Yes, you can use it, but you'll have to put some gas in it. The tank's almost empty.
    A: Can you lend me some money for the gas? I'm broke. I've got just enough for a couple of sodas.
    B: I can lend you five dollars, but you'll have to give it back on payday.
    A: OK. That's a deal.

14. **A:** Could I borrow Tuesday's newspaper, please?
    B: I'm sorry. I just threw it out. Did you want to look up anything in particular?
    A: There was an ad for a tour to Bermuda at reduced rates, but I'm confused about the dates.
    B: Let's look in today's paper. Those tours are usually advertised more than once.

useful expressions

Asking for a favor

"Can you lend me _____?"
"Can you call me _____?"
"Could you lend me _____?"
"Could you call me _____?"

Requesting permission

Informal: "Can I use your _____?"
            "Can I sit _____?"

More polite: "Could I speak _____ ?"
Very polite: "May I come in _____ ?"
                "May I borrow _____ ?"
                "May I sit _____ ?"

Here are other polite expressions you may use when asking for a favor or requesting permission. Even if your request is denied, always remember to say "thank you."

"Is it all right if I use this pen?"
"Do you mind if I take a piece of paper?"
"Would it be all right if I sat here?"
"Would you mind lending me your notebook?"
"I wonder if I could borrow your hair dryer?"

practice

1. Using the word *can*, ask the person who sits next to you to lend you something of his or hers: a book, a dictionary, a pen, etc. He or she will give an appropriate answer, either affirmative or negative. Each person must ask for a different item.

2. Your instructor will ask you to get together with another student and pretend that you are an instructor, a secretary, a postal worker, a police officer, a doctor, a security guard, a lab technician, etc. Your partner will request your permission to do various things such as using the phone, taking a paper, leaving the room, smoking, etc.

example: A: Mr. Wood, may I leave the class a little early today?
               B: Why certainly.

The High Central Vowel [ɚ]

The Sound [ɚ]

description of the sound

[ɚ] is a high central vowel. In order to produce the sound, bring the blade of the tongue high up in the center of the mouth and very close to the hard palate. Round the lips and touch the upper back teeth with the sides of the tongue. (The IPA uses the symbol [ɝ] to represent this sound in stressed syllables.) The vowel chart and the diagram show the tongue position used to produce the sound [ɚ].

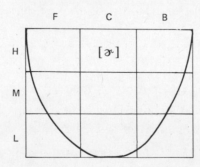

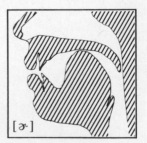

Pronounce these words after listening to your instructor. Notice that in the first two words the sound [ɚ] appears in a stressed syllable and in the last two in an unstressed syllable.

vérb   wórk   láter   dóllar

The sound [ɚ] is lengthened before a voiced consonant. Listen to the following examples, then pronounce these words yourself.

Voiceless	*Voiced*
hurt	heard
surf	serve

listening exercises and oral practice

1. Your instructor will read some of the words from the following sections. Circle the words you hear. Then pronounce all the words in each section after your instructor reads them again.

Distinguishing [ɚ] from [ɪr]

[ɚ]	[ɪr]	[ɚ]	[ɪr]
her	hear	per	pier
fur	fear	bird	beard
stir	steer	purse	pierce

Distinguishing [ɚ] from [ɛr]

[ɚ]	[ɛr]	[ɚ]	[ɛr]	[ɚ]	[ɛr]
her	hair	were	wear	stir	stare
fur	fair	per	pear		

Distinguishing [ɚ] from [ɑr]

[ɚ]	[ɑr]	[ɚ]	[ɑr]	[ɚ]	[ɑr]
fur	far	burn	barn	heard	hard
stir	star	firm	farm	hurt	heart

2. As your instructor reads these sentences, underline the syllables in which you hear [ɚ]. Each sentence will be read twice.

    1.   Bob took his sister to the circus last Thursday.
    2.   The young doctor bought some comfortable furniture from her neighbor.
    3.   The actors couldn't find work in the theater.
    4.   The girl looked up the meaning of the third word in the first sentence.
    5.   I bought a dollar's worth of sugar cookies.
    6.   This merchant offers courteous service to everyone.

3. Your instructor will read these sentences using one of the words in parentheses. Circle the word that you hear. Each sentence will be read twice.

    1.   She told me to (steer, stir) it carefully.
    2.   How long has he had that (bird, beard)?
    3.   All the (furs, fares) are more expensive this year.
    4.   His father manages a large (firm, farm).
    5.   I always confuse the word (her, hair) with the word (her, hair).

4. Read the following sentences after listening to your instructor. Be sure you make a distinction between the boldface words.

    1.   The man with a **beard** has a **bird** in a cage.

2. The girls **were** going to **wear** new skirts.
3. I couldn't **hear her**.
4. She **stared** at me as I **stirred** the custard.
5. **Her hair** is very curly.
6. Those shoes cost thirty dollars **per pair**.
7. That music is **hardly heard** at all any more.

spelling hints

The Sound [ɚ] in Stressed Syllables

Stressed [ɚ] appears initially as in *early*, medially as in *nurse*, and finally as in *fur*. Stressed [ɚ] is most often represented in writing by:

er or *er* + consonant: prefer, fern, clerk
ur or *ur* + consonant: occur, church, Thursday
ir or *ir* + consonant: stir, first, confirm

The combination of *w* plus *or* is almost always pronounced [wɚ] as in *word, work*. However, the past tense and past participle of wear are pronounced *wore* [wɔr] and *worn* [wɔrn].

Some troublesome words containing stressed [ɚ]

or	er		ur		ir	
word	term	nurse	húrry	stir	círcle	
work	verb	hurt	húrricane	firm	circus	
world	sérvice	burn	occúr	bird	dirty	
worm	certain	church	Thúrsday	thírty	virgin	
wórry	person	púrpose		thirsty	birthday	
worse	nervous	púrple				
worst	dessért					
	emérgency					

ear	*our*
earn	cóurage
learn	courteous
heard	courtesy
earth	colonel [kɚnəl]
search	journey
eárly	journalist

The Sound [ɚ] in Unstressed Syllables

Unstressed [ɚ] appears medially as in *surprise* and finally as in *súgar*. It does not appear initially.
[ɚ] is usually represented in writing by:

er or *er* + consonant: father, exercise
ar or *ar* + consonant: dollar, forward
or or *or* + consonant: color, comfort
ure   : picture, nature

Some troublesome words containing unstressed [ɚ]

er		ar			or	
páper	módern	sólar	súgar	fórward	cólor	góvernor
murder	exercise	grammar	similar	backward	doctor	senator
zipper	manager	collar	regular	standard	favor	scissors
perháps	understánd	dollar		standard	flavor	comfort

ure

pícture	fúture	tréasure	árchitecture
nature	pleasure	législature	líterature
culture	measure	ágriculture	témperature

Unusual Spelling for Unstressed [ɚ]

cupboard [kə́bɚd]   soldier [so^wldʒɚ]   acre [e^ykɚ]   iron [áɪɚn]

> **NOTE:**   [ɚ] is often added to nouns and verbs to form new nouns ending in *er* or *or*. Can you add some to the list?

love	lóver		compóse	compóser
jog	jogger		act	áctor
play	player		sail	sailor
sing	singer		góvern	governor
swim	swimmer		diréct	diréctor

Oral Practice

These exercises have been made very simple to allow you to concentrate on producing a good [ɚ] sound and on practicing blending and correct stress. Make the necessary substitutions in the following exercises.

1. In this exercise one student will read the statement that appears after Student A. The next student will then add *er* or *or*, both pronounced [ɚ], to the basic form of the verb and place it after the noun to form a compound noun. Notice in the example below how the noun *cigarettes* is changed from plural to singular; that is, the *s* is dropped. Do not forget to add the indefinite articles *a* or *an*.

example: Student A: If he smokes *cigarettes*, then . . .
Student B: He's a *cigarette* smoker.

designs fashions	keeps a zoo
tells fortunes	pays taxes
plays baseball	teaches languages
collects garbage	keeps books
plays the piano	directs a bank
sings opera	lifts weights
keeps house	wins prizes
conducts orchestras	

Can you think of any other combination of verb and noun that may become a compound noun? Now try the next exercise.

2. If it *cleans rugs*, then it's (a, an) *rug cleaner*.

records tapes	sharpens pencils
plays records	lights cigarettes
opens cans	washes dishes
makes ice	conditions air
blows hair	dries clothes
cuts paper	removes spots
holds keys	dries hair

Can you add others to the list?

dialogues containing troublesome words with the sound [ɚ]

1. **A:** What's Gertrude's address? I'd like to look her up.
   B: She lives at 530 West 33rd Street.

2. **A:** I heard you were both sick this summer.
   B: We were, but we're both feeling much better now, thank you.

3. **A:** Who's that girl sitting in the third seat in the first row?
   B: Her name is Shirley. She's a nursing major.

4. **A:** Have you ordered yet, Colonel Richards?
   B: Yes, I ordered a cheeseburger and a side order of French fries.
   A: What're you having for dessert?
   B: Vanilla custard.

5. **A:** How much did you earn last summer, Bertha?
   B: Thirty dollars a week, and I worked only on Thursdays and Saturdays.

6. **A:** The shirts weren't dirty, were they?
   B: Yes, they were, and so were the skirts.

7. **A:** Do you work in the afternoons?
   B: Yes, I work as a clerk in a furniture store.

8. **A:** Where are you working now?
   B: I'm working as a clerk in a personnel office.
   A: Are you happy there?
   B: No, I was happier when I was working at the supermarket.

oral reading

Read the following sentences which contain troublesome words with the sound [ɚ].
Make correct use of stress, rhythm, intonation, and blending.

1. Gertrude bought that skirt in the Virgin Islands.
2. There's an old proverb that says that the early bird catches the worm.
3. The third hurricane last November was the worst ever.
4. The nurses showed great courage during the emergency.
5. Life in this modern world is full of surprises.
6. She's a senator in the New Jersey state legislature.
7. That's her daughter standing by the mirror.
8. Do you need another pair of scissors?
9. Herman's a popular singer and band director.
10. We need thirty-five dollars for the party favors.

Written Exercise: Review of Front and Central Vowels: [i], [ɪ], [eʸ], [ɛ], [æ], [ɑ], [ə], [ɚ]

Write the correct symbol for the sound of the boldface vowel in each of these words. Where there are two lines, write the first symbol on the line to the left of the word and the second symbol on the line to the right.

1. ____ wear
2. ____ great
3. ____ bread
4. ____ sweat
5. ____ decrease (v) ____
6. ____ lead (v)
7. ____ heartily
8. ____ fear
9. ____ bear
10. ____ earth
11. ____ beard
12. ____ dollar ____
13. ____ lovely ____
14. ____ column
15. ____ colonial
16. ____ opinion ____
17. ____ come
18. ____ commerce ____
19. ____ commercial
20. ____ concert
21. ____ control
22. ____ page
23. ____ image
24. ____ imagine
25. ____ honest ____

26. ____ work
27. ____ effort
28. ____ flood
29. ____ private
30. ____ dictate
31. ____ military ____
32. ____ nation
33. ____ national
34. ____ serious ____
35. ____ liquor ____
36. ____ recent ____
37. ____ represent ____
38. ____ receipt ____
39. ____ feel
40. ____ been
41. ____ key
42. ____ they
43. ____ survey (v)
44. ____ experiment
45. ____ experience
46. ____ development ____
47. ____ developmental ____
48. ____ servant ____
49. ____ terrible ____
50. ____ filled

51. ____ field
52. ____ manage
53. ____ workman
54. ____ standard ____
55. ____ please
56. ____ pleasure ____
57. ____ success ____
58. ____ actress ____
59. ____ husband ____
60. ____ grammar ____
61. ____ marry
62. ____ marine ____
63. ____ pays
64. ____ says
65. ____ said
66. ____ paid
67. ____ atom ____
68. ____ atomic
69. ____ soda
70. ____ foreign
71. ____ holiday
72. ____ the
    ____ orphan
73. ____ the
    ____ hurricane
74. ____ encourage
75. ____ subtract ____

Homework

Select one of the following:

1. Be prepared to discuss in class the type of work you would like to do after you finish school.

2. If you are working now or have worked before, describe briefly your responsibilities. If you do not have any working experience, tell the class what kind of work you would enjoy doing.

Appropriateness: Making Requests and Asking People to Do Things

dialogues

1. **A:** Do you happen to have an eraser you could lend me?
   B: Sure, I do. Here it is.
   A: Thanks a lot. I'll return it right away.
   B: Take your time. There's no hurry.

2. **A:** Could you bring me that book on the table, please?
   B: Of course. I'd be glad to.
   A: Thank you very much.

3. **A:** Could you hand me that red pen over there. I can't reach it.
   B: Certainly. Do you need anything else?
   A: No, thanks. That'll be fine.

4. **A:** Please pass me the candy.
   B: Certainly. But don't eat too much of it. You'll spoil your appetite for dinner.
   A: Thank you. I won't.

5. **A:** Would you please pass the peanuts?
   B: Yes, of course. Help yourself.
   A: Thank you.

6. **A:** Will you please hand me the matches?
   B: Surely.
   A: Thanks.

7. **A:** Would you please direct me to the municipal art museum?
   B: I'd be glad to, but I'm not sure where it is myself. Let's look it up in the tourist guidebook.

8. **A:** Would you do me a favor, please? Help me pull this suitcase off the shelf.
   B: Certainly. I'd be glad to. Oh, my! This suitcase is heavy. No wonder you couldn't get it down by yourself.
   A: Thank you, I really appreciate your help.
   B: You're welcome. Don't mention it.

9. **A:** Would you mind opening this window, please? It's too hot in this room.
   B: Not at all. The humidity is terrible today.

10. **A:** Could you possibly move your chair a little? I can hardly see the instructor.
    B: Of course. There, is that better?
    A: Yes, thank you. That's much better.

11. **A:** Would you please put away that dictionary if you're through using it?
    B: I'm still using it. I'll put it away when I finish reviewing for a quiz. I have to look up a lot of words.

12. **A:** I know you're very crowded today, but would it be possible to get a table for two near the window?
    B: Certainly. There'll be one available in just a few minutes. Please wait here in the meantime.

useful information

The dialogues above demonstrate a number of expressions you can use when you want a person to do something for you. The expression you use will depend on your relationship with the person you are addressing. Analyze the dialogues with your instructor and identify the type of relationship that exists between the speakers. Also discuss the tone of voice used in making various requests. Examine the different expressions as to the degree of politeness and notice the variety of possible answers.

practice

Below are a series of requests and a list of different people who could be asked to fulfill these requests. Study the list carefully at home. Your instructor will assign you to act the part of one of the people listed. The student on your left must select an appropriate request from the list and ask for your assistance. You will make an appropriate response to his request.

The requests are often not appropriate to the person listed directly opposite. Study the list and find an appropriate request for each person listed. Sometimes more than one request is appropriate for a particular person, and sometimes a particular request may be appropriate for more than one person.

Ask

a professor (instructor)	to give you a cigarette
a police officer	not to speak so quickly because you can't understand
a waiter or waitress	to show you a table for four in the nonsmoking section
a friend	to open or close a window or a door
a student	to move his chair to the left or the right
a salesperson	not to smoke because you are allergic to smoke
your boss	to turn on the light because the room is too dark
a stranger	to explain the meaning of a word or an expression
a librarian	to repeat what he or she has said because you didn't hear it
a classmate	to help you carry something heavy to your car
a tourist guide	to call a tow truck for you because your car has broken down
your father or brother	to help you locate a particular reference book
a sister or mother	to help you move a heavy desk or chair
your English instructor	to reach something for you from a high shelf
	to help you change a flat tire
	to bring you another cup of coffee
	to get something for you from the bookstore
	to show you a silk shirt like the one in the show window

This time the person listed will ask you to do something. For example:

Officer: Are you the owner of the blue Chevrolet that's parked across the street?
  Man: Yes, I am, officer. What's wrong?
Officer: I'm sorry but you'll have to move the car. It's blocking a driveway.
  Man: Oh. I'm sorry, officer. I'll move it right away.

The High Back Vowels [u] and [ʊ]

The Sounds

description of the sound [u]

[u] is called a **tense, high back** vowel. To produce this sound, push the back of the tongue upward and backward toward the soft palate (the velum). The back of the tongue is higher for the [u] sound than for any other vowel. Round your lips and push them forward. The [u] is the most rounded vowel sound. The muscles of the lips and tongue should be tense. The vowel chart and the diagram show the tongue position used to produce the sound [u].

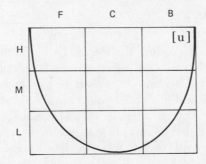
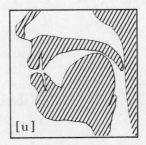

Pronounce these words after listening to your instructor. Remember to round your lips and push them forward. [u] is a long sound. You can hold it as long as you have breath.

too   blue   moon   fool   root

Pronounce the following words after listening to your instructor. Remember that vowels are lengthened before voiced consonants.

Voiceless	*Voiced*
root	rude
hoot	who'd
proof	prove
loose	lose

description of the sound [ʊ]

[ʊ] is a lax, high back vowel. To produce this sound, place your jaw and the tongue slightly lower than for [u]. Move your tongue slightly more forward. Your lips should be less rounded. [ʊ] and its variant [jʊ] are the only lax vowels among the back vowels. The vowel chart and the diagram show the tongue position used to produce the sound [ʊ].

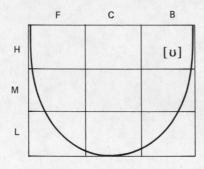
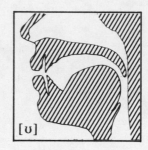

Pronounce these words after listening to your instructor.

book   foot   full   put   push

Now, pronounce the following words after listening to your instructor. Remember to lengthen the vowel before the voiced consonant.

Voiceless	*Voiced*		*Voiceless*	*Voiced*
shook	should		book	bull
cook	could		putting	pudding

description of the sounds [ju] (see also p. 202)

In order to know how to produce the sounds [ju], you must first learn how to make the consonant sound [j], which is called a voiced, palatal glide. To form this sound, spread your lips apart. The muscles of your tongue and lips as well as those at the corners of your mouth and just under your chin should all be tense. The articulation of the sound [j] varies according to the lip and tongue position used to produce the particular vowel sound that follows. That is, for the front vowels, the lips move back, in varying degrees, toward the corners of the mouth, and the tongue moves forward, while for the back vowels, the lips move forward in varying degrees of roundness, and the tongue moves back.

Watch your instructor's mouth as he or she pronounces these words. Notice how the shape of the mouth changes with the pronunciation of each successive word.

yeast	year	Yale	yell	yam	yard
[ji]	[jɪ]	[jeʸ]	[jɛ]	[jæ]	[jɑ]

Now pronounce the words. You will feel the changes in the shape of your lips and the position of your tongue as you produce the different vowels that follow [j]. Those are the front vowels preceded by [j]. Now listen and watch as your instructor pronounces the following words containing the central and back vowels.

yucca	yearn	you	your	yoke	yawn
[jə́kə]	[jɚn]	[ju]	[jʊr]	[joʷk]	[jɔn]
or					
[júkə]					

Now pronounce the words. Again, notice how your mouth changes shape as you pronounce the words in order.

As with the other vowels, the sounds [ju] are lengthened before voiced consonants. Pronounce these words after your instructor says them.

Voiceless	*Voiced*
use (n)	**use** (v)
juice	**Jews**
réfuse (n)	refúse (v)

Listening Exercises and Oral Practice

Your instructor will read some of the words from each of the following sections. Circle the words that you hear. After each section, your instructor will pronounce all of the pairs of words in that section and then ask you to pronounce them.

Distinguishing [u] *from* [ʊ]

fool	full	who'd	hood	suit	soot
pool	pull	stewed	stood	food	foot
Luke	look	cooed	could		

Distinguishing [ʊ] *from* [ə]

put	putt	look	luck	shook	shuck
stood	stud	took	tuck	book	buck

Distinguishing [u] *from* [ju]

ooze	use (v)	fool	fuel	moot	mute
food	feud	coo	cue	who	hue

Your instructor will read one word from each of the following pairs of words. Put a check (✔) next to the word you hear. Each one will be read twice.

1. who'd ____
   hood ____

2. shut ____
   shoot ____

3. look ____
   Luke ____

4. pool ____
   pull ____

5. Q ____
   coo ____

6. shoot ____
   should ____

7. poor ____
   pure ____

8. but ____
   boot ____

9. fuel ____
   fool ____

10. stood ____
    stewed ____

Your instructor will read the following sentences. Listen carefully to the pronunciation of the vowel sounds in the boldface words.

1. Only a **fool** would fill the tank so **full**.
2. **Pull** that man out of the **pool**.
3. **Look** at **Luke** play ball!
4. There's black **soot** all over your white **suit**.
5. **Who'd** like to wear this **hood**?
6. You **should shut** the door.
7. I need another **buck** to buy that **book**.
8. Jane **took** a **tuck** in her shirt.
9. **Look** what bad **luck** we had.
10. Luis taught his pet dove to **coo** on **cue**.

Now practice reading the sentences making a clear distinction between the vowel sounds in the boldface words. Observe correct stress, intonation, and blending.

Spelling Hints and Troublesome Words

the sound [u]

Since [u] is a long sound, it most often appears in strongly stressed syllables. It may occur initially as in *ooze*, medially as in *move*, or finally as in *threw*. [u] is represented in writing by:

u: especially after the letter *j* or *r* or a consonant + *r* or *l* as in *June*, *rule*, *true*, *blue*
oo: in final position or before a voiced consonant as in *too*, *choose*
oo: before the voiceless consonants *t*, *th*, *f*, *s*, as in *boot*, *tooth*, *proof*, *loose*

exceptions: *good*, *hood*, *stood*, *wood*, *wool*, *foot*, and *soot*, in which *oo* is pronounced [ʊ].

ui: fr**ui**t
o: pr**o**ve, d**o**
ou: gr**ou**p
ew: especially after the letter *j* or after a consonant + *r* or *l* as in *crew*, *flew*, *jewelry*

Some troublesome words containing the sound [u]

rule	Julý	fruit	lose	blew
true	conclude	suit	tomḅ	flew
blue	include	juice	impróve	chew
clue	pool	rúin [rúɪn]	group	crew
June	tool		through	jéwelry
	afternóon			

the sound [ʊ]

[ʊ] is a short vowel and occurs in both stressed and unstressed syllables. It appears medially as in *book*, *cushion*, and finally in unstressed syllables as in *to* [tʊ] before a word beginning with a vowel. [ʊ] does not appear initially.

> **NOTE:** Before an *r* the sound [u] is usually shortened to [ʊ] as in *sure* [ʃʊr], *tour* [tʊr], *and poor* [pʊr].

[ʊ] is represented in writing by:

u: push, áctual
u + ll: full, pull
u + sh: push, bush
oo + k: look, took
ou: could, should

Some troublesome words containing the sound [ʊ]

bull	búllet	grádual	good	understóod
pull	jury	gráduate (n)	wood	poor
push	insúre	situátion	stood	tour
súgar	insurance	Jánuary	book	could
cushion	cásual	Fébruary	took	should
pudding	actual		look	would
butcher	factual		shook	wóman

the sounds [ju]

The sounds [ju] appear initially as in *use*, medially as in *music*, and finally as in *review*. They occur mainly in strongly stressed syllables.

[ju] are represented in writing by:

u: únit
u:
iew: } following the sounds [p], [b], [f], [v], [m], [k], and [h] as in *pupil, beauty,*
eau: } *few, view, music, cute, human*

NOTE: Before an *r*, the [ju] is usually shortened to [jʊ] as in the following:

Eúrope	pure	cúrious	cúrable	your
Européan	búreau	furious	secúre	you're
Eurásia	bureáucracy	cure	secúrity	

Some troublesome words containing the sounds [ju]

use (n) [jus]	fúel	munícipal	huge
use (v) [juz]	amúse	community	húman
únit	refuse	cube	humídity
uníte	confuse	Cuba	húmor
úniverse	confusion	cute	you*
univérsity	transfusion	Q	you'll*
únion	fúneral	accúse	you've*
uniform	music	excuse (n)	you'd*
usual	musícian	excuse (v)	youth
future	muséum	peculiar	béautiful

*In stressed position only.

Some words may be pronounced with either [u] or [ju].

example: *new* may be pronounced [nu] or [nju].

New Yórk	tune	stúpid	stúdio	cóstume
tube	dúty	student	Tuesday	altitude

| **Oral Practice**

substitution exercises using the sound [u]

In these simple exercises concentrate on producing a good [u] sound and on using correct stress and blending.

1.   Choose one of the words from the list and ask the student next to you a question using rising-falling intonation. He or she will answer using an appropriate name with a possessive *s*.

example: Whose *tomb* is it?   It's *Lincoln's* tomb.
Whose _____ is it?   It's _____ _____.

tool	food	pool
room	group	spoon
broom	suit	fruit

2.   In this exercise, be sure to use rising-falling intonation in the question and to put the stress on the first element of the compound noun. Do not choose a word already chosen by a classmate until all the words have been used.

A: What shall I use?   B: Use (a, the, some) _____
    [ʃəl]

toothpaste	newspaper
toothbrush	chewing gum
toothpick	food coloring
sugar spoon	fruit juice
soup spoon	shoe box

substitution exercises using the sound [ʊ]

In these simple exercises, concentrate on producing the [ʊ] sound. Be sure to stress the first element of the compound nouns. As usual, Student A will ask the question and Student B will answer.

1.   In this exercise be sure to pronounce the past tense of the verb *look* correctly. To help you make the correct blending, we have written the word in phonetic symbols.

A: What did he look at?   B: He *looked at* the wood.
     [lúkæt]   [lúkt ət]

wolf	búll's-eye
wool	bulldozer
bull	bulletin board
bullet	news bulletins
	footprints

2.   What did the woman take Sue? She _____ her (a, some, the) _____ .

súgar bowl	nótebook
sugar cubes	bankbook
pudding	checkbook
cushions	cookbook
pussycat	textbook

sentences containing troublesome words with the sounds [u], [ju], and [ʊ]

Practice reading these sentences aloud using correct pronunciation, phrasing, and blending. All of the sentences call for rising-falling intonation.

1. Judy bought some beautiful and unique handmade jewelry.
2. At first, Stuart refused to apologize for his rude behavior, but later we shook hands.
3. Please put the cushions back on the sofa after you vacuum them.
4. Ruth always listens to the latest news bulletins at noon.
5. Many groups of university students will be touring Europe during July.
6. Don't make a fool of yourself by putting your foot in your mouth.
7. Some of the students don't look at the bulletin board as often as they should.
8. What foolish, inconsiderate person put chewing gum on the bottom of this chair?
9. We'll review all of the vowels as soon as we're through with the next two lessons.
10. The hurricane blew the roof off our beach house, and all our new furniture was ruined.
11. Who was on duty on Tuesday when the young woman was rescued?
12. Junior was born in Cuba, but he grew up in Utah.
13. In the confusion at the baggage pickup, a tourist mistook my suitcase for his.
14. Why do you always try to pull a door when the instructions say "push"?
15. After several blood transfusions, Gertrude's condition improved gradually.

mini-dialogues

1. **A:** Suzy, I like that cute bathing suit. Where did you get it?
   B: It's not new. I got it a few months ago in New York.

2. **A:** Is your cousin Lucy a student at the municipal university?
   B: Yes, she's a junior. She'll be graduating a year from next June.

3. **A:** Have you seen the new mural which the art students contributed to the Community Center?
   B: Yes. It's really beautiful. What a great opportunity for those students who painted it!

4. **A:** Where did you put your new uniform?
   B: I hung it on a hook in the bathroom. There's no room in my closet until I put up some more hooks.

5. **A:** We've signed up with a special tour group for a trip to New York in January. Would you like to go with us?
   B: I'm not sure. New York is such a huge and confusing city. I always lose my way and some friend has to rescue me. I know it's a wonderful opportunity, but let me think about it for a day or two.

Written Exercise: The Sounds [u], [ju], and [ʊ]

Write the symbol for the sound of the boldface vowel on the line next to the word.

1. ___ choose	18. ___ good	35. ___ human
2. ___ through	19. ___ gradual	36. ___ blue
3. ___ youth	20. ___ food	37. ___ butcher
4. ___ would	21. ___ foot	38. ___ union
5. ___ peculiar	22. ___ uniform	39. ___ amuse
6. ___ include	23. ___ cook	40. ___ funeral
7. ___ museum	24. ___ lose	41. ___ bullet
8. ___ rule	25. ___ jewelry	42. ___ ruin
9. ___ pudding	26. ___ Tuesday	43. ___ stood
10. ___ suit	27. ___ music	44. ___ fool
11. ___ blew	28. ___ pupil	45. ___ full
12. ___ few	29. ___ unit	46. ___ cube
13. ___ tomb	30. ___ improve	47. ___ future
14. ___ cushion	31. ___ movie	48. ___ juice
15. ___ woman	32. ___ usual	49. ___ municipal
16. ___ fruit	33. ___ cruel	50. ___ huge
17. ___ could	34. ___ confusion	

Homework

questions using irregular verbs containing the sounds [u], [ju], and [ʊ]

Be prepared to give oral answers to these questions. Remember to look up the form or the meaning of any verb you don't know. You should answer in complete sentences. As usual, Student A will ask a question, Student B will answer and then ask the next student the following question and so on.

1. In what year did the astronauts first fly to the moon?
2. When did you last take out a book from the library?
3. When you were a child, did you ever lose your way in an unfamiliar place?
4. Did you know most of the people in your hometown?
5. When you were in high school, did you or your parents choose your clothes?
6. When did you last blow up a balloon?
7. How much of the last movie you saw did you really understand?
8. How long did you stand in line when you registered for this course?
9. When you were at home, who usually put out the garbage at your house?
10. What sort of things did you throw away yesterday? (last week, last month.)

Appropriateness: Addressing People and Asking for Information

dialogue

Tourist: Excuse me, sir. I wonder if you could help me. Which way is the Modern Art Museum?

Man: I'm sorry. I've no idea. I'm new here myself. Why don't you ask the traffic cop?

Tourist: Officer, I wonder if you could tell me the shortest way to the Modern
Art Museum.
Police Officer: It's about twenty blocks from here. You'd better take a bus or a taxi.
Tourist: Where can I get a taxi?
Police Officer: Just stand right here and . . .   There's one heading this way. (Signals
to the taxi.) Here you are, Miss. Driver, take this lady to the Modern
Art Museum.
Tourist: Thank you very much, officer. You've been very helpful.
Police Officer: Not at all. Glad to help you.

useful expressions

Addressing People

When you want to get someone's attention, you usually do so by using the person's
name. This may be preceded by the expression "Excuse me" which in itself is a means
of getting someone's attention.

"Joe!"   "Betty!"
"Excuse me, Mrs. Brooks!"   "Excuse me, professor."

If you do not know the person you should use *sir, miss*, or *ma'am* (short for Madam).
You may also use the terms "young man" or "young lady" (but only of course if you are
considerably older).

If a person has a title, you should address him or her by that title.

"Doctor, . . . "
"Senator, . . . "

In some cases you add *Mr.*, *Miss* or *Madam* before the title.

"Mr. President, . . . "
"Madam Chair, . . . "

Look at the list of people below and notice the appropriate expression used to address
each one.

To get the attention of a:		*To speak to a:*	
waiter	"Waiter"	judge	"Your Honor"
porter	"Porter"	clergyman	"Reverend" (Protestant)
bus or taxi driver	"Driver"		"Father" (Catholic)
nurse	"Nurse"		"Rabbi" (Jewish)
policeman	"Officer"	nun	"Sister"
policewoman		teacher*	

*Never *address a teacher as "Teacher."* A high school teacher is addressed as *Mr., Miss, Mrs., Ms. A
person who teaches in a college or university is referred to as an instructor or professor. This
person may be addressed as *Dr., Miss, Mrs. Ms., Mr.,* or Professor, *according to his or her personal preference.*

Be careful not to use the expressions below. They are considered very rude.

"Hey!"   "Hey, you!"   "Hey, listen!"   "Hey, miss," (mister, etc.)

Asking for Information

In Lesson 3 we talked about the appropriate expressions used to ask for the time. Those expressions can also be used to ask for other types of information. For example:

"Do you know Sue's phone number?"

"Do you know where I can get a taxi?"

"Could you please tell me how much this costs?"

"Do you know whether the stores are open tomorrow?"

"I wonder if you could help me. How far is the post office?" (very polite)

"I wonder if you could show me the way to the bank." (very polite)

"I hope you don't mind my asking, but I'd like to know if you're coming to the party." (very polite)

In Lesson 3 we also talked about possible answers to these questions. In addition to those mentioned you could also say:

"Let me think for a second . . . (minute)"

"Just a second . . . (minute)"

"I'm not sure, but . . . I think . . . "

practice

Look at the list of situations below. According to your instructor's directions, get together with another student and work out a dialogue for one or more of these situations. Use an appropriate expression to get a particular person's attention. Your instructor will ask you to present your dialogue or dialogues to the class.

example: You are addressing someone you don't know.

A: Excuse me, Nurse. Is the doctor in?

B: No, he hasn't come in yet.

A: What time are you expecting him?

B: He said he'd be here around five o'clock.

A: Thank you very much.

Situations

1. Ask an instructor about making up a test you have missed.
2. Ask a police officer the location of the nearest post office.
3. Ask a salesperson the price of an article you would like to buy.
4. Ask a flight attendant the time of arrival of your flight, or ask for a pillow or a magazine.
5. Ask a stranger at a bus stop how long he or she has been waiting for the bus. Then ask how often the bus runs.
6. Ask a professor whether he or she knows another professor's teaching schedule or where you can find out that information.
7. Ask a secretary whether the boss (whom you want to see) is in. If he or she isn't in, ask when that person is expected.

The Back Vowels [oʷ] and [ɔ]

The Sound [oʷ]

description of the sound

[oʷ] is a tense, mid-back vowel. In order to produce the sound [oʷ], push the lips forward and round them closely. At first, the position of the jaw should be lower than the position for [u]. But as you move the back of the tongue back and upward, raise the jaw slightly. This movement of the tongue and jaw produces a gliding effect. [oʷ] is a long sound. You can hold it as long as you have breath. The vowel chart and the diagram show the tongue position used to produce the sound [oʷ].

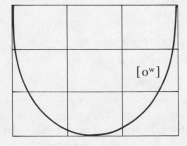

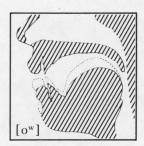

Pronounce these words after listening to your instructor.

105   go   boat   low   own

Repeat the following words after listening to your instructor. Remember that the sound [oʷ] will be lengthened before a voiced consonant.

Voiceless	*Voiced*
coat	code
close (adjective)	close (verb)
rope	robe

listening exercises and oral practice

Distinguishing [oʷ] and [ə]

Your instructor will read one word from each pair of words. Circle the word you hear. Then repeat the pairs after your instructor.

[oʷ]	[ə]		[oʷ]	[ə]		[oʷ]	[ə]		[oʷ]	[ə]
soak	suck		coat	cut		hole	hull		cope	cup
robe	rub		wrote	rut		boat	but		cloak	cluck
note	nut		comb	come		home	hum		mode	mud

Distinguishing [oʷ] and [ɑ]

Your instructor will read one word from each pair of words. Circle the word you hear. Then pronounce the pairs after your instructor says them.

[oʷ]	[ɑ]		[oʷ]	[ɑ]		[oʷ]	[ɑ]
coat	cot		comb	calm		soaks	socks
note	not		robe	rob		won't	want (also [ɔ])
wrote	rot		cloak	clock		tote	tot

Read the following sentences after listening to your instructor. Make sure you make a distinction between the boldface words.

1. **Come** here and **comb** your hair.
2. There was a **hole** in the ship's **hull**.
3. Don't **suck** your finger; **soak** it in cold water.
4. My cat likes to **rub** against my soft **robe**.
5. Joe wanted to go by **boat**, **but** the boat wasn't running.
6. I often **hum** a tune while I'm working at **home**.
7. I **cut** two inches off my **coat**.
8. Please **note**: the coconut is a fruit, not a **nut**.
9. **Calm** down and **comb** your hair.
10. You did **not** write me a **note**.

spelling hints

[oʷ] is used in both strongly stressed and weakly stressed syllables. It appears initially as in *owe*, medially as in *note*, and finally as in *toe*.

[oʷ] is represented in writing by:

o: go, open, smoke
oa: coat, toast, road
ow: show, row, window

ou: soul, though
oe: toe, Joe
ew: sew (unusual spelling)

Some troublesome words containing the sound [oʷ]

go		yolk	won't	lócal	ópen	dóughnut
so		comb	most	notice	only	contról
toe		both	home	soldier	lonely	hotél
old	[kloz]	clothes	tow	moment	total	woke úp
told		don't	sew	ocean	social	énvelope

oral practice

Student A will ask the question and Student B will answer, making the necessary substitution. These exercises have been made very simple to allow you to concentrate on producing a good [oʷ] sound. Also give careful attention to stress and blending.

1. Will they go to the *hotél*? No, they won't go.

    stúdio
    road
    ocean
    show
    boat
    TV́ program
    post office
    radio station
    polo game

2. Do you want to go to the *móvies*? No, I don't want to go.

    opera
    ballet
    theater
    party
    concert
    beach
    park
    library
    circus
    gym

3. What did you show her? I showed her a *comb*.

    [ʃoʷɚ]   [ʃoʷdɚ] rose
                            coat
                            bow
                            pony
                            radio
                            hotél
                            raincoat
                            (an) overcoat
                            photograph

4. In this exercise be careful to pronounce the past tense *-ed* ending correctly as [t], [d], or [ɪd], and blend the consonant ending with [ɪt].

    Did you *sew* it? Yes, I *sewed* it.

load	smoke
roll	roast
fold	enclóse
open	propose
close	postpone
toast	prógram
own	phótograph
notice	contról

The Sound [ɔ]

description of the sound

[ɔ] is a low back tense vowel. In order to produce this sound push the lips slightly forward. Lower the jaw from the position for [ʊ]; move the tongue back into a low back position. Tense the muscles at the corners of the mouth and those in the throat. [ɔ] is a long sound. You can hold it as long as you have breath. The vowel chart and the diagram show the tongue position used to produce the sound [ɔ].

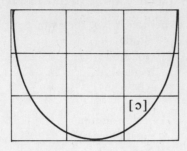
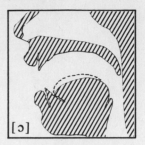

Pronounce these words after your instructor says them.

saw   ball   song   bought

Repeat the following words after listening to your instructor. Lengthen the [ɔ] before a voiced consonant.

Voiceless	*Voiced*
loss	laws
sauce	saws
brought	broad

listening exercises and oral practice

The following section is divided into two parts. Your instructor will first read one word from each pair. Circle the word you hear. Then pronounce the pairs of words after listening to your instructor. Next read the sentences that follow. Be sure you make a distinction between the boldface words.

Distinguishing [ɔ] *from* [oʷ]

[ɔ]	[oʷ]	[ɔ]	[oʷ]	[ɔ]	[oʷ]	[ɔ]	[oʷ]
bought	boat	ball	bowl	called	cold	walk	woke
caught	coat	tall	toll	pause	pose	jaw	Joe

Distinguishing [ɔ] *from* [ʊ]

[ɔ]	[ʊ]		[ɔ]	[ʊ]
Paul	pull		ball	bull
wall	wool		talk	took

Distinguishing [ɔ] *from* [ə]

[ɔ]	[ə]
bought	but
dawn	done
boss	bus

1. The boy threw the **ball** and broke the **bowl**.
2. Her **coat** got **caught** in the car door.
3. She'll **pause** a minute to **pose** for photographs.
4. Rose **called** to say that she has a **cold**.
5. The ball hit **Joe** on the **jaw**.
6. Paul **bought** a **boat** yesterday.
7. A **tall** man collected the **toll**.
8. When he **woke** up he went for a **walk**.
9. **Paul** will **pull** the rope.
10. They hung the small **wool** rug on the **wall**.
11. She **took** a few minutes to **talk** to us.
12. The boy hit the **bull** with his **ball**.
13. Paul **bought** coffee **but** he didn't drink it.
14. The job was **done** before **dawn**.
15. I saw the **boss** on the **bus** this morning.

spelling hints

[ɔ] usually occurs in stressed syllables. It may appear initially as in *off*, medially as in *lost*, and finally as in *saw*.

[ɔ] is represented in writing by:

o: song, boss,* cost
a: ball,* salt, war*
au: August, pause*
aw: saw, draw*
ou: thought, bought*
oa: broad, board

The following combinations of letters are almost always pronounced [ɔ].
consonant + *o* + *ss:* boss, loss, toss
consonant + *a* + *ll:* ball, call, tall
w + *ar:* war, warn, wart
consonant + *au:* sauce
consonant + *aw:* lawn
all other past forms ending in *ought, aught,* such as *fought, caught*

Some troublesome words containing the sound [ɔ]

sword	false	warn	sauce	automátic	dráwer
corps	talk	wash*	pause	bróadcast	pour**
fóreign*	wállet	wáter*	taught	aboárd	court**
office*	war	quarrel	aúthor	law	cough
coffee*	warm	quart	August	lawn	thought
towárd		appláud		láwyer	bought
salt					

*also [ɑ]
**also [oʷ]

Oral Practice

1. Student A will ask the questions and Student B will answer in a complete negative sentence. Concentrate on making a good [oʷ] in the word *won't*. Make sure to use correct stress and blending.

Will they *fold* it? No, they won't *fold* it.

    close
    open
    hold
    load
    toast
    control
    notice
    oppose
    propose
    photograph

2. Concentrate on the [oʷ] and [ɔ] sounds.

What're you going to order? I'm going to order some *toast*.

    soda
    oátmeal
    doughnuts
    tomatoes
    potatoes
    corn
    coffee
    stráwberries
    roast pórk
    meátballs

3. Read the following sentences. Be sure to use correct stress, rhythm, blending, and intonation.

    1.   How much do I owe you for the potatoes?
    2.   I left all my old clothes at home.
    3.   It's very cold; it's three below zero.
    4.   When will they open the new hotel?
    5.   Which show did you enjoy most?
    6.   Joe was born on August 4, 1945, just before the war ended.
    7.   I lost my wallet at the shopping mall this morning.
    8.   Her daughter is the author of a new book on indoor plants.
    9.   Give me the ball; I won't throw it at you.
    10. Our car was stolen yesterday morning.

mini-dialogues

1. **A:** What did you order?
    B: Oh, I ordered a chocolate malted.

2. **A:** Hi, Laurie. Have you seen my daughter?
    B: Yes, she just went in that clothing store.

3. **A:** It's almost ninety-four degrees outside, and it's very warm in here.
    B: I'll open the door to the porch. We'll get a breeze from the ocean.

4. **A:** Do you wash your delicate clothes yourself?
    B: No, I always send them to the laundry.

5. **A:** Would you like a bowl of soup?
    B: No, thanks. I just had doughnuts and coffee.

6. **A:** Don't forget to put those folders in the brown envelope.
    B: I already did. They should be on top of your desk.

7. **A:** Do you watch any local TV programs?
    B: I don't watch TV, period.

Written Exercises

exercise on the sounds [oᵂ] and [ɑ]

Identify the [oᵂ] [ɑ] sounds in the following words in which both sounds are spelled with the letter *o*. Write the symbol [oᵂ] or [ɑ] on the line. If a word contains both of the sounds, write both symbols.

1.	___	dollar	14.	___	postal	27.	___	goes
2.	___	close	15.	___	soldier	28.	___	popular
3.	___	closet	16.	___	holiday	29.	___	don't
4.	___	notice	17.	___	ocean	30.	___	economics
5.	___	doctor	18.	___	politics	31.	___	Protestant
6.	___	October ___	19.	___	comb	32.	___	protest (n)
7.	___	honor	20.	___	social	33.	___	spoken
8.	___	open	21.	___	coconut	34.	___	clothes
9.	___	coma	22.	___	promise	35.	___	shot
10.	___	comma	23.	___	rob	36.	___	alone
11.	___	hot	24.	___	told	37.	___	both
12.	___	body	25.	___	job	38.	___	so
13.	___	won't	26.	___	hope	39.	___	radio

exercise on the vowels [ə], [ɑ], [ɔ], and [oᵂ]

Write the symbol for the sound of the boldface vowel.

1.	___	dawn	11.	___	author	21.	___	lunch
2.	___	done	12.	___	want	22.	___	launch
3.	___	bus	13.	___	won't	23.	___	custom
4.	___	boss	14.	___	must	24.	___	costume
5.	___	oven	15.	___	most	25.	___	know
6.	___	dozen	16.	___	moment	26.	___	knowledge
7.	___	frozen	17.	___	rough	27.	___	note
8.	___	doesn't	18.	___	cough	28.	___	nothing
9.	___	collar	19.	___	though	29.	___	comb
10.	___	color	20.	___	thought	30.	___	come

Homework

Be prepared to give your opinion on one of the following:

1. smoking in public places
2. home computers
3. TV programs (talk shows, for example)
4. Use of coffee or salt in your diet

Appropriateness: Asking for and Giving Directions

1. Tourist: Excuse me. How can I get to the municipal stadium?
Young Man: Take Bus No. 37. It goes all the way to Central Park. The stadium is right across from the park.
Tourist: How long does it take to get there?
Young Man: Around thirty-five minutes, if you go by bus.
Tourist: Then I'd better take a taxi. Where is the taxi stand?

Young Man: At the next corner.
  Tourist: Thanks a lot.
Young Man: Don't mention it.

2. **Larry:** Excuse me. I'm lost. Where's the nearest post office?
    Man: I'm sorry. I really don't know. I don't live here.
  Larry: . . . Excuse me, ma'am. Could you please tell me where the post office is?
  Lady: Of course. It's on Lake Drive.
  Larry: Where's that? Is it far from here?
  Lady: Well, let's see . . . It's about half a mile from here.
  Larry: What's the best way to get there?
  Lady: Take any bus at the corner and get off after the third traffic light. You'll find the post office right there.
  Larry: Thank you; you've been very helpful.
  Lady: Not at all.

useful expressions

Asking for Directions or Information

"Where's _____ , please?" (the library)

"What street is _____ on?" (the University Museum)

"(Could) Can you tell me where _____ is?" (the Pearl Hotel)

"On which side is it?"

"Do you have a map?"

"Do you happen to know where I can get _____ ?" (a bus)

"How far is it from here?"

"What's the best way to get (of getting) to _____ ?" (Vernon Street)

"Which way is _____ ?" (the bank)

"Where's the nearest (closest) _____ ?" (church)

"How can (do) I get to _____ ?" (the supermarket)

"Is this the right way to _____ ?" (New Jersey)

"Would you mind repeating that?"*

"Where do I get _____ ?" (a taxi)

"Where does the bus stop?"

"How much is the fare?"

"Does this bus go to _____ ?" (Liverpool)

"Is this where I get off?"

"How far is it from _____ to _____ ?" (Atlanta, Miami)

"How long does it take to get there?"

"I need some information about _____ ."

"Is this a one-way street?"

"Can I catch a taxi here?"

"Where is the taxi stand?"

Showing Concern, Giving Directions, and Expressing Regret for Inability to Help

"What seems to be the problem?"

"What's the matter? Can I help you?"

"Do you need any help?"

*to answer affirmatively you say, "Not at all . . . ."

"Of course. I'll try to. It's at the next corner."

> down the block
> near that sign
> to the right
> straight ahead
> around the corner
> down the street (towards lower numbers)
> up the street (towards higher numbers)

If you do not know the answer to a question concerning directions you may answer by using one of the following expressions.

> "I'm sorry. I don't know."
> "Sorry, I don't live here."
> "Sorry, I don't know. I'm new here myself."
> "I'm not sure. You'd better ask somebody else."

Once people give you directions then you should say:

> "Thanks a lot."
> "Thanks a million." (informal)
> "Thank you."
> "You've been very helpful."
> "Thanks for your help."
> "Very kind of you."

practice

Structured Dialogues

In the following short dialogues, Student A will select an item from Column 1 to complete the question. Student B will then select an appropriate item from Column 2 to complete his or her response.

1. **A:** I beg your pardon. Where's the _____1_____ ?
   B: It's _____2_____ .
   A: Thank you.
   B: Don't mention it.

1	2
cafeteria	around the corner
main office	on the first floor
cashier	that way
ticket office	just past the main door
phone booth	across the street

2. **A:** Excuse me. Where's the _____1_____ ?
   B: It's in this building.
   A: How can I get there?
   B: _____2_____ .
   A: Thank you very much.

1	2
newsstand	Walk straight ahead.
reception desk	Turn right.
main entrance	Turn left over there.
barber shop	Walk all the way down.
doctor's office	Go down the hall.

3. **A:** How far is it to _____1____ ?
   B: It's only ____2____ .
   A: Thanks a lot.
   B: You're welcome.

1	2
the center of town	about half a mile away
the shopping mall	two blocks from here
the next gas station	a mile away
City Hall	three streets from here
Al's Studio	two doors away

Semistructured Dialogues

1. **A:** Where's the student cafeteria?
   B:
   A:
   B:

2. **A:** On which side of the street is the _____ ?
   B:
   A:
   B:

3. **A:** What's the best way to get to the _____ ?
   B:
   A:
   B:

4. **A:** What's the matter? You look lost. Can I help you?
   B:
   A:
   B:

5. **A:**
   B: Turn left at the next corner.
   A:
   B:

6. **A:**
   B: It's in the next block next to the police station.
   A:
   B:

Unstructured Dialogues

Prepare a dialogue with another student in which one of you asks for directions and the other one responds appropriately. Use some of the expressions you have studied in this lesson.

The Diphthongs [aɪ], [aʊ], and [ɔɪ]

A diphthong is the blending of two vowel sounds within a syllable. The tongue, the lips, and the jaw move from the position of the first vowel to the position of the second vowel in a smooth, continuous, gliding movement. The first vowel is accented.

The Diphthong [aɪ]

description of the sound

The diphthong [aɪ] begins with a low front vowel similar to the Spanish [a] and ends with the lax, high front vowel [ɪ]. The vowel chart and the diagram show the two tongue positions used to produce the sound [aɪ].

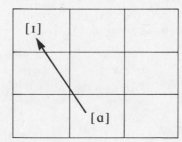

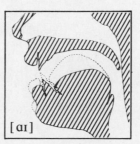

Pronounce these words after listening to your instructor. Notice how your mouth changes shape as you produce the sound [aɪ].

115   my   buy   tie   die   guy   kite

Like all other vowel sounds [ɑɪ]* is lengthened before voiced consonants. Repeat the following pairs of words after your instructor.

Voiceless	*Voiced*		*Voiceless*	*Voiced*
sight	side		rice	rise
height	hide		price	prize

*The IPA symbol for this sound is [aɪ]. However, since students often confuse the symbol [a] with [ə], we have used the symbol [ɑɪ] to represent the diphthong in this text.

listening exercises and oral practice: distinguishing [ɑ] from [ɑɪ]

Your instructor will read some of the words from the following columns. Circle the words that you hear. Then repeat all of the words after your instructor.

[ɑ]	[ɑɪ]	[ɑ]	[ɑɪ]	[ɑ]	[ɑɪ]	[ɑ]	[ɑɪ]
fond	find	lot	light	top	type	hot	height
blond	blind	not	night	lock	like	spot	spite

Read the following sentences, making a clear distinction between the boldface words.

1. I don't **like** that **lock**.
2. The **blond** girl is **blind**.
3. Those plants need a **lot** of **light**.
4. **Type** the title on the **top** line.
5. Tonight is **not** the **night** to leave.
6. **I'd** find it **odd** if he didn't come.
7. The air is not as **hot** at this **height**.
8. I'll try to **find** the wine you're so **fond** of.

spelling hints

The sound [ɑɪ] appears initially as in *item*, medially as in *rise*, and finally as in *deny*. It almost always occurs in stressed syllables. [ɑɪ] is represented in writing by:

> *i:* island, sign, bicycle
> *i* + consonant + *e:* side, quite, glide
> *y:* my, cycle
> *i* + *gh:* high, night
> *ie:* lie, tie

Troublesome words containing the sound [ɑɪ]

eye	twice	island	vítamin	alíve	óccupy
I'll	climb	iron	triangle	arrive	magnify
while	sign	item	typewriter	advice	satisfy
child	wind (v)	private	socíety	advise	multiply
wild	pint	climate	varíety	decide	recognize
hide	quite	title	aisle	resígn	analyze
rise	wire	diet	type	invite	sacrifice
price	stripe	quiet	éyebrow	surprise	
prize	wipe	science	guide	excited	
knife	choir	height		entirely	
	[kwɑɪr]				

exercises: the contractions *I'm, I'll* and *I'd*

The purpose of these simple exercises is to concentrate on the correct pronunciation of the contractions *I'm, I'll,* and *I'd.* In the first two exercises make sure that you bring your lips together to form the [m] and say: [ɑɪm].

1. Watch your instructor's mouth as he or she reads each sentence. Then repeat the sentences carefully according to your instructor's directions. Where possible, blend *I'm* with the initial vowel of the following word.

I'm glad I'm here.   I'm glad I'm alíve.
I'm glad I'm right.   I'm glad I'm inside.
I'm sorry I'm late.   I'm glad I'm fínished.
I'm sorry I'm behind.   I'm glad I'm outside.
I'm glad I'm in time.   I'm glad I'm not dríving.

2. Student A will ask a question using one of the words in the list. Student B will answer. Be sure to pronounce the endings of the past participles correctly.

Aren't you _____ ?   Yes, I'm _____ .

surprísed   delíghted
excited   invited
quálified   fríghtened
occupied   satisfied

3. In this exercise, one student will ask the question, and the next student will answer. Make sure to pronounce the contraction *I'll* correctly, and blend the final consonant of the verb with the pronoun *it*.

A. Will you *wind* it?   B. Yes, I'll _____it.

buy   write   describe
try   price   strike
type   drive   advise
sign   climb   grind

4. In this next exercise, make sure you say [ɑɪd lɑɪk] and not [ɑɪ lɑɪk]. Again, Student A will ask the question and Student B will answer it.

A. What would you like to do?   B. I'd like to _____it.

[ɑɪd]

try   hide   órganize
buy   guide   analyze
climb   desígn   advertise
drive   divide   revíse

The Diphthong [ɑʊ]

description of the sound

To produce the diphthong [ɑʊ] begin with the low front vowel [ɑ] and let your tongue glide upward and backward to the position of the lax, back vowel [ʊ]. The vowel chart and the diagram show the two tongue positions used to produce the sound [ɑʊ].

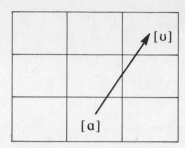 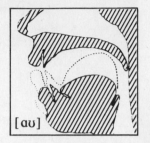

Repeat these words after your instructor. Notice how your mouth changes shape as you produce the diphthong [ɑʊ].

how   now   aróund

Like all the other vowels, [ɑʊ] is lengthened before voiced consonants. Pronounce these words after listening to your instructor.

Voiceless	*Voiced*
bout	bowed
clout	cloud
house (n)	house (v)

listening exercises and oral practice

Your instructor will read some of the words from each of the pairs of words below. Circle the words that you hear. Then pronounce all of the words after your instructor says them.

***Distinguishing* [ɑ] *from* [ɑʊ]**

[ɑ]	[ɑʊ]	[ɑ]	[ɑʊ]	[ɑ]	[ɑʊ]
fond	found	prod	proud	spot	spout
pond	pound	dot	doubt	Scot	scout
bond	bound	shot	shout	are	hour, our

***Distinguishing* [ɑʊ] *from* [ɑɪ]**

[ɑʊ]	[ɑɪ]	[ɑʊ]	[ɑɪ]	[ɑʊ]	[ɑɪ]
bow (v)	buy	loud	lied	found	find
how	high	proud	pride	wound (v.)	wind (v.)
down	dine	crowd	cried	ground	grind

Listen carefully as your instructor reads the sentences below. Then practice reading the sentences aloud, making a clear distinction between the boldface words.

1. We **found** out that she was **fond** of flowers.
2. The magician **wound** a scarf around his magic **wand**.
3. We heard a **shout** and then a **shot**.
4. **Are** these **our** seats?
5. I caught a ten-**pound** fish in the **pond**.
6. Whenever he sang, the **crowd cried** for more.
7. Let's go **down** and **dine** right now.
8. **Grind** the grain and set the bag on the **ground**.
9. He's **proud** of his son and really shows his **pride**.
10. **How high** is that mountain?

spelling hints

The sound [ɑʊ] appears intially as in *ounce*, medially as in *about*, and finally as in *allow*. It occurs only in stressed syllables. [ɑʊ] is represented in writing by:

ow: **h**o**w**, sh**o**wer
ou　**o**ut, sh**o**ut

Some troublesome words with the sound [ɑʊ]

now	flówer	loud	shout	announce	coúncil
plow	shower	cloud	doubt	pronounce	mountain
crowd	coward	proud	blouse	amount	fountain
drown	powder	wound (v. pt.)	south	around	thousand
tówel	anyhow	ounce	tróusers	surround	boundary
vowel	allów	alóud			

oral exercises

In this exercise, concentrate on producing a good [ɑʊ] sound. Be sure to pronounce the past tense *ed* ending correctly. (If you have forgotten the rules, refer to Lesson 6.) As usual, one student will ask a question and another will answer it.

Did he pound it?　　B. Yes, he pounded it.
[dɪd i]

doubt	shout
sound	plow
count	announce
allów	pronounce

In the next exercise, Student A will ask a question using one of the words from list 1. Student B will answer by choosing an **appropriate** word or phrase from list 2. (List 2 is not arranged in any particular order.) **Do not repeat** words or phrases that have been used by other students.
(Notice that some of the words are plural and, therefore, you will need to use the pronoun *them* in your answer.)

A. Where did you find the ____ ?   B. I ____ it ____ .
                                             (them)

1	2
tówels	outside the house
flowers	outdoors
clowns	indoors
mouse	insíde the house
blouses	around tówn
trousers	downtown
scouts	in the tówn
shower	on the móuntain
powder	near the fóuntain
fountain	on the gróund
accoúnts	in the tówer
	south of tówn
	downstairs

The Diphthong [ɔɪ]

description of the sound

To produce the diphthong [ɔɪ], begin with the low, rounded back vowel [ɔ] and let your tongue glide upward and forward to the position of the lax, front vowel [ɪ]. The vowel chart and the diagram show the tongue positions necessary to produce the sound [ɔɪ].

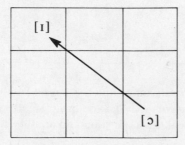

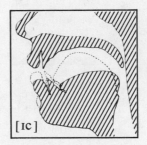

Pronounce these words after listening to your instructor. Notice how your mouth changes shape as you produce the sound [ɔɪ].

oil   noise   boy

Like all the other vowels and diphthongs, [ɔɪ] is lengthened before voiced consonants. Repeat these pairs of words after your instructor.

Voiceless	*Voiced*
joint	joined
Boyce	boys
Joyce	joys

listening exercises and oral practice: distinguishing [ɔ] from [ɔɪ]

Your instructor will read one of the words from each of the following pairs. Circle the words you hear. Then repeat all the words after your instructor.

[ɔ]	[ɔɪ]	[ɔ]	[ɔɪ]	[ɔ]	[ɔɪ]
all	oil	call	coil	jaw	joy
ball	boil	tall	toil	pause	poise

Your instructor will read the following sentences aloud. Practice reading them, making a clear distinction between the vowels in the boldface words.

1. The instructions **call** for a **coil** of wire.
2. I just used up **all** the **oil**.
3. Put the meat**balls** in the sauce, and bring it to a **boil**.
4. **Toil** is a noun or verb, and **tall** is an adjective.
5. The actress was very **poised** when she **paused** to speak.

spelling hints

The diphthong [ɔɪ] occurs mainly in stressed syllables. It appears initially as in *oil*, medially as in *boil*, and finally as in *enjoy*. [ɔɪ] is represented in writing by:

oi: **noise**
oy: **boy, loyal**

Troublesome words containing the sound [ɔɪ]

oil	point	lóyal	annóy	annóyance
boil	noise	royal	enjoy	enjoyment
coil	poise	voyage	employ	employment
coin	voice	poison	destroy	unemplóyment
join	choice	toilet	avoid	appóintment
joint			appoint	disappóintment
			disappóint	

exercise

This exercise has been made very simple to allow you to concentrate on producing a good [ɔɪ] sound. As usual, one student will ask a question and the next student will answer.

A: What shall I give the boy?
    [ʃəl]

B: Give him _____ .
    [gɪvɪm]

a coin

some óil

his chóice

a toy

emplóyment

five póints

an appóintment

some óil

Oral Practice Using All the Diphthongs

questions using irregular verbs with the sounds [ɑɪ] and [ɑʊ]

Student A will ask a question beginning with *what* and using one of the verbs listed. Student B will give a logical answer. If you don't remember the past tense form of the verb or its meaning, look it up; otherwise, you won't be able to answer the question.

A: What did (he, she) ____ ?   B: (He, She) ____ (a, an, some) ____ .

find	write
fly	drive
ride	strike
wind	grind

questions using regular verbs with the sounds [ɑɪ] and [ɔɪ]

Student A will ask a question beginning with *who** or *what* and one of the verbs listed. Student B will give a logical answer. Be sure to pronounce the past tense *ed* endings correctly.

**Who* *is used in speaking,* whom *in writing.* What *is for things.*

A: Who did you ____ ?   B: I ____ .
   (What) (he, she)

invíte	surpríse
emplóy	fríghten
avóid	descríbe
appóint	récognize

mini-dialogues

Read the following dialogues with a classmate, observing the rules of intonation, stress, and blending. Your instructor may ask you to memorize some of them.

1. **A:** What is the price of that toilet water?
   B: This bottle is a $9.98 value specially priced at $5.95.
   A: Thank you.

2. **A:** Where have you been? I've been trying to find you all afternoon.
   B: I was trying to buy a nylon blouse, but I couldn't find anything in my size.

3. **A:** Were you able to buy any tickets for Friday night's concert?
   B: Yes, I was very surprised. I got two, right on the center aisle downstairs.

4. **A:** Are you sure we're on the right highway? I don't recognize any landmarks.
   B: Well, the sign a while back said Route 195, and that's the road we have to take.

5. **A:** I need a sharp knife to cut this fine wire, and I can't find one.
   B: Here — use my pocket knife. It's quite sharp.

6. **A:** Excuse me, do you know the height of the observation tower?
   B: I'm sorry, I don't. Why don't you ask the guide at the information booth?

7. **A:** Our toilet has a broken pipe. Do you know of a good plumber?
   B: Yes, my friend Jim Boyce. He lives behind you — right next to the highway. I'll call him for you. I'm sure he'll give you a good price.
   A: Thank you. I appreciate your help.

incomplete dialogues

Construct the questions for which the following sentences would be logical answers. One student will ask a question, and the person sitting next to him or her will give the answer given below.

1. **A:** Where _____ last week?
   B: They flew to England.

2. **A:** How fast _____ ?
   B: He drove ninety miles an hour.

3. **A:** How many _____ ?
   B: We invited twenty-five people.

4. **A:** What _____ ?
   B: She bought a child's bicycle.

5. **A:** What kind of books _____?
   B: She wrote three novels and a biography.

6. **A:** How long _____ the apartment?
   B: We occupied it for a month.

7. **A:** What _____ the fire _____?
   B: It destroyed five houses in my town.

8. **A:** What _____?
   B: She designs women's blouses.

9. **A:** What kind of _____ ?
   B: I like pineapple juice best.

10. **A:** How many _____ ?
    B: I typed nineteen pages.

oral reading: sentences

These sentences use many of the troublesome words containing diphthongs. Read them carefully.

1. My political science professor announced his retirement last Friday.
2. Please buy me a pint of olive oil and a five-pound bag of white rice.
3. Joyce has an appointment with her faculty adviser on Friday afternoon at five-fifteen.
4. If that light is too bright for your eyes, why don't you turn it around the other way?
5. I was disappointed to find out that I had such a small amount of money in my bank account.
6. That microscope magnifies the eye of a fly a thousand times.
7. The temperature sometimes rises to ninety in the daytime, but it's always cool at night.
8. The announcement said that the final concert had been sold out since last Friday.
9. Greenland, an island in the North Atlantic, is the world's largest island.
10. I was late to my nine o'clock class because I forgot to wind the clock last night.

Written Exercise: Practice with the Diphthongs [ɑɪ], [ɑʊ], and [ɔɪ]

Write the symbol for the sound of the boldface diphthong on the line next to each word.

1. ___ wind (v)	15. ___ down	29. ___ private
2. ___ tower	16. ___ mountain	30. ___ coward
3. ___ title	17. ___ voice	31. ___ quite
4. ___ sour	18. ___ flower	32. ___ point
5. ___ time	19. ___ climb	33. ___ child
6. ___ file	20. ___ sound	34. ___ eyebrow ___
7. ___ brown	21. ___ ice	35. ___ crowd
8. ___ fire	22. ___ allow	36. ___ avoid
9. ___ vowel	23. ___ variety	37. ___ destroy
10. ___ write	24. ___ shower	38. ___ plow
11. ___ round	25. ___ excited	39. ___ annoy
12. ___ house	26. ___ ounce	40. ___ vitamin
13. ___ blind	27. ___ loyal	41. ___ poison
14. ___ enjoy	28. ___ diet	42. ___ towel

Homework

questions for class discussion

Give some thought to the following questions and prepare an oral answer to each one of them. As usual, one student will ask a question and another student will give an appropriate answer. (Your instructor may ask everyone to answer some of the questions.)

1. What kind of people do you enjoy most?
2. What sort of people annoy you?
3. Which do you enjoy more—being by yourself or being in a crowd? Can you tell why?
4. What do you do when you're feeling down (depressed) or in a bad mood?
5. Are you satisfied or dissatisfied with your present life style? If you are dissatisfied, what aspects of your life would you like to change?
6. If you could relive the most recent years of your life, what things would you do differently?
7. What do you consider an ideal home or apartment? Mention such things as location, size, type, etc.
8. What kind of climate do you consider ideal?
9. If you had more time, what sports, hobbies, projects, or community work would you become involved in?
10. If you had $5,000 to spend on a vacation, where would you go?

class presentation

Choose a place with which you are familiar and that you think other students would enjoy visiting. **Do not choose a museum or an art gallery.** Be sure to think of a second and third choice in case someone else chooses the place you have in mind.

Prepare to speak for 2 to 5 minutes about the place you have chosen. Besides giving a description, try to get some information about its history, importance, and so on. Be sure that you can give a clear explanation of its location and explain how to get there.

Appropriateness: Asking for Assistance and Saying Thank You

dialogues

1. **A:** Thank you for trying to understand my problem.
   B: Not at all. I'm sorry I can't help you.

2. **A:** Thanks for letting me borrow your dictionary.
   B: Don't mention it. Any time you want it, just ask for it.

3. **A:** Thank you very much for lending us the cash. We really appreciate your kindness.
   B: Think nothing of it. I'm glad I could help you out.

4. **A:** Thanks a million for carrying the package for me.
   B: It was a pleasure.

5. **A:** Thank you very much for reserving the tickets.
   B: You're welcome, I'm sure. Any time I can be of help, just call me.

6. (More formal) (Elsa knocks on the door which is half open and looks in.)

Prof. Stevens: Good morning, Elsa. Come on in.
        Elsa: Good morning, Professor.
Prof. Stevens: What can I do for you?
        Elsa: I've been having trouble getting the book you told me to read for my term paper.
Prof. Stevens: Have you tried the Graduate Library?
        Elsa: Yes, they've ordered the book, but they haven't received it yet.
Prof. Stevens: Well, in that case, I'll lend you my own copy.
        Elsa: Oh, thank you very much, Professor. It's really kind of you to lend me your personal copy. I'll take very good care of it.
Prof. Stevens: I'm sure you will. Is there anything else I can do for you?
        Elsa: No, I don't think so. Anyway, I've already taken up enough of your time. I really appreciate your lending me your book. You have no idea how worried I was when I couldn't get the book from the library.
Prof. Stevens: I'm glad I could help you out.
        Elsa: You certainly have. Goodbye, Professor, and thank you again.
Prof. Stevens: You're welcome, Elsa. See you.

useful expressions

The most often used expressions to show gratitude are "Thanks," "Thanks a lot," "Thank you", and "Thank you very much." But appreciation can also be expressed through use of one of the following expressions, depending on whether a situation is formal or informal.

"I don't know how to thank you, . . . "

"I'm very grateful for all you've done."

"I'm very grateful to you."

"Thanks very much for your help."

"It really is very kind (good, nice) of you to help me."

"That's very kind of you."

"I certainly do appreciate all you've done for me. I hope I can return the favor some time."

Sometimes you may want to add the reason for your gratitude. In that case, you can say:

"I've had a wonderful time (at the party, dance, dinner, weekend, etc.)"

"Thank you so much for inviting me."

In some instances you may want to add what might have happened if you had not received help. You can say:

"Thanks a million for your help. I would never have been able to do it by myself."

"Thank you so much for the ride. I would have been late to class otherwise."

If you wish to thank someone for all the time you've taken up, you can say:

"Thanks a million for all your help. I really appreciate your spending so much time with me."

"Thank you very much. I'm sorry to have bothered you."

What is an appropriate response when someone thanks you for something? You can use one of these expressions:

"That's all right."

"Don't mention it." or "Not at all."

"Think nothing of it." or "It's nothing."

"You're welcome." or "You're very welcome."

"It's been a pleasure." or "It was a pleasure."

"I enjoyed helping you."

"I'm glad I could be of help to you." or "Any time you need help, just ask me," or "(let me know)."

practice

Listed below are some situations. With the classmate who sits next to you, choose two situations and practice saying "thank you." You may add an expression to explain why you are grateful or what would have happened if you had not received assistance. Depending on the situation, you may also add an expression to thank the person for taking up his or her time. Your classmate will respond with an appropriate expression. Then, for the second situation, reverse the roles you play. Be prepared to present your dialogues to the class. (Your instructor may wish to assign particular situations to each group of two students.)

Situations

1. An instructor has given you a make-up examination.
2. It was almost time for the store to close, but a salesperson kindly waited on you.
3. You dropped your books and a passerby helped you pick them up.
4. Someone you don't know has helped you carry a heavy package to your car.
5. A friend has gotten you tickets for a concert because you didn't have time to pick up the tickets yourself.
6. A friend has spoken well of you to your boss (or to another professor).

7. A friend's mother has just given you a ride home on a rainy day.

8. It is raining and someone has shared an umbrella to help you get to the next building.

9. A classmate helped you study for a test by lending you his or her notes.

10. You have just gotten someone's phone number from another friend.

11. A police officer has helped you change a tire.

12. Your boss has given you a day off to attend a seminar or to attend to personal business.

13. You were sick and a friend sent you a get-well card.

14. A neighbor has just shared some delicious homemade food (you decide upon the dish).

15. You forgot your wallet and a classmate has lent you money for lunch.

16. A relative of yours died recently and a friend sent you a sympathy card.

Review:
Lessons 1–13

Vowel Recognition: Listening

The following sentences will be read twice by the instructor using one of the words in parentheses. Circle the word that you hear.

1. The (boss, bus) was here on time.
2. Does he know the (man, men)?
3. I'd like a large (ball, bowl).
4. Bob (leaves, lives) here in February.
5. Where is the (beer, bear)?
6. Where did you put the (beads, bids)?
7. I like that (collar, color) very much.
8. The (cop, cap) was lost.
9. Doesn't that woman have any (fears, furs)?
10. I bought some new (shirts, shorts).
11. Do you like this kind of (soup, soap)?
12. How much is the (toll, towel)?
13. Can you lend me a (buck, book)?
14. We heard the men (shouting, shooting).
15. That (wool, wall) cost a lot of money.
16. The men couldn't move the heavy (rock, rack).
17. That black (soot, suit) should be removed from the show window.
18. Please (taste, test) this medicine.
19. Put the (pen, pin) in the drawer.
20. We (laughed, left) when she came in.

128

21. Please put (this, these) away.
22. Do you know how Jim (cut, caught) the fish?
23. You have to (steer, stir) it carefully.
24. Everyone heard the (shot, shout).
25. That kind of (floor, flower) is expensive.

Your instructor will read the following pairs of words. If the two vowels sound the same to you, write *S* on the line. If the two vowels sound different, write *D* on the line.

1.	seen	6.	threw	11.	flower	16.	now
____	scene	____	through	____	flour	____	know
2.	wear	7.	sun	12.	sleep	17.	so
____	were	____	soon	____	slip	____	sew
3.	calm	8.	stood	13.	lunch	18.	war
____	comb	____	stewed	____	launch	____	wore
4.	bought	9.	seat	14.	goat	19.	laid
____	boat	____	sit	____	got	____	led
5.	pair	10.	bear	15.	been	20.	he'll
____	pear	____	beer	____	bin	____	heel

Vowel Recognition: Written Exercises

stressed and unstressed vowels

Write the symbol for the sound of the boldface vowel and mark the primary stress. Remember, vowels in unstressed syllables are reduced to [ə] or [ɪ].

1. ____	be	____	beside	11. ____	lent	____	silent
2. ____	can't	____	canary	12. ____	band	____	husband
3. ____	ate	____	private	13. ____	face	____	surface
4. ____	man	____	woman	14. ____	ant	____	merchant
5. ____	men	____	women	15. ____	ledge	____	knowledge
6. ____	land	____	island	16. ____	cycle	____	bicycle
7. ____	age	____	message	17. ____	rent	____	different
8. ____	able	____	vegetable	18. ____	sand	____	thousand
9. ____	ice	____	practice	19. ____	fast	____	breakfast
10. ____	era	____	camera	20. ____	fort	____	effort

vowels and diphthongs

Write the symbol for the sound of the boldface vowel or diphthong. The same combination of letters may have more than one pronunciation.

1. ____	now	13. ____	ounce	25. ____	radio	37. ____	shoot
2. ____	know	14. ____	once	26. ____	native	38. ____	shout
3. ____	allow	15. ____	wound (v.)	27. ____	national	39. ____	shot
4. ____	aloud	16. ____	wound (n.)	28. ____	dozen	40. ____	tomb
5. ____	alone	17. ____	towel	29. ____	frozen	41. ____	comb
6. ____	along	18. ____	owe	30. ____	oven	42. ____	come
7. ____	quit	19. ____	crowd	31. ____	cough	43. ____	stood
8. ____	quite	20. ____	wind (v.)	32. ____	enough	44. ____	blood
9. ____	quiet	21. ____	wind (n.)	33. ____	though	45. ____	food
10. ____	item	22. ____	sew	34. ____	through	46. ____	good
11. ____	floor	23. ____	height	35. ____	thought	47. ____	sign
12. ____	flour	24. ____	eye	36. ____	shut	48. ____	signal

vowel sounds and diphthongs followed by *r*

Write the phonetic symbol ([ɪr], [ɛr], [ær], [ɑr], [ɝ], [ʊ], [jʊ], [ɔ], [ɑɪ], or [ɑʊ]) for the sound of the boldface vowel or diphthong + *r*. Notice that the same combination of letters may have more than one pronunciation.

1. ____ y**ear**	17. ____ v**ir**gin	36. ____ **ar**ticle
2. ____ p**ear**	18. ____ ent**ire**	37. ____ w**ere**
3. ____ f**ire**	19. ____ p**oor**	38. ____ w**ear**
4. ____ b**ir**d	20. ____ fl**oor**	39. ____ w**e're**
5. ____ **air**	21. ____ slow**er**	40. ____ w**eir**d
6. ____ h**eir**	22. ____ tow**er**	41. ____ f**ir**m
7. ____ s**er**ious	23. ____ b**ur**n	42. ____ **ir**on
8. ____ c**ir**cle	24. ____ c**ure**	43. ____ engin**eer**
9. ____ d**ur**ing	25. ____ **Eur**ope	44. ____ b**ear**d
(3 possibilities)	26. ____ d**ir**ty	45. ____ f**ur**ious
____	27. ____ adm**ire**	46. ____ h**ur**ry
____	28. ____ f**or**eign	47. ____ h**ear**d
10. ____ qu**ar**rel	(2 possibilities)	48. ____ h**ear**
11. ____ squ**are**	____	49. ____ h**ear**t
12. ____ liqu**or**	29. ____ w**ar**m	50. ____ f**ur**
13. ____ **or**ange	30. ____ w**or**n	
(2 possibilities)	31. ____ w**or**m	
____	32. ____ requ**ire**	
14. ____ h**ar**bor	33. ____ th**ir**ty	
____	34. ____ ch**ar**acter	
15. ____ c**are**ful	(2 possibilities)	
16. ____ c**our**age	____	
	35. ____ d**oll**ar	

Communication Exercises

1. Here is a list of some everyday situations. What would you say in each of them? There is more than one way to express yourself in these situations. Your instructor will provide information about the age, sex, and status of the person to whom you will be talking and will also specify the relationship between the two speakers.

1. Someone asks you for the time.
2. Ask someone for the time.
3. Someone asks you where you live.
4. Someone introduces an older person to you.
5. Ask about a friend's health.
6. Introduce a friend of yours to your instructor.
7. Ask someone to come with you to the movies.
8. Someone asks you to spell your last name.
9. Ask someone for the name of a friend of his.
10. Ask someone where she was born.
11. Ask someone where he comes from.
12. Ask someone to repeat what she has just said.
13. Tell someone your age.
14. Ask how long a particular trip takes.

15. Ask what time a particular flight leaves.
16. Ask someone whether a book belongs to him or her.
17. Someone asks you the number of students in your class.
18. Ask your instructor about your grade on a test.
19. Ask someone what size he or she wears.
20. Ask a salesperson to show you a particular article of clothing.
21. You call the salesperson and ask where the men's umbrellas are.
22. You want to try on an article of clothing; ask where the dressing room is.
23. Ask someone to do you a favor.
24. Ask someone where the bank is.
25. Tell someone where the library is.
26. Offer a ride to a friend.
27. Offer a drink to an acquaintance.
28. Refuse an alcoholic drink and request something else.
29. Ask your instructor to repeat the instructions given.
30. Thank someone for helping you change a tire.

2. With a classmate, choose one of the situations listed above and make up a dialogue of about 6 or 8 lines. Show it to your instructor for suggestions and/or corrections. Then memorize it and act it out in a future class meeting as the instructor indicates. You may also choose a situation not included in the list that you think would be appropriate for a dialogue to be presented to the class.

The Consonants: The Bilabial Stops [p] and [b]

A consonant is a speech sound which is produced by a complete or partial obstruction of the air stream in the vocal tract. The speech organs responsible for this obstruction are called **articulators**. The articulators are the **lips, teeth, tongue, hard palate, soft palate** (or **velum**) and the **uvula**. (Look at the diagram of the parts of the speech mechanism on page 2.)

There are various ways of classifying the consonants. Basically, they may be identified according to:

1. the state of the vocal cords
2. the place of articulation — where the obstruction of the airstream occurs
3. the manner of articulation — how the stream of air is blocked

In Lesson 1 we explained voiced and voiceless sounds and gave you a list of these consonant sounds in English with their corresponding phonetic symbols. Review Lesson 1 so that you have the concept of voiced and voiceless sounds clearly in mind. The consonants, classified according to their place of articulation, will be taken up individually in this order: stops, fricatives, affricates, glides, liquids, and nasals.

Description of the Sounds [p] and [b]

[p] and [b] are called bilabial stops because the articulators used to produce them are the two lips. To produce [p] and [b], close the lips completely, thus blocking the passage of air and creating a build-up of pressure. When you suddenly open your lips to produce the [p] sound, there is an explosion of air. This explosion is called **aspiration**. If you put your fingers in front of your mouth as you pronounce [p], you will feel this puff of air. In the production of [p], the **vocal cords do not vibrate**. Therefore, [p] is a **voiceless** sound. [b] is produced in exactly the same way, but the **vocal cords**

vibrate, and there is **no aspiration**. Therefore, we say that [b] is a **voiced** sound. The diagram shows the position of the speech organs in the production of [p] and [b].

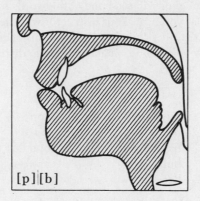

Both [p] and [b] appear initially as in *pin*, and *be*, medially as in *simple* and *above*, and finally as in *top* and *cab*. Repeat the words after your instructor.

Important Hints about the Sounds [p] and [b]

Notice the following hints and listen carefully as your instructor reads the examples.

1. Strongly aspirate [p] and strongly explode [b] in stressed syllables.

| pen | appéar | step úp | big | obéy |

2. Do not aspirate [p] when it is preceded by [s].

| space | spoon | whisper |

3. It isn't necessary to explode final [p] and [b]. However, you **must** put your lips in position to produce the sounds. If you do release the sounds, explode [p] with little aspiration and [b] with little or no voicing.

| up | Pull her up. | lab | He's in the lab. |
| stop | Don't stop. | club | Call me at the club. |

4. Both [p] and [b] form combinations with other consonants. These combinations are called **clusters**. A cluster may consist of two, three, or four consonants. Clusters appear in both initial and final position. Here are some of the most common ones.

[pr]	price	[pt]	slept	[bl]	blow
[sp]	speak	[mpt]	jumped	[br]	bread
[spl]	splash	[mpts]	tempts	[bd]	rubbed
[spr]	spray	[ps]	stops	[bz]	rubs

5. *p* is silent in the following words: *receipt, corps, cupboard, psychology, psalm, pneumonia*, and all other words beginning with *pn* and *ps*.

b is usually silent when preceded by *m* or followed by *t*: for example, *comb, tomb, climb, dumb, thumb, bomb, plumber, doubt, debt*.

Some Exceptions: timber, remember, slumber, lumber, number

Listening Exercises and Oral Practice: Distinguishing [p] from [b]

Your instructor will read one of the words from each of the following pairs. Circle the words that you hear. Your instructor will then read all the words and ask you to repeat them. Next, he or she will read the sentences. Listen carefully. Then practice reading the sentences aloud, making a clear distinction between the [p] and [b] in the boldface words.

[p]	[b]		[p]	[b]		[p]	[b]
pie	buy		mop	mob		simple	symbol
pit	bit		cup	cub			
pay	bay		rope	robe			
pull	bull		cap	cab			
pet	bet						

1. Please **buy** some **pie** for dessert.
2. I broke a tooth when I **bit** a cherry **pit**.
3. You have to **pay** for a tour of the **bay**.
4. That **bull** will **pull** on the rope.
5. He **bet** ten dollars that his **pet** would win the contest.
6. We'll have to **mop** up after that **mob** leaves.
7. The lion **cub** drank a **cup** of milk.
8. She wore a **rope** of pearls with her **robe**.
9. The **cab** driver was wearing a **cap**.
10. This **symbol** is quite **simple** to draw.

Your instructor will read the following sentences using one of the words in parentheses. Circle the word that you hear.

1. I'm so hungry I could eat a big (pear, bear).
2. I put a (punch, bunch) of grapes in the fruit (punch, bunch).
3. You need a bigger (pole, bowl).
4. The (palm, bomb) fell on the house.
5. The doctor gave her a (pill, bill).
6. I'll hang the (rope, robe) on a hook.
7. Bob needs a (cap, cab) immediately.
8. You'll find a (mop, mob) outside.
9. That (cup, cub) is very small.
10. She put the beer in the (pack, back).

Frequently Used and Sometimes Troublesome Words Containing [p] and [b]

This list will serve as a short review of the vowels and diphthongs. Repeat the words after your instructor.

Initial [p]		*Medial* [p]		*Final* [p]	
piece	pool	péople	púpil	keep	pulp
pink	pull	simple	input	dip	burp
play	pole	paper	hoping	tape	soup
pear	Paul	separate (adj)	postpóne	step	soap
past	pie	happy	impórtant	tap	type
part	pound	operate	múltiply	pop	
puff	point	couple	compound		
perháps		purpose	pinpoint		

Initial [b]		*Medial* [b]		*Final* [b]	
beach	booth	sýmbol	públic	rib	verb
big	book	baby	distúrbance	Babe	tube
bay	both	rebel	cúbicle	lab	robe
bear	bowl	habit	baseball	job	tribe
back	boss	robber	soupbowl	tub	
bódy	bought	rubber	describíng	bulb	
bottle	bícycle				
birth	bound				
	boil				

Oral Practice

sentences with strongly aspirated [p] and strongly exploded [b]

Read these short sentences aloud. Remember to strongly aspirate [p] **only** before a stressed vowel. Otherwise aspirate it weakly. **Do not** aspirate [b].

1. Give me a piece of pie, please.
2. Please pass the pepper, Paul.
3. Put your passport in an envelope.
4. Do you suppose you could pick me up at the park?
5. She bought a pair of pants for her little boy.
6. Where did you buy the boat?
7. My boss is away in Belgium.
8. Is the bowling alley above the bank?

sentences with unreleased [p] and [b]

These sentences contain [p] and [b] in final position. Be sure to close your lips to form the sounds even if you do not release the explosion.

1. Did he stop?
2. I have a new job.
3. Hurry up!
4. Call a cab.
5. Let's meet at the club.
6. Would you like some soup?
7. Be careful you don't slip.
8. I have to go to the lab.
9. Will you be able to sleep?
10. I'll take a nap.

questions containing words with final [p] and [b]

Student A will ask a question and Student B will answer in a complete sentence, blending the final [p] and [b] with the initial vowel of the next word.

1. Have you ever mailed a letter without putting a stamp on it?
2. In your room, is there a lamp on a table or on a desk?
3. Would you prefer to have a job in a laboratory or in the library?
4. What do you use to pump up a tire?
5. What may happen if you step on a banana peel?

6. Do you sleep in a single bed or in a double bed?
7. Would you prefer a ripe apple or a ripe orange?
8. Would you rather type a paper or prepare an oral report?
9. Do you prefer your soup in a bowl or in a cup?
10. Why is it dangerous to fall asleep in the sun?

sentences with [p] and [b] in clusters

In these sentences, practice reading the words with the boldface clusters first. Then read the sentences. Be careful not to add a vowel before words beginning with *sp*.

1. **Pl**ease he**lp** me **br**ing the soup **sp**oons to the kitchen.
2. The baby sle**pt** with the lam**ps** on.
3. The **pr**esident faced several atte**mpts** on his life.
4. The **pr**ice of **br**ead increased very shar**pl**y.
5. Don't ju**mp** and **pl**ay on the bed while I'm sleeping.
6. He often ru**bs** his eyes when he **sp**eaks.
7. She put five sta**mps** on that letter.
8. His car bum**ped** into a **bl**ack truck.
9. The gang ro**bbed** a bank last **spr**ing.
10. The **bl**ock of cement hit the water with a big **spl**ash.

sentences with silent [p] and [b]

Read these sentences. Be sure not to pronounce silent *p* and *b*.

1. Is there a Peace Corps camp in this area?
2. Do you have a comb in your pocket? I lost mine in the cab.
3. Pat came down with pneumonia.
4. What's the plumber's telephone number?
5. She sent me the receipt promptly.
6. Peter cut his thumb on the soap dish in the bathtub.
7. Paula, are you taking psychology?
8. I have no doubts about his lab grades.
9. Please put these bottles in the captain's cupboard.
10. I've paid all my debts.

mini-dialogues

1. **A:** Would you please bring me a soupspoon?
   B: Why certainly. I have a couple of them here.
2. **A:** Aren't you going in the pool, Bobby?
   B: I think I'll take a nap first.
3. **A:** Look at all the bubbles this soap makes.
   B: It's a special bath soap.
4. **A:** Why don't you put Paul in the playpen?
   B: Because I have to bathe him first.
5. **A:** Betty, please pass the bread and butter.
   B: Sure. Here's the bread. I'll pass the butter as soon as Peter's through using it.
6. **A:** Could you buy me some corn on the cob?
   B: Of course. Would you care for a hamburger or a roast beef sandwich too?
   A: Just the corn will be fine, thank you.

7. **A:** Where's the Speech Lab?
    B: It's at the bottom of the stairs.

8. **A:** Can I park near the post office?
    B: Yes. There's a parking lot a block away.

9. **A:** I'd like a piece of apple pie.
    B: How about some coffee with your dessert?
    A: Splendid!

10. **A:** What's her business?
    B: It's a publishing business. She prints all types of paperback books.

Homework

Make a list of five things you have never done but would like to do. For example, "I would like to visit Paris in the summer." Write these things down on a piece of paper and bring them to class. Be prepared to explain why you chose **one** of these particular things and to tell the class how you would go about accomplishing it.

PARTS OF THE TELEPHONE*

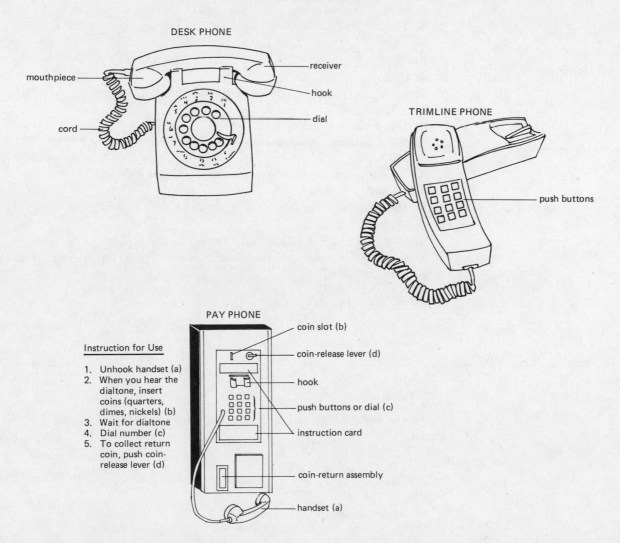

DESK PHONE

mouthpiece

receiver

hook

dial

cord

TRIMLINE PHONE

push buttons

PAY PHONE

Instruction for Use

1. Unhook handset (a)
2. When you hear the dialtone, insert coins (quarters, dimes, nickels) (b)
3. Wait for dialtone
4. Dial number (c)
5. To collect return coin, push coin-release lever (d)

coin slot (b)

coin-release lever (d)

hook

push buttons or dial (c)

instruction card

coin-return assembly

handset (a)

*The appropriateness sections of the following lessons deal with various types of telephone conversations. Therefore, you should learn the names of the parts of the telephone.

Appropriateness: Greetings, Leave-takings, and Other Expressions Used in Telephone Conversations

dialogues

1. **A:** Hello, Petersen residence.
   B: Hello. This is Peter Borg. May I speak to Paula, please?
   A: Just a minute. I'll get her.
   (calls Paula)
   C: Hello.
   B: Hi, Paula. This is Peter.
   C: Oh! Hi, Peter. How are you?
   B: Fine, thank you, and you?
   C: All right, I guess. I'm just getting over a bad cold.
   B: Oh, I'm sorry to hear that. I was wondering if you could lend me your biology notes from last week's class.
   C: Hold on a second. Let me check to see if I have them here . . . Yes, I do. When do you need them?
   B: Can I pick them up tonight? I can return them to you before class tomorrow morning.
   C: Sure. Come on over.
   B: Thanks, Paula. I'll be over right away.
   C: 'Bye!
   B: 'Bye!

2. **A:** Hello.
   B: Hello, this is Sara speaking. May I speak to John?
   A: Who?
   B: May I please speak to John?
   A: What number are you calling?
   B: 436-1053.
   A: I'm sorry, you have the wrong number. This is 435-1053.
   B: I'm sorry.
   A: That's all right.

3. **A:** Hello.
   B: Hello. This is Bob calling. May I speak to Mary, please?
   A: I'm sorry you must have the wrong number. There's no one here by that name.
   B: Is this 616-5987?
   A: No, it's 616-5978.
   B: I'm sorry, I must have dialed wrong.
   A: That's quite all right.

useful expressions

Greetings

When you are making a call, it is always appropriate to identify yourself to the other person.

"Hello. This is Barbara Parks."
"Good morning. This is Pat speaking."

If you are answering a call you say:

"Hello."
"Hello, Bill Pond speaking."

"Hello, Pierce residence." (more formal)
"Mrs. Bates' residence, Bob speaking."

If you know the person who is answering your call, follow the initial greeting with the usual expressions.

A: Hello.
B: Good morning, Pete. This is Joe speaking. How are you? (Recognizes voice of Speaker A.)
A: Hi, Joe, I'm just fine, thanks.

Asking for a Person and Responding

If you wish to speak to someone in particular, you use one of the following expressions after you have identified yourself.

"May I speak to Pete, please?"
"Is Pete in?"
"Is Pete home?"
"I'd like to speak to Pete, please."
"Could I please speak to Pete?"

An appropriate answer to any of these expressions is one of the following.

"Certainly."
"Just a minute. I'll call him."
"Hold on a minute. I'll get him."

If the person is not available you say:

"I'm sorry. He's not in."
"I'm sorry. He isn't home."
"Sorry, he can't come to the phone right now. Can you call back a little later?"
"Can he call you back?"

Leave-taking

The following expressions are appropriate for ending a conversation.

Informal

A: So long.   **A:** Thanks for calling.   **A:** 'Bye.
B: 'Bye.   **B:** Not at all. Goodbye.   **B:** 'Bye.
A: 'Bye.

A: Nice to hear from you.   **A:** It was good talking to you. Goodbye.
B: Same here. 'Bye.   **B:** Goodbye.
A: 'Bye.

Formal

A: Thank you very much for calling, Mr. Parks.
B: You're welcome, Brenda. Goodbye.
A: Goodbye.

A: Goodbye, Mrs. Post. It was nice of you to call.
B: Goodbye, Helen. I hope you feel better.
A: Thank you.

Getting the Wrong Number.

If you happen to get a wrong number, do not hang up without a word of explanation. It is appropriate to say one of the following expressions.

"I'm sorry. Is this 725-8132?"
"I'm sorry; I must have dialed wrong."

If you are on the other end of the line receiving the wrong call you might say:

"What number are you calling?"
"I'm sorry; you must have the wrong number."
"Sorry, there's no one here by that name."

As soon as the caller apologizes for getting the wrong number, then you add:

"That's all right."

practice

Select one of the following situations.

1. Student A was absent from a class today and calls Student B for the assignment. Student C answers the phone. Student A and Student C exchange greetings and then Student C calls Student B to the phone. Student A and Student B carry on a short conversation about the assignment.

2. Student A would like to get together with Student B to study for an important examination. Student A calls Student B to make arrangements to meet, but someone else, Student C, answers the phone. Student A and Student C do not know each other. They carry on a short conversation.

3. Student A was absent from a class. Student B finds out that Student A is sick and calls to inquire about his health. The mother of Student A answers the phone, and she carries on a conversation with Student B.

4. Student A calls Student B. Student C answers the phone and both Student A and Student C exchange greetings. Student A asks for Student B, but Student C explains that Student B is busy right now, cannot answer the phone, and would like Student A to call back later.

5. Student A must be hospitalized during the semester and he calls Professor Spring at the English Department to explain why he will be absent from a class for two weeks. The secretary answers and calls Professor Spring.

6. Student A calls Student B, but gets a wrong number.

7. With one or two other students, make up a dialogue using some of the expressions presented in this lesson. Practice it and be prepared to act it out in class.

The Consonants: The Alveolar Stops [t] and [d]

Description of the Sounds [t] and [d]

[t] and [d] are postdental, alveolar stops. [t] is **voiceless**, and [d] is **voiced**. To produce these sounds, place the tip of the tongue against the alveolar ridge*, and the curved border of the tongue against the entire alveolar ridge, thereby stopping the flow of the air stream. Then suddenly release the air by pulling the tongue back, thus causing the sound to explode with a puff of air (aspiration). To make sure that you are aspirating the [t], put your fingers to your lips; if you are producing the sound correctly, you should be able to feel the puff of air with your fingers. [d] is produced in exactly the same way as the [t] except that when the air is released, the vocal cords vibrate, and there is no aspiration.

the ridge of the gums behind the upper front teeth

> **NOTE:** In the production of [t] and [d] **do not allow the tongue tip to touch the upper front teeth at any time.** The diagram below shows the position of the speech organs in the production of [t] and [d].

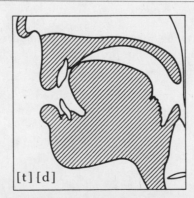

[t] [d]

141

[t] and [d] may appear initially, as in *tea* and *day*, medially as in *attain* and *medium*, and finally as in *meet* and *bed*. Repeat the words after your instructor.

Important Hints about the Sounds [t] and [d]

1. In stressed syllables, strongly aspirate [t] and strongly explode [d]. Repeat these words after your instructor.

táble	atténtion	tear dówn	Aunt Ánna
dóllar	addítion	dówntówn	bend óver

2. Whenever [t] falls between a stressed vowel and an unstressed vowel, many American speakers substitute a sound that is produced by a quick movement of the tongue tip against the alveolar ridge (for instance, the words *water* and *city*). In fact, many Americans do not distinguish between the words *latter* and *ladder*. Some do make a distinction by shortening the vowel in *latter* and lengthening it in *ladder*. It is best to rely on the context in which the words are used to determine which word a speaker is using, as in:

> The *latter* is easier than the former.
> I'll need a *ladder* to reach the window.

3. Do not release (explode) final [t] and [d] at the end of a sentence or phrase, or when there is no opportunity for blending with the following word.

Pet the cat.
Read the third word.

4. Do not aspirate [t] when it is preceded by the sound [s].

steam	still	stay	step	stamp	stop

5. Notice how [t] and [d] combine with other consonants to form both initial and final clusters.

[tr]	tree	[kt]*	act	[nt]*	want	[dr]	dream
[tw]	twenty	[kst]	next	[rst]*	burst	[dw]	dwell
[str]	street	[mpt]*	prompt	[st]*	beast	[nd]*	find
						[rd]*	card
						[ld]*	hold

See Lesson 5 for the pronunciation of these final clusters with the addition of the s ending.

The following final clusters are formed when the regular past tense ending *ed* is added to a verb. For pronunciation rules for this ending, review Lesson 6.

[pt]	stopped	[kst]	fixed	[nd]	burned	[ŋd]	banged
[mpt]	jumped	[ft]	laughed	[rd]	tired	[ld]	failed
[st]	kissed	[ʃt]	washed	[bd]	rubbed	[zd]	pleased
[kt]	walked	[tʃt]	watched	[gd]	begged	[dʒd]	damaged
				[vd]	loved		
				[ðd]	bathed		

6. In the following words, do not pronounce the letters *t* and *d*. They are silent.

lísten	ballet	whístle	hándkerchief
fasten	buffét	castle	Wednesday
soften	crochét	Christmas	
often*	dépot	mortgage	
christen	bouquét		

Many people pronounce the t in this word.

Listening Exercises and Oral Practice

1. Distinguishing [t] from [d]

Your instructor will read one word from each of the pairs of words in the following exercise. Circle the words that you hear. Then the instructor will read all of the words in each exercise and ask you to repeat them. Next, he or she will read the sentences in each exercise. Listen carefully and then read the sentences aloud, making a clear distinction between the boldface words in each sentence.

[t]	[d]	[t]	[d]	[t]	[d]	[t]	[d]
tear	dare	tip	dip	heart	hard	sat	sad
tan	Dan	town	down	wrote	rode	cart	card

1. I **dare** you to **tear** up that paper.
2. **Dan** has a good **tan**.
3. **Dip** the **tip** of the brush in the paint.
4. I'm going **downtown**.

2. Your instructor will read the following sentences. Listen to the length of the vowel and the blending with the following vowel to determine whether the present or the past tense of the verb is used in a sentence. Circle the word that you hear. At the end of the exercise, practice reading the sentences first in the present tense and then in the past. Be sure to make the correct blending.

1. My parents (travel, traveled) all over the world.
2. We (walk, walked) along the river every night.
3. The boys often (talk, talked) about their cars.
4. He told me that you (study, studied) at night.
5. We (dance, danced) every Saturday afternoon.
6. They (entertain, entertained) a great many people.
7. I frequently (stop, stopped) at the market on my way home.
8. The children usually (wash, washed) all the supper dishes.
9. Those men (train, trained) animals for the circus.
10. I (dream, dreamed) almost every night.

Frequently Used and Sometimes Troublesome Words

These frequently used words contain the sounds [t] or [d] in initial, medial, or final positions. Notice that the lists serve as a review of all the vowel sounds.

	Initial [t]		*Medial* [t]		*Final* [t]
teach	Tuésday	fatígue	opportúnity	sweet	shoot
tícket	took	sýstem	fóotstep	quit	foot
tape	total	native	motor	great	throat
terrible	taught	attémpt	autumn	sweat	bought
talent	tight	láughter	delíghtful	flat	quite
target	tower	Octóber	accountant	shot	shout
touch	toilet	cóuntry	oíntment	shut	joint
turn		curtain		hurt	

	Initial [d]		*Medial* [d]		*Final* [d]
deep	dúplicate (n)	idéa	redúce	lead (v)	food
dig	durable	window	endure	lid	stood
dánger	don't	radio	ólder	grade	load
delicate	drawer	index	audience	said	appláud
dramátic	diet	adápt	upside dówn	bad	wide
dóllar	doubt	bódy	inside óut	guard	round
dozen	destróy	índustry		blood	avoid
dirty				heard	

Oral Practice

These exercises contain the sounds [t] and [d] in initial, medial, and final positions and serve to illustrate the various features of the sounds which were taken up on pages 142–43 of this lesson. Be aware of the various degrees of aspiration, voicing, and de-voicing of the [t] and [d] sounds in the sentences below. Also practice blending. Watch for silent *t*s and *d*s, which occur in some of the sentences.

sentences

1. We watched an interesting television program last Tuesday night.
2. Dan had worked in the textile industry for almost twenty years when he quit last September.
3. We bought tickets for the ballet for the first Wednesday in October.
4. Donna turned her good skirt inside out when she put it in the laundry basket.
5. Betty taught her oldest daughter to crochet, and she made some very attractive Christmas gifts.
6. Donald typed a letter and handed it to me to read.
7. The storm destroyed a watch tower of the ancient castle.
8. The Park Department dug holes along the east side of Front Street to plant trees.

questions

Answer the following questions using the past tense as in the example. Be sure to substitute the correct pronoun for the noun subject. Sometimes more than one pronoun is correct. Remember to blend the *-ed* ending with *it*.

example: "Did you answer the question?" "Yes, I answered it."

Student A will ask Student B. Student B will answer and ask Student C and so on.

1. Did Tom accept your apology?   Yes, he ____ it.

2. Did Tina attend the party?   Yes, she ____ it.
3. Did the men connect our telephone?   Yes, they ____ it.
4. Did the dentist treat your infected tooth?
5. Did you taste the dessert?
6. Did the little girl touch that wet paint?
7. Did you notice our new television set?
8. Did Tony drop his towel?
9. Did the teacher dismiss her class?
10. Did the dean's assistant address the letter?
11. Did you step on that rusty nail?
12. Did you fasten the lock on the gate?
13. Did Don learn that new tune?
14. Did you and Talma study today's assignment?
15. Did the dealer guarantee the radio?

dialogues

Practice reading these dialogues with another student, observing all you have learned about intonation, stress, and blending. Your instructor may ask you to memorize one or two.

1.　**A:** Your car looks so shiny! Have you had it painted recently?
　　B: No, I just washed it and waxed it. It took me all day yesterday.
　　A: You haven't used it much lately, have you?
　　B: No, I haven't needed it since I stopped attending night school. I live near the school where I teach so I've been walking to work.

2.　**Prof:** Hello, Tom. How are you? How are your classes going?
　　Tom: Fine, thanks, but I'm glad this semester is almost over. I'm very tired.
　　Prof: Why is that? Have you studied unusually hard this semester?
　　Tom: Well, I've studied a lot. So far I've passed all my exams with good grades.

3.　**Prof:** David, I've noticed a big improvement in your pronunciation lately.
　David: Thank you, Professor. This semester I've really worked on it, and I've learned a lot from my American roommate, too.

4.　**A:** I just met Ted. He looked terrible! And he was sweating a lot, too. What's wrong with him? Do you know?
　　B: I just talked to him, too. He told me he had a bad cold and a sore throat. He said he ached all over. He has an appointment with his doctor tomorrow morning.

5.　**A:** I heard about your Aunt Tillie's accident. I understand she shut a door on her left hand. Did she hurt it badly?
　　B: No, fortunately she didn't. The doctor gave her a shot and put some ointment on her hand. Then he taped it up and told her to avoid using it as much as possible for the next ten days.

6.　**A:** Tony's overweight. He'd better watch out. He's apt to have a heart attack.
　　B: He's on a diet and he's already lost twenty pounds. He said he still has another fifteen to lose, but he's determined to take off all that extra weight before Christmas.

7.　**A:** Terry, I didn't know you weren't attending night classes any more. Have you finished all the courses you need for your M.A.?
　　B: Oh, yes. I finished all but one course last May. I attended summer school and worked on my thesis at the same time.
　　A: Have you completed your thesis already? You must have worked on it day and night!
　　B: I did! I finished it and it was accepted last fall. I received my Master's in December. I'm all through—at last!

Written Exercise: Reviewing the Past Tense Ending of Regular Verbs

Before you do this exercise, review the rules for the pronunciation of the past tense of regular verbs in Lesson 6. The words listed below contain the sounds [t] or [d] in initial, medial, or final position. Write the correct phonetic symbol for the pronunciation of the *ed* ending—[t], [d], or [ɪd], and then practice reading the words out loud. Some of the words contain a silent letter *t*. Watch for them.

1. ___ discovered	17. ___ mortgaged	33. ___ dished
2. ___ doubled	18. ___ touched	34. ___ trusted
3. ___ taxed	19. ___ listened	35. ___ deserted
4. ___ divided	20. ___ dented	36. ___ dressed
5. ___ denied	21. ___ detected	37. ___ studied
6. ___ graduated	22. ___ tripped	38. ___ contributed
7. ___ watched	23. ___ fastened	39. ___ started
8. ___ practiced	24. ___ stepped	40. ___ guaranteed
9. ___ delayed	25. ___ tempted	41. ___ ditched
10. ___ detested	26. ___ whistled	42. ___ tipped
11. ___ traveled	27. ___ stopped	43. ___ avoided
12. ___ continued	28. ___ addressed	44. ___ accepted
13. ___ attacked	29. ___ softened	45. ___ destroyed
14. ___ imitated	30. ___ dusted	46. ___ dipped
15. ___ astonished	31. ___ treated	47. ___ doubted
16. ___ descended	32. ___ christened	48. ___ defeated

Homework

Prepare to tell the class about the most frightening experience you have had in your life or about a very exciting experience. Plan to speak for **not less than 2 minutes** and **not more than 5 minutes**.

Appropriateness: Leaving a Message or Taking a Message

dialogues

1. **A:** Hello.
   B: May I speak with John, please?
   A: I'm sorry he isn't home. Who's calling, please?
   B: Bill Smith. May I leave a message for him, please?
   A: Yes, of course, Mr. Smith. May I have your telephone number?
   B: Yes. It's 763-7140.
   A: 766-7140.
   B: No. It's 763-7140.
   A: I'm sorry. 763-7140. Bill Smith, right?
   B: Yes, that's right.
   A: All right, I'll have John call you as soon as he comes in. Goodbye.
   B: Thank you, goodbye.

2. **A:** Hello, Lopez residence. José speaking.
   B: Hello. May I speak to Maria, please?
   A: I'm sorry, Maria isn't home right now. Who's calling?
   B: This is Martin Levy. When do you expect her?

A: I'm not sure; she said she'd be home late this afternoon.

B: Will you please take a message?

A: Certainly. Wait until I get a pencil and paper. OK. Now, what's your name again?

B: Martin Levy. Please tell Maria to call me as soon as she comes in. It's very important. My number is 753-7983.

A: Please call Martin Levy—important. 753-7983. OK. I'll see that she gets the message.

B: Thank you very much. Goodbye.

A: Goodbye.

3. **A:** Good morning, Dr. Wilson's office.

B: This is Mrs. Jones. Is the doctor in, please?

A: No, he isn't. Do you wish to make an appointment?

B: No, I don't. When will the doctor return? I wish to speak to him.

A: He'll be back in the office at about 5:30. Do you wish to leave a message? I'll have him call you when he comes in.

B: Yes, I must speak to him about a prescription he gave me. It's very important.

A: What is your number, please?

B: 765-7650.

A: 765-7650?

B: Yes.

A: And your name?

B: Mrs. Jones, Mrs. Doris Jones.

A: Thank you, Mrs. Jones. I'll have the doctor call you as soon as he returns.

B: Thank you very much. Goodbye.

A: You're very welcome. Goodbye.

useful expressions

As you noticed in the preceding dialogues, when you make a call to someone and that person is not at home or in his office, there are different ways to leave a message. You can say:

"May I leave a message?"
"Will you take a message, please?"
"Please take this message." (more formal)
"Will you please ask ____ to call me?"

Always give your full name. If it is a difficult name, be prepared to spell it slowly. Leave the message and then give your telephone number—slowly. If the person answering the phone doesn't repeat the name and number, ask him or her to do so, so that you can be sure that they have the correct information.

If you are taking a message for someone, always ask the person calling for the full name. If you have difficulty understanding, ask that person to spell his or her name. After you have written down the name, the telephone number, and the message, always repeat it back to the caller. You can use one of these expressions to ask a person if they want to leave a message.

"Do you want (wish) to leave a message?"
"Would you like to leave a message?"

practice

In each of these situations, the person being called is not available. The person answering the phone will take a message. Following your instructor's directions, get together with another student and work out a dialogue for a particular situation, and then present it to the class. Use some of the expressions from the dialogues above.

1. You call a friend and ask to have him call you back in the evening. The person answering has trouble understanding your name and telephone number.

2. Call your lawyer and ask the secretary to have him or her call you between six and eight o'clock in the evening at your home. Explain that it is very important that you speak to your lawyer at that time.

3. Call your doctor's office and ask the secretary to have the doctor call you when he or she arrives. You have a question about some medicine he or she asked you to take.

4. Make up a situation in which one person calls for someone who is not available. The person who answers will make the appropriate response.

The Consonants: The Velar Stops [k] and [g]

Description of the Sounds

[k] and [g] are velar stops. [k] is **voiceless**, and [g] is **voiced**. [k] and [g] are called velar stops because the firm contact of the back of the tongue with the soft palate (velum) completely blocks the air stream. To produce the [k] sound, raise the back of the tongue against the soft palate. (The tongue tip usually rests slightly below the lower front teeth.) Suddenly release the air by pulling the back of the tongue away from the soft palate, thus causing an explosion of the air (aspiration).

[g] is produced in exactly the same manner as [k] except that there is vibration of the vocal cords and no aspiration. The diagram below shows the position of the speech organs during the production of [k] and [g].

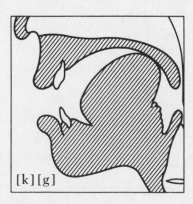

[k][g]

Both [k] and [g] appear initially as in *cold*, and *gold*, medially as in *become* and *begin*, and finally as in *pick* and *pig*.

Repeat these words after your instructor.

Important Hints about the Sounds [k] and [g]

1. Aspirate [k] and explode [g] strongly in stressed syllables and when the following word begins with a stressed vowel.

keep	becaúse	gold	begín	plug ín
cótton	peculiar	ghest	engage	dig up
character	account	look úp	pick óut	
kick	recórd			

2. Do not release final [k] and [g] at the end of a sentence or phrase, or when there is no opportunity for blending.

Bake the cake.	Please tag that rug.	Don't drag the flag.

walk fast	make things	black socks	make sure
take vitamins	take these	black zipper	make change

3. When [k] is preceded by [s], do not aspirate [k] (or aspirate it weakly).

ski, skip, skate, skeptic, scatter, Scot, scoot, scope, scald, sky, scout, skirt

4. Notice how both [k] and [g] form clusters with other consonants. Below are some troublesome clusters.

[kr]	cry		[lk]	silk*
[kw]	quiet, equal		[rk]	cork, dark
[skw]	square		[sk]	desk, ask
[skr]	scream, inscription		[sks]	risks, asks
			[ŋk]	think

*l *is silent before* [k] *in these words:* walk, talk, chalk, balk, folk, yolk

[gl]	glass, England
[gr]	group, regret
[gw]	language, distinguish

The following clusters are formed with the addition of the s ending and regular past tense ending. (See Lessons 5 and 6, respectively.)

[lkt]	milked		[ks]	makes
[skt]	risked, asked		[sks]	asks
[rkt]	parked		[rks]	parks
[gd]	drugged		[gz]	drugs
[kst]	fixed, next			

Listening Exercises and Oral Practice: Distinguishing [k] from [g]

Your instructor will read one of the words from each of the following pairs. Circle the words you hear. Then your instructor will pronounce all the words and ask you to repeat them. Next, he or she will read the sentences. Listen carefully. Then read the sentences, making a clear distinction between [k] and [g] in the boldface words.

[k]	[g]	[k]	[g]	[k]	[g]
came	game	decree	degree	pick	pig
could	good	bicker	bigger	back	bag
coat	goat			tack	tag
card	guard			Dick	dig
cage	gauge				

1. Gary **came** home after the **game**.
2. You **could** get **good** grades if you tried.
3. The **goat** chewed up my green **coat**.
4. I showed the **guard** my ID **card**.
5. The **bigger** the prize, the more they'll **bicker** over it.
6. **Pick** out the **pig** you want to buy.
7. He carried the **bag** on his **back**.
8. **Tack** up the notice while I **tag** the furniture.

Your instructor will read the following sentences using one of the words in parentheses. Circle the word that you hear. Each sentence will be read twice.

1. There's a (tack, tag) on this chair.
2. You can see the (coast, ghost) from here.
3. I bought a (coat, goat) at the market.
4. There are some (racks, rags) in the closet.
5. Put the food in the (back, bag).
6. This (cage, gauge) is useless.
7. You need a (guard, card) to enter the parking lot.
8. Everyone thought it was (cold, gold).
9. We didn't get the (goal, coal) we needed.
10. How did he get the (gash, cash) he has in his hand?

Spelling Hints

[k] is represented in writing by:

k: kind, booklet, joke
c: come, second, topic
ck: kick, pocket
ch* Christmas, christen, chemistry, mechanic, ache, stomach, chorus, character, echo, monarch, architect, epoch, choir [kwaɪr]
qu: conquer, liquor, technique
qu: [kw] quick, frequent, liquid
cqu: [kw] acquire, acquaint
x: [ks] six, mixture

1. The letter k is silent in knock, knee, knit, knowledge, knight, know, knew, knife, knob.
2. The letter c is silent in muscle, scene, scissors, scent.
3. The letters cc are sometimes pronounced [ks] as in *accept, success.*

*ch *is usually pronounced* [tʃ] *as in* church [tʃɚtʃ].

[g] is represented in writing by:

g: give, tiger, leg
gg: egg, bigger*
gu: guest, fatigue

The letter g is silent in the following words:

gn: **g**nat, **g**nome, si**g**n, forei**g**n, champa**g**ne, campai**g**n, assi**g**nment
gh: diaphra**g**m
gh: althou**gh**, thou**gh**, thorou**gh**, dou**gh**nut
gh: before t in final position:
ni**gh**t, kni**gh**t, hei**gh**t, fi**gh**t; also in all the past tense verbs ending in **gh**t: fou**gh**t, cau**gh**t, tau**gh**t, etc.

The words suggest and suggestion may be pronounced [səgdʒɛ́st] *or* [sədʒɛ́st]; [səgdʒɛ́stʃən] *or* [sədʒɛ́stʃən].

Frequently Used and Sometimes Troublesome Words

These frequently used words contain sounds [k] and [g] in initial, medial, or final positions. Notice that they review all the vowel sounds.

Initial [k]		*Medial* [k]		*Final* [k]	
key	cool	fréquent	pecúliar	speak	uníque
kítchen	cube	liqúor	cróoked (adj)	sick	cook
cable	cúshion	bacon	vócal	ache	joke
chemist	curious	record (n)	recórd (v)	techníque	chalk
character	coast	ankle	áwkward	crack	bike
quality	cause	doctor	requíre	lock	óutlook
culture	caution	uncle	account	luck	
curve	kind	turkey	bóycott	clerk	
	couch				
	coin				

Initial [g]		*Medial* [g]		*Final* [g]	
grease	group	légal	árgue	league	diálogue
guílty	good	signal	sugar	fatígue	brown-bag
gain	goal	engáge	agó	dig	
guess	gone	again	Áugust	maílbag	
gather	guide	wágon	disguíse	egg	
guard	gown	regárd	pláyground	tag	
govern		drúgstore		rag	
girl		hámburger		flag	
				cátalog	

Oral Practice with [k] and [g]

strongly aspirated [k]

Remember to aspirate [k] strongly before stressed vowels. In two-word verbs, blend final [k] of the first element with the initial vowel of the next word. Notice the various spellings of [k].

1. Take off your coat and then take a seat in the corner.
2. The cushions were covered with a fine quality cotton.
3. Back up and park in back of that car across the street.
4. Think over that question carefully.
6. Let's talk about the chemistry assignment.
7. My cousin Kathy's cat has peculiar character traits.
8. Jackie asked us to look over our accounts.

strongly exploded [g]

1. Dig up the garden gradually.
2. Plug in the electric sandwich grill.
3. The group will gather at the front gate.
4. Gilda announced her engagement two weeks ago.
5. It'll be good to see the Goldmans again.

words with unreleased final [k] and [g]

1. Take this big piece of chalk.
2. Doug broke the clock.
3. I'll be back soon to pack my bag.
4. When Greg comes back, ask him to walk the dog.
5. There's a big black bug climbing up the table leg.

The Prefix ex

pronunciation

1. *ex* is pronounced [ɛks] in a **stressed syllable** before both vowels and consonants as in *éxercise, extra,* and *èxpedítion*. (*Ex* has secondary stress in a four-syllable word ending in *ion*.)
2. *ex* is pronounced [ɪks] is an **unstressed syllable before a consonant** as in *excépt, explósion*.
3. *ex* is pronounced [ɪgz] in an **unstressed syllable before a vowel** as in *exámple, exhibit*.

> **NOTE:** The prefix ex meaning former or out as in *ex-president* or *ex-communicate* is always pronounced [ɛks].

frequently used words beginning with ex

1. Words in which *ex* is pronounced [ɛks]

éxcellent	éxpert (n)	explanátion	exhibítion
exercise	export (n)	exclamation	exploration
excise tax	exploit (n)	expedition	execution
extra	extract (n)	exposition	expiration
exhale	excerpt (n)		

2. Words in which *ex* is pronounced [ɪks]

excúse (n)	expláin	explóre	excítement	expérience
excuse (v)	expense	extend	excessive	expensive
exclaim	expect	extreme	explosion	explanatory
except	express	exchange	experiment	expression

3. Words in which *ex* is pronounced [ɪgz]

exáctly	exémpt	exhíbit	examinátion
example	exist	exotic	exháustion
examine	exhaust	executive	

> **NOTE:** The words *exile* and *exit* may be pronounced [ɛ́ksaɪl] or [ɛ́gzaɪl]; [ɛ́ksɪt] or [ɛ́gzɪt]

Additional Oral Practice

dialogues using words with the sounds [k] and [g] and the prefix ex.

1. **A:** What's the matter? Did you forget the car keys again?
    B: Nooo — I want to cash a check and I forgot to take my identification card.

2. **A:** How many sugar cubes would you like in your coffee? It's extra strong.
    B: I don't take any sugar, thank you. I prefer to drink my coffee black.

3. **A:** Where does your grandfather keep his legal records?
    B: I guess he keeps them locked up in the bank. He's a very peculiar character; he never discusses things like that except with his lawyer.

4. **A:** When I woke up this morning I had a terrible headache and I felt sick to my stomach.
    B: You should've gone to the doctor. The way you're coughing it sounds like you have bronchitis. I asked my professor to excuse me and went home.

5. **A:** Good morning. May I help you?
    B: Where can I exchange this skirt for a larger size?
    A: Was it cash or credit?
    B: I bought it with my credit card.
    A: Leave the skirt and your credit card receipt with the cashier and select another skirt. We still have an excellent selection.
    B: Thank you very much.
    A: You're welcome.

sentences using the sounds [k] and [g] and the prefix ex

1. Dr. Gates gives an excellent course in experimental psychology.
2. Please explain the exercise again; I find it extremely complex.
3. Clark was exasperated by the extra expenses which he had not anticipated.
4. An expert chemist gave us an explanation of the exhibit.
5. The explosion caused extensive damage to the liquor store.
6. After my uncle broke his ankle, climbing stairs was extremely difficult for him.
7. I skinned my knuckles opening the back of the station wagon.

8. When you enter a theater, do you ever look to see where the fire exits are located?
9. The executives filled out questionnaires concerning their expense accounts.
10. The polio vaccine was perfected by Dr. Jonas Salk in the early 1950s.

homework: questions containing words with the sounds [k] and [g]

Student A will ask Student B a question based on the information requested in a particular item. Student B will answer in a complete sentence. Be prepared to answer all the questions. You instructor may ask everyone to answer the same question.

Item:	What time he or she goes to bed
Student A:	What time do you go to bed?
Student B:	I go to bed around eleven o'clock.

1. when he or she expects to graduate
2. his or her plans after receiving a college degree
3. what he or she expects to have accomplished by his or her fiftieth birthday.
4. how he or she reacts when someone disagrees with him or her
5. his or her favorite ice cream concoction (a mixture of flavors and syrups)
6. how he or she feels about keeping up with the lastest fashion in clothes
7. his or her favorite family custom
8. who does the cooking in his or her house
9. in his or her house, who usually gets up the earliest? the latest?
10. how many flights of stairs he or she climbs every day

Written Exercises

Write the symbol for the sound of the boldface letter or letters. If the letter is silent, write *S* and draw a slash (/) through the letter. When there is a cluster, write the symbols for the cluster. (Review spelling hints, pages 151-52.)

example: S **k**nit   [kw] **qu**ick

1. ___ **ch**emistry	9. ___ **g**uide	17. ___ **g**uest
2. ___ **ch**aracter	10. ___ si**gn**al	18. ___ me**ch**anic
3. ___ **kn**owledge	11. ___ stoma**ch**	19. ___ li**qu**id
4. ___ tau**gh**t	12. ___ si**gn**	20. ___ s**c**issors
5. ___ assi**gn**ment	13. ___ **kn**ife	21. ___ langua**g**e
6. ___ li**qu**or	14. ___ uni**qu**e	22. ___ thou**gh**
7. ___ **qu**iet	15. ___ **c**ir**c**uit	23. ___ **qu**ality
8. ___ ac**c**ept	16. ___ mus**c**le	24. ___ si**gn**ature

In the following words write the symbol for the *ex:* [ɛks], [ɪks], or [ɪgz]

1. ___ **ex**ecutive	9. ___ **ex**ercise	19. ___ **ex**hibit
2. ___ **ex**planation	10. ___ **ex**change	20. ___ **ex**hibition
3. ___ **ex**plain	11. ___ **ex**pression	21. ___ **ex**asperate
4. ___ **ex**tra	12. ___ **ex**amination	22. ___ **ex**treme
5. ___ **ex**ample	13. ___ **ex**hale	23. ___ **ex**port (v)
6. ___ **ex**it	14. ___ **ex**ploration	24. ___ **ex**ist
(2 pronunciations)	15. ___ **ex**cellent	
	16. ___ **ex**citement	
___	17. ___ **ex**cavation	
7. ___ **ex**periment	18. ___ **ex**plosion	
8. ___ **ex**pert (n)		

Homework

Choose one of these topics and prepare a two-minute talk. You may use notes if you wish, but please **do not read** your report.

1. The Most Unusual Person I Have Ever Met
2. A Very Unusual Old Person Whom I Know

An example of an unusual person might be a handicapped person who has a successful career, a very talented friend or relative, and so on.
  Here are a few examples of unusual old people.

An eighty-three-year-old woman in Florida became an expert water skier.
A lawyer in Salt Lake City still practiced full-time at eighty-six.
A man in California was a full-time flight instructor at eighty-four.
An eighty-eight-year-old woman in California ran a 1,000 acre farm.

Appropriateness: Using the Telephone — Extending, Accepting, or Refusing an Invitation

dialogues

1. **A:** Hello!
   B: May I speak to Mary, please?
   A: Who's calling, please?
   B: This is Luis Gómez.
   A: Just a minute. I'll call her.
   B: Thank you.
   C: Hello!
   B: Hello, Mary. This is Luis Gómez.
   C: Oh, hello. How are you?
   B: Fine, thank you, and you?
   C: Just fine, thanks.
   B: I was wondering if you'd like to go to the movies this weekend.
   C: Oh, that sounds like fun. Do you have any particular one in mind?
   B: I was thinking about "The Devil's Friend."
   C: Oh, I'm sorry. I saw that last week. It was very good.
   B: That's too bad. Do you know what else is playing?
   C: How about "The Space Machine"? It's playing at the theater just around the corner from my house.
   B: All right. That sounds great! How about Saturday night? Are you free?
   C: Oh, I'm sorry, Luis, I'm busy on Saturday. Could we go on Friday instead?
   B: OK. I'll pick you up about 8 o'clock.
   C: Great! I'll see you then.
   B: Okay. That's fine. So long.
   C: So long, Luis. Thanks for calling.
   B: Bye.

2. **A:** Hi, Jackie, How are you?
   B: Annie? Where've you been? I haven't seen you for a long time.
   A: I've been working on a big project, but I've finally finished it. That's why I'm calling. Bill and I are having a barbecue next Saturday afternoon to celebrate. Can you come?
   B: Oh, I'd love to. Is it all right to bring a date?
   A: Of course. Come about 4 o'clock. We'll have cocktails and grill some steaks.

B: It sounds great. 4 o'clock on Saturday. I'll be there.

A: I'm so glad you can make it. See you on Saturday. Bye now.

B: Bye, bye.

3. **A:** Hello, Betty. This is Cathy Brown.

B: Oh, hello, Cathy. How are you?

A: Just fine, thanks. Betty, Tom and I are celebrating our tenth anniversary next Sunday and we're inviting some friends over for dinner. Are you and Bob free that night?

B: Yes, we are. What time would you like us to come?

A: Come about 6:30. It's informal. Don't dress up.

B: OK. See you on Sunday about 6:30. Bye now.

A: Bye.

4. **A:** Hi, Jim. How've you been doing?

B: OK, I guess; nothing special.

A: Would you like to spend the day at the beach on Saturday? My parents are having a bunch of people out.

B: Gee, Fred, I won't be able to make it. My brother's graduating from medical school that day, and the whole family is going to the ceremony. I'm sorry.

A: Don't worry. We can do it some other time. Congratulate your brother for me. So long.

B: So long. Thanks for asking me anyway. Give my regards to your folks.

A: I will.

useful expressions

1. Whenever you extend an invitation over the telephone, be sure to mention the date, the time, and the place where the affair is to be held. Also, make it clear to the person you're inviting whether the invitation is for him (or her) alone, or whether it includes others. For instance, if it's an affair where you don't plan to have children present, you can say "It's an adults-only party." Or if it is to be a family affair, you may say, "Bring the children along."

Also, depending on the nature of the affair, you may need to tell the person whether to dress casually or formally. For instance, if you're giving a barbecue, obviously, it's to be informal, but if you are giving a dinner party, you should mention whether it's to be a formal or an informal affair.

2. When you accept an invitation, never invite another person to go with you without first checking with your host or hostess. Otherwise, you could cause an embarrassment for everyone involved. If you aren't sure just whom the invitation includes, you can ask:

"May I bring a date?"

or

"Is it all right if I bring my friend, cousin, sister, etc.?"

Always repeat the date, time, and place so there are no misunderstandings.

3. If you refuse an invitation, you may or may not wish to explain why you must refuse, depending on how well you know the person who is extending the invitation.

You can simply say:

"I'm sorry, I have another engagement."

or

"I'm terribly sorry, I'm busy that night."

or

"I'd love to come, but _____ and I won't be able to."

You may want to add, "Perhaps some other time."

4. If you do accept the invitation you can say:

"I'd love to. Thank you for the invitation."

"It'll be a pleasure."

"That sounds great. Thanks." (informal)

practice

According to your instructor's directions, get together with another student and prepare a dialogue on one of the following situations. Present it to the class.

1. A close friend whom you haven't seen for a long time calls and invites you to his graduation party. Ask whether you can bring someone else.

2. A person whom you don't know very well invites you to a dinner party. You don't know whether it's to be formal or informal, so you ask.

3. A friend invites you to a movie, but you've already seen it. Suggest another movie instead and agree on a time to meet.

4. A friend invites you to a party, but you already have another invitation. Respond appropriately.

5. Make up a situation of your own involving an invitation, and accept or refuse following the examples given in the dialogues.

The Fricatives [f] and [v]

In Lessons 15, 16, and 17 we talked about the different kinds of stop consonants in English. In this lesson we will begin to talk about another category of consonants best known as **fricatives** because of the manner in which they are produced. Fricatives are continuous sounds resulting from the coming together of two articulators through which the air stream flows with a frictionlike quality. There are nine fricatives in English.

[f]   fish
[v]   voice
[θ]   thin
[ð]   this
[s]   see
[z]   zoo
[ʃ]   shoe
[ʒ]   vision
[h]   hello

There are two sounds related to the fricatives called affricates, but these will be taken up later.

Description of the Sounds [f] and [v]

[f] and [v] are labio-dental oral fricatives. The articulators involved in producing these sounds are the lower lip and the upper teeth; thus the term labio-dental. [f] is **voiceless**, and [v] is **voiced**. To produce these sounds, bring the lower lip in contact with the upper teeth. Then let a stream of air flow through the small opening made by the two articulators. In the case of [v], there is a vibration of the vocal cords

together with the expulsion of air. There is no such vibration for the production of [f]. The diagram shows the position of the mouth during the production of [f] and [v].

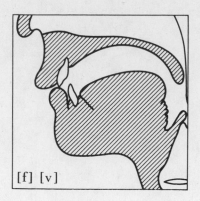

[f] [v]

Both [f] and [v] appear initially, as in *free* and *vote*, medially as in *office* and *even*, and finally as in *if* and *love*. Repeat these words after your instructor.

Important Hints about [f] and [v]

1. When [f] is in a final position, pronounce it forcefully so that the escaping air can be clearly heard. Repeat these words after your instructor.

beef   if   safe   clef   laugh   off   surf   cuff   roof

2. In informal speech the expression "I have to" as in "I have to go" becomes [ɑɪ hæf tə go] or "I have to eat" [ɑɪ hæf tʊ it].

3. Strongly enunciate final [f] and [v] when the following word begins with a stressed vowel. Blend both sounds with the vowel. Listen and repeat after your instructor.

cough úp   láugh at   move óver   give ín

4. Notice that both [f] and [v] form clusters with other consonants. Below are some of the more troublesome clusters.

[fr]	fruit, afraid	[ft]	left	[vj]	**view, review**
[fj]	**few, in**fuse	[fs]	graphs	[rv]	serve, marvel
[sf]	**sphere, sphinx**	[fθ]	fifth	[lv]	involve, solvent

The clusters below are formed with the addition of the *s* endings and the regular past tense ending. (See Lessons 5 and 6, respectively.)

[fts]	gifts*	[rvz]	serves	[vd]	proved
[fθs]	fifths*	[lvz]	solves	[lvd]	solved
[ft]	lau**ghed**, photogra**phed**			[rvd]	served

These endings are often reduced to [fs] in everyday speech.

5. The following words have two spellings—one for the noun or adjective form, and the other for the verb form. The **noun** or **adjective** form ends in the letters *f* or *fe* while the **verb** form ends in the letters *ve*. Each pair of words is related in meaning.

Noun	Verb		Noun	Verb
proof	prove		safe	save
belief	believe		serf	serve
relief	relieve		life	live
grief	grieve			

6. Nouns ending in *f* usually form their plurals by changing *f* to *v* and adding *es*.

shelf   shelves   self   selves   knife   knives   wife   wives

exceptions: chiefs, roofs, proofs, *chefs* (the *ch* in *chefs* is pronounced like the *sh* in *shell*).

Listening Exercises and Oral Practice

Your instructor will read one word from each of the pairs of words in the following exercises. Circle the words that you hear. Then the instructor will read all of the words in each exercise and ask you to repeat them. Next, he or she will read the sentences in each exercise. Listen carefully and then read the sentences aloud, making a clear distinction between the boldface words in each sentence.

distinguishing [f] from [v]

few	view		define	divine		safe	save
feel	veal		rifle	rival		leaf	leave
face	vase					relief	relieve

1. Only a **few** of us could see the **view**.
2. Don't you **feel** that **veal** is too expensive?
3. The **vase** had a **face** painted on one side.
4. Can you **define** the word **divine**?
5. What kind of **rifle** did his **rival** have?
6. Is it **safe** to **save** money nowadays?
7. **Leave** that silver **leaf** where you found it.
8. What a **relief** to have the doctor **relieve** her pain.

distinguishing [v] from [b]

[v]	[b]		[v]	[b]		[v]	[b]		[v]	[b]
veil	bail		vote	boat		marvel	marble		rove	robe
very	berry		vest	best		covered	cupboard		curve	curb
vase	base									

1. This **berry** comes from a **very** rare plant.
2. Do you have a **base** for this **vase**?
3. She went to **vote** while I stayed on the **boat**.
4. This **vest** looks **best** with that shirt.
5. I sometimes **marvel** at his **marble** collection.
6. The **cupboard** is all **covered** with dust.
7. He likes to **rove** around in a Japanese **robe**.
8. The car hit the **curb** on that dangerous **curve**.

Spelling Hints

1. [f] is represented in writing by:

   f: for, often, leaf
   ff: off, different
   ph: phone, orphan, Ralph
   gh: enough, laughter

2. [v] is represented in writing only by the letter *v*. It appears initially as in *voice*, medially as in *service*, and finally as in *love*.

exception: The letter *f* in the word *of* is pronounced [v]

Frequently Used and Sometimes Troublesome Words with [f] and [v]

Remember that in this section we are also reviewing the English vowel sounds.

Initial [f]		*Medial* [f]		*Final* [f]		
feel	food	deféat	confúse	beef	enoúgh	proof
fear	foot	official	bárefoot	if	tough	roof
faith	phone	afraid	telephone	safe	rough	wolf
fare	fought	affair	befóre	deaf	surf	loaf
fast	file	unfasten	define	half		off
father	foul	grándfather				cough
fun	foil					knife
fur						

Initial [v]		*Medial* [v]		*Final* [v]	
veal	view	évil	sérvice	leave	love
víllage	válue	civil	revíew	live (v)	serve
vacátion	vote	favorite	November	shave	prove
vélvet	vítamin	heavy	divorce	twelve	stove
van	vowel	travel	revise	have	alíve (adj)
volume	voice	invólve	ínvoice	solve	
vegetable	voyage	óven	devoút		
virtue					

Oral Practice

forceful pronunciation of [f]

Read the following sentences carefully. Remember to pronounce [f] forcefully when it appears in final position or at the beginning of a stressed syllable.

1. Take your foot off the wall.
2. Do you feel safe in here?
3. I'll stay if the food here is good.
4. My father had a rough day today.
5. Please have faith in me.
6. Wrap the half loaf of bread in foil.
7. Don't unfasten your seatbelts until the sign is turned off.
8. Phil answered the phone immediately.

strongly enunciated [v]

Read the following sentences carefully. Remember to blend final [v] with the initial vowel of the following word.

1. Would you please move over?
2. We'll visit Vivian in November.
3. Don't give in now.
4. You must live up to your reputation.
5. Review the vowels for the final test.
6. Do you think he'll drive off with the van?
7. I prefer to try the veal and vegetables.
8. That violet-colored velvet is very beautiful.

[v] and [b]

In these sentences be sure to use the proper mouth positions for these two sounds: both lips for the [b], and upper teeth on the lower lip for the [v]. Make a clear distinction between these two voiced sounds.

1. Vivian put on her very best dress.
2. Where did you buy such good vegetables?
3. The Governor believed all the votes were in his favor.
4. Bobby and Bess are going to play volleyball.
5. Do they serve beer here?
6. This is the best vocabulary list I've seen.
7. Are you nervous about the voyage?
8. Next November I plan to take a vacation in the Caribbean.
9. Would you prefer roast beef or veal stew?
10. What time does the boat arrive in Vancouver?

clusters with [f] and [v]

As you read these sentences, be aware of the various clusters of [f] and [v].

1. Are you afraid of being photographed here?
2. This is the fifth gift I've gotten since this morning.
3. I put the scarf back on the shelf.
4. They laughed at us for being frightened.
5. The view from the top of the volcano is marvelous.
6. I've proved it could be done frequently.
7. Have they involved Ralph's friends, too?
8. Fred solves one problem at a time.
9. Vivian says she serves ice cream and fruit often.
10. A few visitors took photographs of the Sphinx.

contractions with *have*

Your instructor will read the following sentences to you. Listen carefully to the pronunciation of the contractions. Then read the sentences aloud.

1. We've announced the lecture five times already.
2. What've we done to deserve this treatment?
3. I haven't seen you for ages. How've you been anyway?
4. Where've you been? I've been calling you all afternoon.
5. I think they've attended all the meetings so far.
6. I've accepted an invitation to read a paper at a convention.
7. You've already paid, haven't you?
8. Why've you been absent from class so frequently?
9. When've you had time to watch television lately?
10. Who've you invited to this evening's buffet?

contractions with *have*

Ask the person sitting next to you a question. He will answer it in a complete sentence and ask the person sitting beside him the following question. Be sure to pronounce the contractions correctly. Use contractions in your answers whenever possible. Your instructor may ask everyone to answer the same questions.

1. Where've you been eating lunch lately, at home or in the cafeteria?
2. How've you been getting along in your studies?
3. Where've you been living for the past five months?
4. Why've some governments become so interested in outer space?
5. How've you been getting to the university this semester?
6. What've you been studying recently in your English class?
7. What've you and your friends been doing in the evenings?
8. Where've you gone during your last two vacations?
9. What've you done recently that you're proud of or happy about?
10. Why've people become concerned about the environment lately?

the expression *have to*

Student A will ask a question, Student B will answer, and so on. Be sure to reduce the words *have to* to [hæftə] or [hæf tʊ]. In some instances your instructor may ask everyone to answer the same question.

1. How long do you have to study every day?
2. If your flight leaves at noon, what time do you have to be at the airport?
3. Where do you have to go tomorrow morning?
4. How many questions do you usually have to answer for your English assignment?
5. Where do people usually have to go to apply for passports?
6. Why does a student have to have a dictionary available?
7. When do you have to register for next semester?
8. What does every student have to do to improve his or her pronunciation?
9. What time do you have to get up on weekdays?
10. What does everyone have to have to drive a car?

dialogues

Practice the following dialogues with a classmate. Give special attention to the pronunciation of words containing the sounds [f] and [v].

1. **A:** What's your favorite vacation spot?
   B: The Virgin Islands, of course!
   A: Is that where you're going in November?
   B: I'm not traveling anywhere in November. I don't have the money.

1. **A:** How much money did you save on the V-neck sweater you bought?
   B: Oh, about five dollars.
   A: Not bad. Do you know if they're going to have a sale again next February?
   B: I have no idea. But Fred's Men's Shop is having one right now.

3. **A:** What are you watching on television?
   B: A volleyball game on channel five.
   A: I thought you didn't like to watch games on TV.
   B: I don't, but this evening there's nothing else good on TV.

4. **A:** Would you please move over a little to the left?
   B: Certainly. The view is definitely not very good from here.
   A: I wonder if we could move a little bit closer.
   B: Let's give it a try. If the usher tells us to move, we'll move again.

5. **A:** Have you bought a lot of new clothes for your vacation?
   B: No, I haven't. I've decided I'm going to travel very light this time.
   A: What does "travel light" mean?
   B: Oh! It means that I'm going to take only a few clothes so I don't have to carry a heavy suitcase.

Written Exercise: [p], [b], [t], [d], [k], [g], [f], and [v]

Write the symbol for the sound of the boldface letter or letters in these words. If the letter is silent, write S and draw a slash (/) through the letter.

1. ____ live	16. ____ ache	31. ____ fasten
2. ____ chemistry	17. ____ knee	32. ____ second
3. ____ castle	18. ____ rough	33. ____ kite
4. ____ whistle	19. ____ ghost	34. ____ guess
5. ____ off	20. ____ although	35. ____ muscle
6. ____ of	21. ____ laugh	36. ____ Wednesday
7. ____ know	22. ____ fight	37. ____ technique ____
8. ____ people	23. ____ doughnut	38. ____ assignment
9. ____ phone	24. ____ accept	39. ____ corps
10. ____ verb	25. ____ stomach	40. ____ biscuit
11. ____ debt	26. ____ remember	41. ____ knob
12. ____ receipt	27. ____ plumber	42. ____ club
13. ____ cough	28. ____ fatigue	43. ____ listen
14. ____ love	29. ____ often	44. ____ slept
15. ____ doubt	30. ____ enough	45. ____ number

Homework

Choose one of the topics below and prepare a two-minute talk. You may use notes if you wish, but please do not read your report.

1. A Famous Person I Would Like to Meet
2. The Person I Most Admire

Appropriateness: Using the Telephone — Getting Information from the Telephone Operator

dialogues

1. **A:** Information. May I help you?
   B: Will you give me the number for Transworld Airlines, please?
   A: Flight information or Cargo?
   B: Flight information, please.
   A: I have several listings for that number. What did you want?
   B: I want to make a reservation for a flight.
   A: The number is 815-6000.
   B: 815-6000. Thank you.
   A: You're welcome.

2. **A:** Information. May I help you?
   B: Can you give me the number of Vera Snider in Forest Hills, please?
   A: Spell that last name, please.
   B: S–N–I–D–E–R.
   A: Is that "S" as in "Sam"?
   B: That's right.
   A: And the first name is Vera?
   B: Yes.
   A: Just one moment.
   B: Thank you.
   A: The number is 656-7891.
   B: 656-7891. Thank you very much.
   A: You're welcome.

3. **A:** Information. Good afternoon, may I help you?
   B: Can you tell me the number of Jack Brown living at 416 61st St., Valley View?
   A: Surely. One moment.
   B: Thank you.
   A: I'm sorry, I have no Jack Brown living at that address?
   B: Do you have any Brown living there?
   A: Yes, I have a J.M. Brown.
   B: That's it.
   A: The number is 717-6859.
   B: 717-6859. Thank you.
   A: You're welcome.

useful expressions

The following are appropriate expressions to use when you call Information* to ask for a telephone number.

"Will you give me the number of the Fox Theater, please?"
"Can you tell me the number of Victor Bovar living on Fair Street?"
"Please give me the number of the Vance Company in Bay View."
"Could you tell me the number of the Social Security office?"
"Would you please give me the number of the Fire Department?"

*In certain areas other terminology is used such as Directory Assistance.

In addition to knowing the expressions used to ask for information about a number, you must also be ready to spell names and understand telephone numbers given to you by the information operator. If you don't understand the number, you can tell the operator:

"Please repeat the number slowly."
"Could you please repeat the number?"

Do not forget to thank the operator at the end of the conversation.

practice

Select one of the following situations. With another classmate, work out a dialogue and present it to the rest of the class.

1. Call Information to find out the phone number of an old friend whose address you know. Spell the name of the person and the name of the street.
2. Call Information to find out the phone number of the Lake View Hotel. You cannot understand the number clearly because there is a lot of noise. Ask the operator to repeat the number.
3. Call Information. Ask for the phone number of a person whose first name you do not know. You only have the family name and the address.
4. With another student, make up a dialogue using some of the expressions presented on pages 166–67 and in the dialogues on page 166. Be prepared to act it out in class.

The Consonants: The Lingua-Dental Fricatives [θ] and [ð]

Description of the Sounds [θ] and [ð]

[θ] and [ð] are lingua-dental fricatives. [θ] is **voiceless**, and [ð] is **voiced**. To produce these sounds, bring the lips nearly together leaving only a narrow space between them. Push the tongue forward so that the tip of the tongue touches the edges of both the top and bottom front teeth. When you look in the mirror, your tongue should be clearly visible between your lips. (To make sure your tongue is in the proper position, we say you should bite the tip of the tongue.) With the tongue in this position, the air is forced between the teeth with considerable pressure, thus causing a rushing sound. (If you place your fingertips in front of your lips, you can feel this rush of air.)

In producing the [ð] you will notice that there is much less air escaping because the vocal cords are vibrating. The diagram below shows the position of tongue and teeth during the production of these sounds.

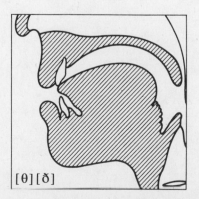

[θ][ð]

Both [θ] and [ð] appear initially as in *thick* and *this*, medially as in *nothing* and *brother*, and finally as in *month* and *bathe*. Pronounce these words after your instructor.

[θ] is represented in writing by *th* and [ð] by *th* and *the*.

Important Hints About the Sounds [θ] and [ð]

the sound [θ]

1. Words ending in this sound are **nouns**, or, rarely, **adjectives** as in *teeth*, *bath*, *breath*, and (adj.) *loath*.
   exception: adj. smooth [smuð].

2. Final *thy* is usually pronounced [θɪ] or [θi] as in *healthy* and *filthy*.

   exceptions: worthy [wɚði] or [wɚðɪ].
   swarthy [swɔrði] or [swɔrðɪ].

3. [θ] appears finally in all ordinal numbers except *first, second, third* and compounds of these numbers: fourth, thirteenth, thirtieth, 3/4 (three-fourths), 2/5 (two-fifths).

4. [θ] combines with other consonants to form clusters both initially and finally.

[θr] th**read**   [lθ] hea**lth**   [rθ] wo**rth**   [nθ] mo**nth**   [ŋθ] le**ngth**
[θs] bir**ths** (See Lesson 6)

the sound [ð]

1. Words ending in *the* are always verbs: breathe, bathe, clothe*, loathe.

The third person singular of the verb clothe *as in "She clothes herself in velvet" is pronounced* [kloðz].

2. Except for the words *ether* [íθɚ] and *author* [ɔθɚ] *medial th + er* is almost always pronounced [ðɚ] as in *either, bather, weather,* and *lather*.

3. [ð] does not form initial clusters. The final clusters [ðz] as in *bathes* and [ðd] as in *bathed* were described in Lessons 5 and 6 respectively.

NOTE: *th* is pronounced [t] in these proper nouns:				
Thomas	Thompson	Esther	River Thames	Thailand

Listening Exercises and Oral Practice

Your instructor will read one of the words from each pair of words in the following sections. Circle the words you hear. Then your instructor will read all the words in a particular section and ask you to repeat them. Next, after each group of words, he or she will read the sentences that follow. Listen carefully and then read the sentences aloud, making a clear distinction between the sounds in the boldface words.

distinguishing [θ] from [ð]

[θ]	[ð]		Noun	Verb		Noun	Verb
thigh	thy		teeth	teethe [tɪð]		bath	bathe*
thistle	this'll		breath	breathe [brɪð]		cloth	clothe*

Remember that when a word ends in a silent e, the vowel "says its name"; hence [beʸð] [kloʷð].

1. **This'll** give you a picture of the **thistle** flower.
2. To **teethe** is to grow one's **teeth**.
3. The verb is **bathe** and the noun is **bath**.
4. **Breathe** in and hold your **breath** for a minute.
5. She'll **clothe** herself in a soft white **cloth**.

distinguishing [θ] from [t]

[θ]	[t]		[θ]	[t]		[θ]	[t]
theme	team		death	debt		faithful	fateful
thin	tin		tenth	tent			
thank	tank		bath	bat			
thought	taught		tooth	toot			
thorn	torn		both	boat			

1. The **tin** plate was so **thin** it bent easily.
2. The **team** has a new **theme** song.
3. **Thank** you for filling the **tank**.
4. I **thought** I **taught** you that song last week.
5. She's **torn** her skirt on a cactus **thorn**.
6. At the time of his **death** he was in **debt**.
7. On the **tenth** day, the **tent** was damaged by a storm.
8. In trying to **toot** the horn, Bill broke a **tooth**.
9. **Both** men rowed the **boat**.
10. The **faithful** dog lost its life in a **fateful** accident.

distinguishing [θr] from [tr]

[θr]	[tr]		[θr]	[tr]		[θr]	[tr]
three	tree		thread	tread		thrill	trill
through	true		thrash	trash		thrust	trust

1. There are **three** birds' nests in that **tree**.
2. Is it **true** that you're **through** with your work?
3. What a **thrill** to listen to that soprano's beautiful **trills**.
4. To prove his **trust** in me, he **thrust** his money into my hand.

distinguishing [ð] from [d]

[ð]	[d]		[ð]	[d]		[ð]	[d]
they	day		those	doze		loathe	load
they'll	Dale					worthy	wordy

1. **They** took the **day** off.
2. **They'll** all visit **Dale** this month.
3. **Those** old men often **doze** in the sun.
4. I **loathe** to **load** the car at night.
5. That theme is too **wordy** to be **worthy** of a prize.

distinguishing [ð], [θ], [d], [t]

Your instructor will read these sentences using one of the words in parentheses. Circle the word that you hear.

1. That's exactly what we've (thought, taught) all along.
2. We were all out of (breath, bread).
3. (They've, Dave) read the newspaper.
4. She kept hoping (they, day) would soon come.
5. Her (faith, face) is known to all of us.
6. The captain gave his (thanks, tanks) to the diving team.
7. That's a good (team, theme).
8. He told us about a mysterious (debt, death).
9. This'll make a good (lather, ladder).
10. The (threads, treads) were very worn.

Frequently Used and Sometimes Troublesome Words

Initial [θ]		*Medial* [θ]		*Final* [θ]	
thief	thigh	cathédral	áthlete	benéath	youth
thick	thésis	fílthy	Catholic	width	booth
thin	théory	aríthmetic	mathemátics	eighth	both
threat	théater	fáithful	nóthing	death	cloth
thread	thérapy	everything	something	breath	north
thank	thirty	anything	sympathy	length	ninth
thumb	thirsty	method	birthday	strength	mouth
third	Thursday	healthy	sympathize	bath	south
through	thermómeter	wealthy	author	birth	
throw	thórough	athlétic	authorize	earth	
thought	thousand	sympathétic	mouthwash		

Initial [ð]		*Medial* [ð]		*Final* [ð]	
these	than	eíther	ráther	smoother	breathe
this	that	neither	lather	clothing	with
they	though	bather	bother	although	bathe
then	those	feather	father	nórthern	soothe
them		leather	farther	southern	smooth
their		weather	further	otherwise	clothe

Oral Practice

sentences in which the sound [d] precedes the sound [ð]

Put the tip of your tongue against the alveolar ridge as if to produce [d]. However, do not release the sound. Instead, immediately move your tongue so that the tip is between your teeth to produce [ð]. [d] is released through the [ð] sound.

1. Who said that?
2. Please guide these tourists around the city.
3. The girls said they're glad they came.
4. The boys told their dad they'd spend their money wisely.
5. Please send those clothes to my brother.
6. I'm afraid they'll demand the money.
7. The farmers said they'll need this land themselves.
8. The men said they'd feed the children.
9. Did they guard the other borders, too?
10. Could that boy load the truck for us?

ordinal numbers

Use ordinal numbers in your answers to these questions. Student A will ask Student B, and so on. Your instructor may ask everyone to answer 1, 2, and 4.

example: A. Which month of the year is April?
B. April is the fourth month.

1. In which month were you born?
2. What will your next birthday be? (i.e. the 19th, the 20th, etc.)
3. Using the months April through December, ask the student next to you, "Which month of the year is _____ month?" (the 4th, the 5th)
4. In which months were your parents born? (the 4th, the 5th, the 6th)
5. In which month does _____ fall?
(Mother's Day, Father's Day, Labor Day, Halloween, Memorial Day, Independence Day, or any other holiday)

words with the sounds [θ] and [ð]

Study these questions and then practice reading them aloud, forming the *th* sounds carefully and using proper intonation and blending. As usual, Student A will ask a question and Student B will respond in a complete sentence. Your instructor may choose some of the questions as the basis for a class discussion.

1. When you take off your clothes, do you throw them on a chair or the bed, or do you hang them up in the closet?
2. What three things are most important to you at this time?
3. Is Alaska in the northern or southern hemisphere?
4. Which is farther away from where you are now, the North Pole or the South Pole?
5. What are three countries in northern Europe?
6. What are three countries in southern Europe?
7. (For the women) Which style of bathing suit do you prefer, a one-piece suit, a two-piece suit, or a bikini?
8. (For the men) Which style of bathing suit do you prefer, boxing trunks or a bikini?
9. Which months of the year have thirty days?
10. What do you like to do during a thunderstorm?

sentences containing [θ]

Read these sentences carefully placing the tongue tip between your teeth to produce the *th* sounds. Use correct, stress, rhythm and blending.

1. Esther wanted to say something thoughtful, but she couldn't think of anything.

2. Beth always thinks she can get something for nothing.

3. Theodore said he'd arrive at nine-thirty on the evening of the thirtieth.

4. Three thousand athletes are participating in the games being held at the new athletic field this week.

5. Those theater tickets that Ruth sent us are for the three-thirty matinée next Thursday.

6. Martha's sixteenth birthday party is on the thirteenth of this month.

7. Although the old man is very thin, apparently he's in good health.

8. We sent Thelma a sympathy card upon the death of her father last month.

9. Nearly three-fourths of the surface of the earth is covered with water.

10. I used these tweezers to remove the cactus thorn from my thumb.

dialogues

1. **A:** Which of these leather purses shall I buy. They're both lovely, aren't they?
   B: Yes, they are. But you'll have to choose either one or the other. We can't afford both of them.

2. **A:** Do you know the length and width of this room?
   B: It's thirty-three feet in length and sixteen feet in width.
   A: And what's the height of the ceiling?
   B: I think it's nine feet.

3. **A:** How wide is this cloth?
   B: It's thirty-six inches wide.
   A: And how many yards long is it?
   B: I think it's about three and a half yards.

4. **A:** What's the weather supposed to be like this afternoon? The sky looks threatening. I wonder whether there'll be rain again.
   B: The weatherman said there'll be thunder showers either this afternoon or this evening.

5. **A:** "True friends stick together through thick and thin." That's one of my favorite proverbs.
   B: I like, "Early to bed, early to rise, makes a man healthy, wealthy, and wise."
   A: How about, "Birds of a feather flock together"? That certainly speaks the truth.
   B: Yes, and so does this one. "The trouble with most people is that they listen with their mouths."

Written Exercise

Write the symbol [θ] for the voiceless *th* sound and [ð] for the voiced *th* sound. Whenever there is a cluster, write the symbols for the cluster. Example: **throw** [θr]

1. ___ bath	14. ___ birthday	27. ___ nothing
2. ___ worthy	15. ___ clothe	28. ___ thousand
3. ___ length	16. ___ lather	29. ___ wealth
4. ___ bathe	17. ___ southern	30. ___ they
5. ___ month	18. ___ south	31. ___ thank
6. ___ thorough	19. ___ clothing	32. ___ Catholic
7. ___ though	20. ___ bather	33. ___ their
8. ___ through	21. ___ thirty	34. ___ farther
9. ___ breath	22. ___ theme	35. ___ leather
10. ___ cloth	23. ___ thigh	36. ___ author
11. ___ three	24. ___ thread	37. ___ mathematics
12. ___ thermometer	25. ___ earth	38. ___ either
13. ___ breathe	26. ___ these	39. ___ healthy

Homework

Make a list of the three or four character traits that you consider most important for a wife, husband, girlfriend, or boyfriend to possess. When the class meets the next time, the instructor will divide the class into groups of three or four students each, who will discuss these characteristics among themselves. One person in each group should be elected to report the opinions of the members to the whole class.

Here are suggestions of characteristics to get you started thinking.

self-confidence, consideration for others, trustworthiness

Appropriateness: Using the Telephone — Requesting Information on the Phone

dialogues

Calling an Airline for Flight Information

A: Transwest Airline. Good afternoon.
B: Can you tell me whether flight #905, which left New York at 11:00 this morning, is on time?
A: No, ma'am. That flight has been delayed. It's due to arrive at 5:00 this afternoon.
B: Thank you very much.

Calling a Movie Theater

A: Bijou Theater. Good afternoon.
B: Can you please tell me what film is playing this week?
A: The feature film is *Space Raiders* starring Geoffrey Lane and Joan Adams.
B: What are the show times on Saturday, please?
A: The feature goes on at 5:45, 7:55, and 10:15.
B: And what are the admission prices.
A: Up until 6 p.m., it's $3.00 for adults, and $1.50 for children under 12. After 6 o'clock it's $4.50 for adults and $2.75 for children.
B: Thank you very much.

Calling a Store

A: Acme Books and Records. Wilkins speaking.
B: I'm looking for information about mainland China. Do you have any books in stock?
A: Yes, sir. What sort of book did you have in mind?
B: Well, I would like to get a book of photographs, and something that will give me basic travel information.
A: Well, sir, we have *Looking at China*, which has about 350 photos, and then we have *China, A Guide for the First-Time Traveler*.
B: What is the price of the book of photographs?
A: Let's see. It's priced at $24.95. The guidebook is $7.95.
B: Thank you very much. I'll stop in sometime this afternoon.
A: Just ask for Wilkins and I'll be glad to help you.
B: Thank you very much, Mr. Wilkins.

Calling a Bus Company

A: Best Way Bus. Good morning.
B: Can you tell me the schedule for buses going to Washington, please?

A: Buses leave every hour on the hour from 7:00 in the morning to 11:00 at night.

B: I see. And what are the fares—one-way and round-trip?

A: A one-way ticket is $35.00, and a round-trip ticket is $60.00.

B: Thank you very much.

A: You're quite welcome, sir.

useful expressions

Calling for Flight Information

When you call an airline office for information about incoming or departing flights, be sure to give the number of the flight you're asking about. If you don't know the flight number, give the cities involved; that is, the destination and/or starting point and the departure or arrival time. Here are some expressions you can use.

"Can you please tell me the arrival time of Flight 316, which left New York City at ten o'clock?"

"When is Flight 11 from Miami due to arrive?"

Calling for Information about Bus or Train Schedules

Here are some other expressions that are useful to know.

"How often do the (buses, trains) leave for Kansas City?"

"Is there an express bus which goes to Reno in the morning?"

"What is the travel time to Boston?" or "How many hours does it take to get to Boston?"

"Are all the buses air-conditioned?"

"Do I have to make reservations ahead of time?"

"Do you accept credit cards?"

Calling for Information about Movies, Shows, and Concerts

Here are some other expressions you can use.

"At what time does tonight's concert begin?"

"Can you tell me the program on tonight's concert?"

"How long will the movie be playing at this theater?"

"What are the ticket prices?"

"How much are the tickets?"

"Do you have half-price tickets for children?"

"Are there special prices for senior citizens?"

Calling a Store for Information about a Particular Item

Here are some expressions you can use.

"Do you have any books about submarines?"

"Do you carry Puerto Rican coffee?"

"Would you have any twenty-five-pound bags of flour in stock?"

If the person who answers does not give his or her name, ask for it. If you do not hear the name clearly, ask the person speaking to repeat it.

"May I have your name, please?"

"To whom am I speaking?"

"Would you please repeat your name?"

If it's a difficult name to remember, ask the person to spell it. Say:

"Would you please spell that?"
or
"How do you spell that, please?"
and then write the name down. It's not necessary to give your name, but you can if you wish.

practice

Following your instructor's directions, choose one or more of the situations below and work out a dialogue with another student, using some of the appropriate expressions discussed above or used in the dialogues.

1. Call a sports store and ask for information about a particular piece of athletic equipment.
2. Call a bookstore and ask whether the store has the latest book by an author of your choice, or ask the price of a current best seller or any other book you want to read.
3. Call a bus company and ask for the schedule and the fare (one-way or round-trip) to a city of your choice.
4. Call an airline and ask for the departure and/or arrival time of a particular flight to or from a city of your choice.
5. Call a local movie theater and ask for the name of the film that's currently playing. Ask for ticket prices and for the times the film is shown.
6. With another student, make up a dialogue using some of the expressions presented on pages 175–76 and in the dialogues on pages 174–75. Be prepared to act it out in class.

The Consonants: The Post-Dental Fricatives [s] and [z]

Description of the Sounds

[s] and [z] are postdental fricative sounds. The [s] is **voiceless**, and the [z] is **voiced**. To produce the [s] sound, bring your upper and lower teeth almost together, with the upper teeth protruding slightly over the lower. Open your lips slightly and pull them back a little toward the corners of your mouth. Place the tip of the tongue behind the lower teeth and arch the blade of the tongue up toward the alveolar ridge. The sides of the tongue should touch the upper back teeth. With the tongue in this position, a narrow groove is formed. The breath stream will flow through this groove and down toward the opening between the lips and front teeth.

Take a deep breath. As you exhale, the air forced through the narrow groove makes a hissing sound as it passes over the cutting edges of your upper and lower teeth. If you put your fingers in front of your mouth, you will feel a rush of air hissing through the opening between your teeth. (The sound resembles that made by a snake.) To produce the [z], the vocal cords vibrate, producing a buzzing sound more like that made by a mosquito. You will notice that in producing the [z], you feel a much smaller amount of air against your fingers. The diagram below shows you the correct tongue position for these two sibilant (hissing) sounds.

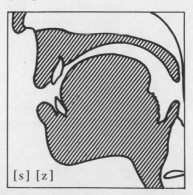

[s] [z]

177

Both [s] and [z] appear initially, as in *say* and *zoo*, medially, as in *listen* and *puzzle*, and finally as in *case* and *boys*. Repeat these words after your instructor.

Important Hints About [s] and [z]

[s] forms the following clusters.

1. Initial clusters

[sp] special	[sw] swim	[sn] sneeze	[skw] square
[st] stone	[sl] slow	[str] street	[spl] splash
[sk] skin	[sm] smoke	[skr] scream	[spr] spread

2. Final clusters

    a. [rs] force, horse   [ns] since   [ks] six

    b. All the following final *s* clusters are formed by the addition of the *s* inflection. (See Lesson 5 for explanation and exercises [ps], [ts], [ks], [fs], [θs], [sks], [sts], [fts]. See Lesson 6 for pronunciation of final *s* clusters formed by the addition of regular past tense endings.)

[z] does not form any initial clusters. All of the following final clusters have been described in Lesson 5: [-bz], [-dz], [-gz], [-vz], [-ðz], [-rz], [-lz], [-mz], [-nz], and [-ŋz]. The final cluster [-zd] is described in Lesson 6.

The following words are used both as nouns (or adjectives) and verbs. As nouns or adjectives, the *s* is pronounced [s]. As verbs the *s* is pronounced [z].

[s]	[z]	
close (adj)	close	A **close** friend will **close** the store for me.
excuse	excuse	**Excuse** me for giving you such a poor **excuse**.
advice	advise	I **advise** you not to take his **advice**.
house	house	They'll **house** the refugees in the fire**house**.
use	use	If the **use** of a certain tool is recommended, we'll **use** it.

Listening Exercises and Oral Practice

In the following exercises, your instructor will read one word from each pair of words in each group. Circle the words that you hear. Your instructor will then pronounce each pair of words and ask you to repeat them. Next, he or she will read the sentences after each group of words. Listen carefully and then practice reading the sentences aloud, making a clear distinction between the boldface words.

distinguishing [s] from [z]

[s]	[z]	[s]	[z]	[s]	[z]	[s]	[z]
seal	zeal	lacy	lazy	cease	seize	loss	laws
sink	zinc	muscle	muzzle	race	raise	price	prize
sown	zone	recent	reasoned	place	plays	ice	eyes
sue	zoo	precedent	president	loose	lose	rice	rise

1. If your belt is **loose**, you may **lose** it.
2. He was at a **loss** to explain the **laws**.

3. They **raise** a flag at the start of a **race**.
4. When your **eyes** are tired, put **ice** on them.
5. The war **zone** was **sown** with land mines.
6. I'm too **lazy** to wash my **lacy** blouse.
7. The **president** set a **precedent** in foreign policy.
8. The director found a **place** to present the new **plays**.
9. For the **price** of a dollar, you have a chance to win a $600.00 **prize**.
10. There's been a **rise** in the price of **rice**.

distinguishing [s] from [θ]

[s]	[θ]	[s]	[θ]	[s]	[θ]	[s]	[θ]
seem	theme	sought	thought	face	faith	use (n)	youth
sing	thing	sum	thumb	pass	path	mouse	mouth
sink	think	sigh	thigh	force	forth	worse	worth
						useful	youthful

1. This **theme** will probably **seem** familiar to you.
2. I can't think of a **thing** to **sing** for you.
3. I don't **think** the boat will **sink**.
4. He pointed to the **sum** with his **thumb**.
5. The poet **thought** she had found the love she **sought**.
6. The girl's **faith** was evident in her **face**.
7. The **youth** made good **use** of his strength.
8. On the way, you'll **pass** a narrow **path** through the woods.
9. You can't **force** him to come **forth** with the truth.
10. This hat makes her look quite **youthful**, but it isn't very **useful**.

distinguishing [z] from [ð]

[z]	[ð]	[z]	[ð]	[z]	[ð]
Z's	these	breeze	breathe	bays	bathe
		close (v)	clothe	teasing	teething
				closing	clothing

1. **These** 7's look too much like **Z's**.
2. When it's hot, it's easier to **breathe** if there's a **breeze**.
3. The baby is **teething**, so stop **teasing** him.
4. My father is **closing** his **clothing** store.
5. When I **bathe**, I can see the **bays** from my window.

recognizing the sounds [s] and [z]

Your instructor will read these sentences using one of the words in the parentheses. Circle the word you hear.

1. She says the (rice, rise) is extraordinary.
2. The (president, precedent) was not unusual.
3. (These, Z's) are the last letters we'll write.
4. We asked him for the (price, prize).

5. At the moment he appears to be (sinking, thinking).
6. Please let me have some (peas, peace).
7. Who owns (this, these) sheep?
8. The new (plays, place) will open next week.
9. You can hear the (bus, buzz) two blocks away.
10. The (mouse, mouth) is very small.

Spelling Hints

1. [s] is represented in writing by:

s: see, sister, this
ss: kiss, message (medial *ss* before an unstressed vowel)
c: (before *e, i, y*) cent, city, cyclone
sc: (before *e, i*) scene, science
x: [ks] box, mixture, extra (See Lesson 17 for explanation of pronunciation of *ex.*)

> **NOTE:** 1. Final **ce** and **ss** (face, pass) are always pronounced [s]. The unstressed ending *ous* is always pronounced [s] as in *dangerous* and *famous*. Initial **s** is always pronounced [s] except in *sugar* [ʃʊgɚ] and *sure* [ʃʊr].
>
> 2. **s** is not pronounced in: iṣland, aiṣle, Illinoiṣ, Arkansaṣ, corpṣ (**s** is silent and **p** is silent also).

2. [z] is represented in writing by:

z: zoo, crazy, quiz
zz: buzz, dizzy
s: is, visit, has, was, does
s + silent *e:* these, please (See Lesson 6 for information concerning the pronunciation of words ending in *s* + silent *e*.)
ss: desssért, possséss (medial *ss* before stressed vowel)

exceptions: esssential, messiah, masságe [s].

x: [gz] example (See Lesson 17 for pronunciation of *ex* in an unstressed syllable preceding a vowel.)

> **NOTE:** When the verb **is** is contracted with a pronoun ending in a voiceless sound, the [z] is completely devoiced: ṭhat's, ẉhat's, ịt's [ðæts/wɑts/ɪts].

Frequently Used and Sometimes Troublesome Words Containing the Sounds [s] and [z]

Initial [s]		*Medial* [s]		*Final* [s]	
scene	school	récent	párcel	peace	nurse
sígnal	sew	listen	muscle	piece	juice
steak	sword	eráser	distúrb	niece	loose
sweat	soil	básin	úseful	six	nótice
said	sour	esséntial	postage	base	boss
scratch	scíence	especially	saucer	nécklace	advíce
circle	sign	ánswer	disappóint	happiness	choice

Initial [z]	*Medial* [z]		*Final* [z]	
zébra	éasy	dessért	peas	lose
zipper	scissors	Tuésday	quiz	amúse
zero	razor	chosen	praise	clothes [kloᵂz]
Zip Code	pleasant	poison	has	laws
zeppelin	magazine	trousers	does	eyes
zoo	closet	resígn	occúrs	advíse
zoólogy	puzzle			noise
				aroúse

Oral Practice

sentences in which the sound [s] is adjacent to the sound [θ]

Place the tongue in the appropriate position for the [s] sound (in back of the lower teeth), and then immediately move the tongue between the teeth for the [θ].

1. This thing costs thirteen cents.
2. Bess thinks things are looking up.
3. Gus thanked us thoughtfully.
4. This theater presents thought-provoking plays.
5. Alice looks thinner than Russ thought she was.
6. This thermometer costs three dollars.
7. This Thursday is Pat's thirty-sixth birthday.
8. This knife cuts through this thick leather strap.
9. This thin little puppy looks thirsty.
10. What's thirty-six plus thirty?

sentences in which the sound [z] is adjacent to the sound [ð]

Place the tongue in the appropriate position for the [z] sound, and then immediately move the tongue between the teeth for the [ð].

1. He says they'll use this theater.
2. Sam feels that this'll cause them problems.
3. It seems they're presenting several plays this season.
4. Stanley raises the flowers that he sends them.
5. He always warns them not to lose their tickets.
6. He says that he often plays that song.
7. Sally refuses these; she prefers those.
8. According to the plans they'll leave the cars there.
9. It seems that these parents often praise their children.
10. They'll refuse these tickets because they've already bought others.

blending the [s], [z], [ɪz] inflection with the initial vowel of the following word

(Refer to Lesson 5 for the pronunciation rules.)

Answer these questions exactly like the sample sentence. As usual, Student A will ask the question, Student B will answer and so on.

example: A: Does Sam run the machine?   B. Yes, he runs it.

1. Does Gus like this cheese?
2. Does Sally recognize the problem?
3. Does Gladys need this soap?
4. Does Seth write a daily newspaper column?
5. Does the professor erase the blackboard after the class?
6. Does Stan play the string bass?
7. Does Janice use the car on Saturdays?
8. Does Alex make the bed every morning?
9. Does Lois wash her car on the weekends?
10. Does Bess watch this TV program every week?
11. Does the painter always mix the paint carefully?
12. Does Lester still owe the rent for his room?
13. Does Sally sometimes miss the bus in the mornings?
14. Does Louis always cut the bread for the sandwiches?
15. Does Tessie announce a sports program on TV?

blending final [s], [z], and [ɪz] endings with initial *s* clusters

Be careful not to let an intrusive [ə] come between the *s* ending and the *s* cluster of the following word. In other words, let the final [s] sound continue into the following *s* cluster. (The [z] and [ɪz] endings will be devoiced.)

1. James speaks Spanish.
2. Alice studies science.
3. Sam teaches school.
4. Alex sleeps soundly.
5. Louis smokes special cigarettes.
6. Charles sometimes sneezes several times.
7. Carlos sometimes has strange dreams.
8. Gladys likes steak sandwiches.
9. Charles's small dog chases squirrels.
10. Louise screams if she sees a mouse.
11. Alex's cats scratch themselves steadily.
12. Bess swims splendidly.
13. This spray can contains sticky glue.
14. Baby Alice smiles as she splashes around in the water.
15. This small rose smells sweet.
16. Bill's school is on this street.

sentences containing *s* clusters

Be sure to pronounce the boldface words correctly. Whenever possible, blend the final *s* sound with the initial vowel of the following word. If you can't figure out the meaning of a word from its use in the sentence, look the word up.

1. Gus sometimes **asks** us for an **ax** to cut wood.
2. There are no writing **desks** on the **decks** of this cruise ship.

3. **Dick's** had two slipped **discs**.
4. Sometimes the **tasks** of the **tax** inspector are not pleasant.
5. Alice **gets** along well with the **guests**.
6. They use **nets** to protect the **nests** of those rare birds.
7. Some people's **pets** are considered **pests** in this neighborhood.
8. Chris says he **wastes** a lot of time when he **waits** around for his friends.
9. The sailors slept on **mats** around the **masts** of the sailing ship.
10. **Rick's** inclined to take dangerous **risks** in making deep sea dives.

oral reading

These sentences contain a variety of [s] sounds. Read them aloud, carefully observing the rules of blending and using the appropriate intonation patterns.

1. Let's exchange this silk dress for the less expensive one.
2. Eating citrus fruits like oranges and tangerines helps one build resistance to some respiratory diseases.
3. Use these scissors to cut the string that's around this package.
4. James keeps his razor in the medicine cabinet above the washbasin in his bathroom.
5. Gus always hangs up his pants, but he leaves his shoes wherever he takes them off.
6. Douglas insists he saw a flying saucer a few nights ago.
7. The zebras are the most popular animals in our local zoo.
8. My Spanish friend is always helpful when her American cousin wants to practice speaking Spanish.
9. Louise discusses her problems with her mother and asks her advice, but then she seldom takes it.
10. Lucy, who's a nurse, sews most of her own clothes.

dialogues

In practicing these dialogues with a classmate, give special attention to all the *s* sounds.

1. **A:** Would you like to taste this sweet and sour pork?
   B: No, thanks. But I'd like a piece of that special dessert you made.
2. **A:** Do you know what the letters Z I P in Zip Code stand for?
   B: As a matter of fact I do. I looked it up one day. Webster's dictionary says that *ZIP* stands for Zoning Improvement Plan.
3. **A:** Tina's so disappointed that she can't solve that puzzle. She's usually a whiz at anything to do with physics or mathematics.
   B: Oh, but that's a very special kind of puzzle. I myself don't know anyone who can figure it out.
4. **A:** Has anyone seen Carlos recently? He seems to have disappeared since the first week of the semester.
   B: Carlos is in Spain. His sister was very sick and his parents sent for him. He's coming back next week.
   A: Thank you, Chris. I'm glad nothing's happened to him.
5. **A:** Have you received any letters from your Japanese friend recently?
   B: Yes, I have. As a matter of fact he wants me to send him some books.
   A: What kind of books does he prefer—novels, short stories, or biographies?
   B: He says he prefers modern novels, but sometimes he enjoys mystery stories and biographies.

Written Exercise

Write the correct symbol ([s], [z], or [ɪz]) for the sound of the final *s* in the third person singular, possessive, or plural forms. (Refer to Lesson 5.)

1. ____ Marie's		19. ____ stays		37. ____ loses
2. ____ Beth's		20. ____ changes		38. ____ stands
3. ____ radios		21. ____ steaks		39. ____ carries
4. ____ raises		22. ____ messages		40. ____ finishes
5. ____ skirts		23. ____ sweats		41. ____ boxes
6. ____ dresses		24. ____ sleeps		42. ____ sews
7. ____ Louis's		25. ____ quizzes		43. ____ clothes
8. ____ discusses		26. ____ alarms		44. ____ notices
9. ____ scissors		27. ____ photographs		45. ____ pleases
10. ____ erases		28. ____ fixes		46. ____ chases
11. ____ baths		29. ____ laughs		47. ____ desks
12. ____ Charles's		30. ____ seems		48. ____ stops
13. ____ uses		31. ____ loses		49. ____ life's
14. ____ bathes		32. ____ breathes		50. ____ doors
15. ____ Alice's		33. ____ goes		51. ____ Bill's
16. ____ studies		34. ____ scratches		52. ____ sings
17. ____ months		35. ____ scenes		53. ____ jobs
18. ____ refuses		36. ____ peas		54. ____ releases

Homework: Interviewing a Classmate

The purpose of this assignment is to help you get to know your fellow students better. Each of you will choose a person whom you would like to know more about and arrange to interview that person. He or she, in turn, will interview you. **These interviews are to be conducted outside of class.** You will present the results of the interview to the rest of the class on the date assigned by your instructor.

The following questions are the type you should ask the person whom you are interviewing. You may add or omit any questions you wish, but please don't substitute any questions that will embarrass the person you are interviewing. Arrange the information you gain from the interview in an interesting manner. Take as many notes as you wish, but do not write the material in paragraph form. **You may not read your presentation.**

1. What is your full name? Do you have a nickname? By which name do you prefer to be called?

2. What is your hometown? Do you still live there? If not, where do you live now?

3. Are you married? Engaged?

4. Do you have any children? (Ask this question only if the person is married.)

5. What are your special interests? Do you have a hobby? If not, how do you spend your leisure time?

6. What sports do you like? Do you participate actively in any sport?

7. Do you have a part-time job? Do you enjoy the work, or do you do it just for the money?

8. What are your plans when you graduate?

9. Have you travelled—around the Caribbean? in South America? in the United States? in Europe? Do you plan to travel in the future? Where?

10. Do you have a favorite TV program or a favorite TV personality?

11. What type of movies do you prefer? Do you go to the movies regularly? Do you have favorite performers?

12. What are your preferences in clothes? What colors do you like most? Is there any color that you particularly dislike?

13. Do you read books, magazines, or newspapers in English? What types of reading material do you prefer? Do you have any favorite authors?

Appropriateness: Using the Telephone—Making Reservations over the Telephone

dialogues

Theater Reservations

A: Civic Theater, good morning.

B: Are there any tickets available for tonight's performance?

A: We have seats at $15.00 in the balcony and some in the mezzanine at $20.00.

B: Are there any center seats in the mezzanine?

A: We have some in the fifth row center. How many would you like?

B: Two, please. The name is Jaime Pérez.

A: Spell the last name, please.

B: P as in Peter–E–R–E–Z as in zebra.

A: First initial?

B: J.

A: Your tickets will be held until 7:30 this evening. Please pick them up at the box office before that time.

B: Thank you very much.

Dinner and Show Reservations

A: Palace Club. Good morning.

B: I'd like to make a reservation for 8:30 this evening, please.

A: Sorry, the only time we have space available is at 9:30. Would that time be OK?

B: I think so. What time is the first show?

A: At 10:30.

B: I think that will be all right. Please make a reservation for two. The name is Sam Zipperling.

A: Please spell the last name.

B: Z–I–P–P–E–R–L–I–N–G.

A: Very well, Mr. Zipperling. That's a reservation for two, at 9:30 this evening. Thank you.

B: Thank you very much.

Flight Reservations

A: Good morning. Globe International Airlines. May I help you?

B: Do you have an evening flight to Caracas, Venezuela?

A: Yes, we have a flight at 7:15.

B: Can I reserve a seat on that flight for tomorrow night?

A: I'm sorry. It's all booked. But we can put you on our next flight which leaves at 11:05. That's flight 310.

B: Please book me on that one. The name is Kay Sanders. S–A–N–D–E–R–S.

A: You can pick up your ticket at the Globe counter an hour before your flight and thank you for flying Globe.

B: Thank you.

useful expressions

When you call to make any kind of reservation, it is a good idea to ask if there is anything available. You can use one of the following expressions.

"Is there any space available?"
"Are there any tickets available?"
"Are there any seats available for tonight?"
"Do you have any tickets left for tonight's show?"
"Do you have any seats available on flight 205?"

If there is something available, you can make a reservation by using any of the expressions below.

"I'd like two tickets, please."
"I'd like to make a reservation for 8:00."
"Please make a reservation for two."
"Can I reserve a seat on that flight?"
"Please book me on that flight."
"Can you hold my reservation until tonight?"

Notice that in making a reservation you must be able to spell your name clearly and understand numbers given over the phone.

If you are calling to change a reservation rather than to make one, then you may say:

"This is Ms. Jones speaking. I have a reservation for tonight's performance, but I'd like to change it for tomorrow. Is that possible?"

practice

Situations

1. Call a local theater and ask for tickets for tonight's performance. Ask specifically for center seats and inquire about the price. Make sure to give your name — and remember to spell it.

2. Call the Concert Hall and ask if there are any tickets left for the evening performance. You need two. The person at the ticket office will tell you that there are seats available, but they are not together. Ask about the location of the seats, the price, and the length of time the tickets will be held in the box office.

3. Call a restaurant to make a reservation for three people. The person answering the phone will tell you that the restaurant has two seatings, one at 7:30 and the other at 9:30. Select one seating and spell your name for the person taking the reservation.

4. Call a nightclub to make a reservation for two for the 11 o'clock show — no dinner. Give your name and spell it. Make sure you ask about the price.

5. You have to go to New York on the first flight available. You call the airline, but the early flight is all booked. You then ask for a reservation on the next flight. Give your name, address, and telephone number.

6. With another student, make up a dialogue using the expressions presented on page 186 and/or in the dialogues on page 185. You may select from making a reservation for a theater performance, a show, a flight, or just for dinner in a restaurant. Present your dialogue to the rest of the class.

The Consonants: The Alveo-Palatal Fricatives [ʃ] and [ʒ]

Description of the Sounds

[ʃ] and [ʒ] are alveo-palatal fricatives. [ʃ] is **voiceless**, and [ʒ] is **voiced**. To produce these sounds, bring the blade of the tongue in a more or less flattened position farther back in the mouth than for [s] and [z]. Round the lips and push them quite forward. Curl the tip of the tongue slightly up and back toward the palate without touching any part of the mouth. Your teeth should be almost closed. The friction of air along the groove of the tongue and between the teeth produces the sound [ʃ]. [ʒ] is produced in exactly the same way except that it is voiced. The diagram shows the correct mouth position for producing these postdental sounds.

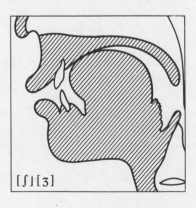

[ʃ][ʒ]

[ʃ] appears initially as in *shore*, medially as in *nation*, and finally as in *push*. [ʒ] appears medially as in *vision* and finally as in *beige*. [ʒ] **never appears initially**. Pronounce the words after your instructor.

Important Hints about the Sounds [ʃ] and [ʒ]

1. Consonant clusters with [ʃ]*

   a. [ʃ] forms only one initial cluster: [ʃr]—shrimp, shrink.
   b. [ʃ] forms only one final cluster by the addition of the *ed* inflection: [ʃt]—pushed, washed.
   (See Lesson 6 for explanation and exercises.)

2. Consonant clusters with [ʒ]*

   a. [ʒ] **does not form any initial clusters** since it does not occur in initial position.
   b. [ʒ] forms only one final cluster by the addition of the *ed* inflection: [ʒd]—massaged, sabotaged. (See Lesson 6.)

*The plurals of nouns ending in [ʃ] and [ʒ], and the third person singular ending in [ʃ] and [ʒ] are pronounced with [ɪz]:—washes, pushes, massages, sabotages. (See Lesson 5 for explanation and exercises.)

Listening Exercises and Oral Practice

Your instructor will read one of the words from each of the pairs in the following sections. Circle the words that you hear. Then repeat all the words after your instructor. Next, your instructor will read the sentences. Listen carefully. Then practice reading the sentences aloud, making a clear distinction between the sounds in the boldface words.

distinguishing [ʃ] from [ʒ]

[ʃ]	[ʒ]	
Aleutian	allusion	He made an **allusion** to the **Aleutian** Islands.
Asher	azure	**Asher** spent his vacation on the **azure** coast.
dilution	delusion	It's a **delusion** to think that the **dilution** of the drug is harmless.
glacier	glazier	The young **glazier** dreamed of exploring a **glacier**.

distinguishing [ʃ] from [s]

[ʃ]	[s]	
shock	sock	What a **shock** to find he kept his money in a **sock**.
shell	sell	Bobby was trying to **sell** his **shell** collection.
fashion	fasten	The **fashion** designer said he would **fasten** the jacket with a large button.
rush	Russ	**Russ** told us to **rush** to the airport.
parish	Paris	She got married in **Paris** in her own **parish**.

Spelling Hints

[ʃ] is represented in writing by:

    sh: shy, fashion, dish
medial *t* + *i:* nation, initial, patience.

exceptions: in question, Christian, and suggestion, *ti* = [tʃ]

medial *ss* + *i:* compassion, permission, profession
medial *ss* + *u:* pressure, issue, tissue
medial *c* + *i:* social, special, delicious, physician
initial *s* + *u:* sure, sugar

Unusual spellings:

ch: **Chicago, Michigan, machine, chaperone, Chevrolet, chef, chauffeur,
champagne**
medial *x* + *i:* anxious, complexion
medial *c* + *e:* ocean

[ʒ] is represented in writing by:

medial *s* + *u:* usual, casual, measure, treasure

exceptions: insurance [ʃ], unsure [ʃ], insurrection [s]

medial *s* + *i:* decision, occasion, television

exceptions: tension and extension; **si** = [ʃ]

final *ge:* beige, massage, mirage, rouge, camouflage, garage

In some American dialects words ending in *ge* are all pronounced [dʒ] as in *jump*
[dʒəmp].

Frequently Used and Sometimes Troublesome Words

Initial [ʃ]		*Medial* [ʃ]		*Final* [ʃ]	
sheet	shirt	machíne	nátional	leash	wash
ship	shérbet	séashore	conscious	Eńglish	pólish
shave	shoe	physícian	commércial	wish	rush
shell	shoot	delicious	musician	fínish	púnish
shelf	should	rácial	tuition	fresh	furnish
shádow	súgar	facial	cúshion	cash	foolish
shop	show	patience	tissue	crash	push
shot	shóulder	nation	ocean	mash	bush
shark	shore	precious	social	flash	Pólish
shut	shine	fashion	caution	Spánish	squash
	shówer	anxious	precáution		Írish

Medial [ʒ]			*Final* [ʒ]	
séizure	tréasure	úsual	beige	garáge
leisure	télevision	visual	éspionage	massage
decísion	transfúsion	casual	cámouflage	rouge
occasion	collision	usually	sábotage	corságe
pléasure	confusion	erósion		
measure	excursion	explosion		

Oral Practice

sentences with the sounds [ʃ] and [ʒ]

Read the following sentences. Be sure to make a clear distinction between the two
sounds.

1. There were many unusual shells in the ocean all along the shore.
2. Your decision to pay cash was very wise.
3. The collision of the pleasure boats on the river caused shock and confusion in the town.
4. The commercial section of the city was shut down as a result of the explosion.
5. The unusually heavy showers caused flash floods and soil erosion.
6. Sheila bought eye shadow, rouge, and some facial tissues.
7. Sherman's hobby is collecting semiprecious stones, which he polishes in his leisure time.
8. Sheldon's father is Polish and his mother is Irish.
9. The physician said it was probably Shelly's poor vision that caused him to crash into the tree.
10. Students from various nations paraded in their national costumes.

regular past tense ending of verbs with final [ʃ] and [ʒ]

Be sure to blend the ending with the initial vowel of the next word.

1. I washed it with soap and water.
2. She cashed a large check.
3. The authorities punished every offender without exception.
4. The men of the special espionage squad sabotaged a great many of the enemy's military installations.
5. We rushed Alice to the hospital for an operation on her shoulder.
6. The guard pushed us into the shelter without an explanation.
7. The plane crashed into the street and a crowd watched it burn.
8. The men camouflaged all the guns with tree branches.
9. I washed and ironed my clothes and shined all my shoes.
10. Shirley finished all her English and Spanish exercises.

[ɪz] ending of verbs and nouns with final [ʃ] and [ʒ]

Be sure to blend the ending with the initial vowel of the next word.

1. Sheila often polishes all the silver herself.
2. The chef specializes in the preparation of native dishes.
3. The physician said massages and hot baths would help James's backache.
4. After Sheldon washes his dog, he takes him for a walk on a leash.
5. The flashes of light from the explosions momentarily blinded us.

questions containing words with the sounds [ʃ] and [ʒ]

Be prepared to answer these questions in complete sentences forming the [ʃ] and [ʒ] correctly and using proper intonation, stress, and blending. As usual, Student A will ask a question and Student B will respond. Your instructor may choose some questions as a basis for class discussion.

1. What color shirts do you usually wear?
2. What kind of shoes do you prefer for everyday casual wear?
3. How much tuition did you have to pay last semester?

4. When was the last time you had your vision checked?

5. How often do you wash and polish your car (or your father's car)?

6. What is the most foolish thing you have done lately?

7. What kinds of things or people or situations cause you to lose your patience? How do you show your impatience?

8. When you watch a television program in English, what percentage of the program do you usually understand?

mini-dialogues

1. A: Do you usually put sugar in your coffee?
   B: No, only occasionally. I really shouldn't use any at all.

2. A: What a shame! I just spilled shoe polish on my new shirt.
   B: Let's wash it out right away before the polish dries.

3. A: Did Sheila park the car in the garage?
   B: I think so. She usually does. Why don't you make sure anyway?

4. A: Last night there was an excellent documentary film about sharks on television.
   B: I saw it. But I wish the program hadn't been interrupted by so many commercials.

5. A: Shall I get you some fresh fruit?
   B: No, thanks. I just had a dish of orange sherbet.

Written Exercise

Write the symbol ([s], [z], [ʃ], or [ʒ]) for the sound of the boldface letters.

1.	____	anxious	15.	____	usually	29.	____	wash
2.	____	message	16.	____	physician	30.	____	house (n)
3.	____	shirt	17.	____	sugar	31.	____	rose
4.	____	scissors	18.	____	pleasant	32.	____	cushion
5.	____	permission	19.	____	pleasure	33.	____	sheet
6.	____	ocean	20.	____	nation	34.	____	extension
7.	____	preface	21.	____	camouflage	35.	____	sure
8.	____	racial	22.	____	machine	36.	____	inspection
9.	____	use (v)	23.	____	complexion	37.	____	beige
10.	____	circle	24.	____	tension	38.	____	rush
11.	____	pressure	25.	____	television	39.	____	corsage
12.	____	measure	26.	____	collision	40.	____	boss
13.	____	patient	27.	____	chef	41.	____	casual
14.	____	easy	28.	____	initial	42.	____	possess

Homework

Imagine that you are making plans for a vacation. Prepare a three-minute talk about the place or places you would like to visit, and the things you would like to do.

Appropriateness: Using the Telephone—Making an Appointment by Phone

dialogues

Calling for an Appointment with the Doctor or Dentist

1. **A:** Good afternoon, Dr. Allen's office.
   B: This is James Brown. I'm a patient of Dr. Allen's. When does the doctor have office hours? I haven't been feeling well and I'd like to come in for a checkup.
   A: On Monday, Wednesday, and Thursday from one to four, and on Tuesday and Friday from six to eight.
   B: May I make an appointment for Friday evening?
   A: Yes; what is the name, please?
   B: James Brown.
   A: All right, Mr. Brown. The doctor will see you at 6:30, Friday evening.
   B: Thank you very much. 6:30, Friday. Goodbye.
   A: You're welcome. Goodbye.

2. **A:** Dr. Mercano's office. Good morning.
   B: My name is Jane Ortiz. I'm a patient of Dr. Liana Wilkins. Dr. Wilkins recommended that I call Dr. Mercano for an appointment. What are the doctor's office hours?
   A: The doctor sees patients on Monday, Wednesday, and Friday from 2:00 to 5:00.
   B: May I have an appointment for sometime on Friday afternoon?
   A: Come at 3:30. May I have your name and telephone number, please.
   B: My name is Jane Ortiz. My phone number is 765-3045.
   A: All right, Miss Ortiz. That's Friday afternoon at 3:30.
   B: Thank you very much. Goodbye.

3. **A:** Dr. Black's office. Good afternoon.
   B: This is Mrs. Watts. I'd like to make an appointment to have my teeth examined. When can the doctor see me, please?
   A: Can you come at 2:30 next Wednesday afternoon?
   B: No, I'm sorry. I can't. Does the doctor have office hours on Saturday mornings?
   A: Yes, he does, from nine to one.
   B: Oh, that's fine. Would it be possible to have an appointment around eleven?
   A: Yes; can you come at 11:15?
   B: Yes, that will be fine.
   A: All right, Mrs. Watts, 11:15, Saturday morning.
   B: Thank you very much. Goodbye.
   A: You're welcome.

4. **A:** Dr. Solomon speaking.
   B: Hello, Dr. Solomon. This is Mary Evans. I have a terrible toothache. May I come in to see you this afternoon?
   A: Yes, I'm free at 1:15. Is that all right?
   B: Yes, that's fine. I'll be there at 1:15. Thank you, doctor. Goodbye.
   A: Goodbye, Mary.

Calling a Garage

A: George's Garage. Joe speaking.
B: I'd like to bring my car in to have the brakes checked as soon as possible. Do you have anything open tomorrow morning?
A: No, sir. The earliest you can bring it in is next Tuesday.
B: That's fine. My name is Harry Miller.
A: OK Mr. Miller. Have your car here by 7:30 in the morning next Tuesday, and we'll check the brakes for you.
B: Thank you very much. Goodbye.

Calling a Beauty Parlor

A: Odette's Beauty Salon. Good morning.

B: Good morning. This is Mary Tomkins. I'd like to come in for a permanent. Do you have anything open this afternoon?

A: No. I'm sorry. We're all filled up today. How about tomorrow afternoon?

B: Can I come at 2:30 or 3:00?

A: Come at 2:30, Ma'am. Your name?

B: Mary Tomkins.

A: OK Mary. See you tomorrow.

B: Thank you very much. Goodbye.

useful information

1. When you call a doctor or a dentist for an appointment, it's a good idea to mention the reason you want an appointment — regular checkup, toothache, etc. If you feel that you have an emergency situation, tell the secretary what it is so that you can have an early appointment.

    If you are calling a doctor or dentist upon the recommendation of a friend or referral by another physician, give your name and the name of the other person.

    When you are given an appointment time, always repeat the day and the hour to make certain that there is no misunderstanding.

2. When you are calling to make an appointment for a service such as those mentioned in the dialogues on pages 192–93, always mention the type of service you need. Again, repeat the hour and day of the appointment.

practice

Following the directions of your instructor, get together with another student and work out a dialogue for one of the following situations, or for a situation you think up yourself. Present the dialogue to the class.

1. A friend has recommended a certain doctor to you. Call for an appointment.

2. You have lost a filling from one of your teeth. Call your dentist and ask for an appointment.

3. You need a shampoo and styling. Call your beauty parlor and make an appointment.

4. Your car needs a tune-up. Call a garage and make an appointment to have it done.

5. Call your personal physician and ask for an appointment for a yearly checkup.

6. Make up a dialogue with some of the expressions used in the dialogues on pages 192–93. Study the suggestions in "useful information." Be prepared to act out the dialogue in class.

The Consonants: The Alveolar Affricates [tʃ] and [dʒ]

Description of the Sounds [tʃ] and [dʒ]

The alveolar affricates [tʃ] and [dʒ] are a combination of two sounds: the stop and the fricative. The [tʃ] is a combination of [t] and [ʃ]. To produce it, let the tip of your tongue make firm contact with the alveolar ridge as for [t], thereby holding back the air stream. Then, move your tongue from the [t] position to the [ʃ] position, simultaneously rounding your lips. The sudden release of air produces the [tʃ], a sound which resembles the last part of a sneeze "a-a-a-chóo." [tʃ] is **voice-less**.

[dʒ], the **voiced** partner of [tʃ], is a combination of [d] and [ʒ]. It is produced in the same way as [tʃ]. Remember that these affricates [tʃ] and [dʒ] are made up of two symbols, but **they represent only one sound**. The diagram shows the correct mouth position for the production of [tʃ] and [dʒ].

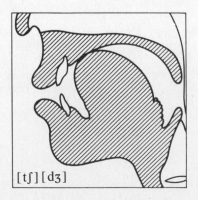

[tʃ][dʒ]

Both [tʃ] and [dʒ] appear initially, as in *church*, and *general*, medially as in *teacher*, and *agent*, and finally as in *match* and *page*.

Important Hints about [tʃ] and [dʒ]

1. [tʃ] forms the final clusters [rtʃ] as in *march* and [ntʃ] as in *lunch*.
The following clusters are formed by the addition of the *ed* ending. (See Lesson 6 for explanation and exercises.)

[tʃt] watched   [rtʃt] marched   [ntʃt] launched

2. [dʒ] forms the final clusters [rdʒ] as in *charge* and [ndʒ] as in *change*.
The following clusters are formed by the addition of the *ed* ending. (See Lesson 6 for explanation and exercises.)

[dʒd] damaged   [rdʒd] charged   [ndʒd] exchanged

3. The plural inflections of nouns, possessives, and the third person of the singular, present tense of verbs ending in [tʃ] and [dʒ] are all pronounced [ɪz]. (See Lesson 5 for explanation and exercises.)

peaches   Blanche's   catches
pages   George's   manages

Listening Exercises and Oral Practice

In the following exercises, your instructor will read one word from each pair of words in each group. Circle the words that you hear. Your instructor will then pronounce each pair of words and ask you to repeat them. Next, he or she will read the sentences after each group of words. Listen carefully and then practice reading the sentences aloud, making clear distinction between the boldface words.

1. Distinguishing [tʃ] from [dʒ]

[tʃ]	[dʒ]	[tʃ]	[dʒ]	[tʃ]	[dʒ]
cheap	jeep	chin	gin	rich	ridge
chest	jest	chain	Jane	etch	edge
chill	Jill	cheer	jeer	batch	badge
choice	Joyce	choke	joke	match	Madge

1. The price of that **jeep** was very **cheap**.
2. Please don't **jest** about the treasure **chest**.
3. **Jill**, please **chill** the fruit salad.
4. **Joyce** made and excellent **choice** of wine.
5. **Jane** bought a new gold **chain** at the jewelry store.
6. Some people **cheered** us, but others **jeered**.
7. Don't make a **joke** while you're eating or you may **choke**.
8. A **rich** family built a house on that mountain **ridge**.
9. We found an old military **badge** and a **batch** of papers.
10. **Madge** lighted a **match** in order to see in the dark.

2. Distinguishing [tʃ] from [ʃ]

[tʃ]	[ʃ]	[tʃ]	[ʃ]	[tʃ]	[ʃ]	[tʃ]	[ʃ]
chip	ship	chair	share	match	mash	much	mush
cheap	sheep	cheese	she's	catch	cash	ditch	dish
cheat	sheet	chop	shop	watch	wash	witch	wish

1. My cat always wants to **share** the arm**chair** with me.
2. Ask someone at the butcher **shop** to **chop** the meat for you.
3. **She's** at the store buying some **cheese**.
4. A **match** fell into the **mashed** potatoes.
5. The sailors' orders were to **chip** the old paint off the **ship**.
6. The child said, "I **wish** I could see a real **witch**."
7. I'm sure the police will **catch** the thief who stole the **cash**.
8. Are you going to **watch** me do the **wash**?
9. How **much** cornmeal **mush** would you like?
10. The wool these **sheep** produce will not be **cheap**.

3. Your instructor will read these sentences using one of the words in the parentheses. Circle the word that you hear. Each sentence will be read twice.

1. Please (catch, cash) it for me.
2. Do you want this (much, mush)?
3. That (dish, ditch) is very deep.
4. You have to (match, mash) them.
5. Are you going to (watch, wash) it?
6. That's quite a big (chip, ship).
7. I'd like to have a (chair, share).
8. I think he's (choking, joking).
9. These (shops, chops) are quite large.
10. The students at the assembly (cheered, jeered) the speaker.

Spelling Hints

1. [tʃ] is represented in writing by:

ch: **ch**op, tea**ch**er, ri**ch**
tch: wa**tch**, ki**tch**en
medial *t + u:* congra**t**ulate, furni**t**ure, cen**t**ury, si**t**uation
medial t + i: ques**ti**on, sugges**ti**on, Chris**ti**an (unusual spelling)
c: **c**ello (unusual spelling)

2. [dʒ] is represented in writing by:

g: **g**eneral, **g**iant, ser**g**eant [sárdʒənt]
j*: **j**oy, pro**j**ect
dge: e**dge**, bri**dge**
final *ge:* pa**ge**, char**ge**
medial *d + u:* gra**d**uate, e**d**ucate, resi**d**ual, indivi**d**ual
d + i: sol**d**ier (unusual spelling)

*The letter j has only one pronunciation in English: [dʒ].

Frequently Used and Sometimes Troublesome Words Containing the Sounds [tʃ] and [dʒ]

Initial [tʃ]

cheek	chícken	chest	choose
cheese	children	chop	chose
cheap	chain	chúbby	chalk
chief	change	church	child
chin	chair	chew	choice
cheer	check		chow

Medial [tʃ]

téacher	céntury	fúrniture
kitchen	temperature	mutual
picture	natural	future
nature	bachelor	butcher
situátion	suggéstion	fortune
quéstion	vírtue	

Final [tʃ]

each	speech	French	watch	such
beach	itch	sándwich	march	lunch
peach	which	catch	much	search
teach	H	scratch	touch	coach
				ouch

Initial [dʒ]

jeep	just
génius	judge
gym	jungle
jail	jóurney
jet	germ
jealous	junior
generous	jewelry
janitor	Julý
January	jaw
jar	join
jump	

Medial [dʒ]

relígion	márgin
indivídual	subject
májor	virgin
stranger	injure
wages	refrígerator
schedule	gráduate (v)
vegetable	gradual
register	educate
imágine	soldier
biology	enjóy
próject	

Final [dʒ]

bridge	páckage
ímage	advántage
age	cóllege
arránge	sponge
page	coúrage
edge	usage
mánage	sausage
damage	lounge
language	mileage
bandage	

Oral Practice

sentences with final [tʃ] and [dʒ]

In reading these sentences aloud, be sure to blend the final [tʃ] or [dʒ] with the following vowel sound wherever possible.

1. Each individual will manage all of her own affairs.
2. If I can arrange it, I'll graduate from college in July.
3. Having a knowledge of the Latin language is an advantage any student of French or German will recognize.
4. Some of these high school graduates will accept the challenge of working their way through college.
5. Fortunately, the explosion did not damage any of the packages of books.
6. Don't scratch or even touch any of your mosquito bites no matter how much they itch.
7. John put the chicken, the sausages, and the vegetables in the refrigerator.
8. Make sure you catch a bus that goes toward the beach.
9. We were allowed unlimited mileage on the jeep we rented in the Virgin Islands.
10. In a speech at the college of education, Jane encouraged all the students to teach before taking graduate courses.

sentences containing clusters with [tʃ] and [dʒ]

Read these sentences carefully making sure to blend the *ed* ending with the following vowel.

1. We watched all the local tennis matches on television.
2. The jeweler charged a lot for the genuine silver chain.
3. The thief who stole Jack's wallet charged a number of items to his credit card and also forged a check.
4. This supermarket chain has branched out all over the country.
5. When we reached Atlanta, we changed our flight to a later one.
6. The salesman exchanged all the furniture damaged in the storm.
7. The jewelry store manager launched a new sales campaign.
8. The names of the composers were arranged in alphabetical order.
9. The children watched and cheered as the soldiers marched along the avenue on the Fourth of July.
10. As the general's jeep approached an open ditch, a sergeant warned him of the danger.

sentences containing [ɪz] endings on words with [tʃ] and [dʒ]

As you read these sentences be sure to pronounce the *s* ending correctly on words ending in [tʃ] or [dʒ]. Refer to the pronunciation rules on pages 43–44.

1. The first pages of this chapter discuss the advantages and disadvantages of controlling wages and prices.
2. My sister Mary, who teaches at the junior college, arranges flowers as a hobby.
3. I don't know how Jane manages to learn two languages at the same time.
4. As a result of his injury, Jim's head was covered with bandages.
5. I can't imagine why George hasn't answered any of my messages.
6. If a sore itches, naturally the child scratches it.

questions containing words with the sounds [tʃ] and [dʒ]

Practice reading these questions aloud using correct pronunciation as well as proper intonation, stress, and blending. As usual, in class, Student A will ask a question and Student B will answer. Be prepared to answer all the questions. Your instructor may decide to use some of the questions as a basis for class discussion.

1. When did you graduate from high school?
2. What's your favorite kind of cheese? Is there any kind you dislike?
3. What was the highest temperature yesterday? The lowest? (Check your local newspaper.)
4. Name and identify three famous men of the nineteenth century.
5. Which other languages besides English would you like to study?
6. What's your favorite kind of sandwich?
7. What are some of your favorite vegetables? Are there any that you particularly dislike?
8. If you had the choice of visiting China or Russia, which country would you choose and why?
9. Have you ever felt that your life was in danger? If so, when?
10. Have you ever tried to teach anyone to do something? Were you successful?

dialogues

Practice these dialogues with a classmate. Your instructor may ask you to memorize one of them.

1. **A:** Did you have a cheese sandwich for lunch today?
   B: No, I didn't. I ate a fresh peach instead. I decided it was less fattening.
   A: That's all you ate for lunch?
   B: Well, not exactly. Later I had a chocolate milkshake.

2. **A:** Rachel, do you have any potato chips? Some friends just dropped in, and I don't have anything to offer them.
   B: I don't have any potato chips, but I can give you some chocolate chip cookies and some orange sherbet.
   A: Thanks, Rachel. You're an angel. I hope I can return the favor.
   B: Don't mention it. I'm glad I could help you out.

3. **A:** What happened to Jerry at the Chamber of Commerce luncheon?
   B: He choked on a piece of chicken and had to be taken to the emergency room.
   A: He's lucky he didn't suffer any brain damage from lack of oxygen.

4. **A:** Does your French teacher speak any other languages?
   B: She also speaks English and Chinese.
   A: That's a strange combination. How come?
   B: She lived in China when she was a young child, but she attended a British school.

5. **A:** Let's have lunch at the shopping center.
   B: I'd rather go to the lunch counter at the corner drugstore. It's much cheaper — and quicker, too.
   A: OK. I just thought it would be nice to eat somewhere else for a change.

6. **A:** This finger itches terribly! I'm dying to scratch it, but the doctor told me not to.
   B: Why don't you put a bandage on it? Then you can't scratch it.

Written Exercise: [tʃ], [dʒ], [ʃ], [ʒ], [s], or [z]

Write the correct symbol for the sound of the boldface letter or letters.

1. ___ situation ___	19. ___ sabotage	37. ___ choose
2. ___ question	20. ___ less	38. ___ orange
3. ___ cheese	21. ___ furniture	39. ___ century
4. ___ machine	22. ___ children	40. ___ genuine
5. ___ scissors	23. ___ finish	41. ___ schedule
6. ___ possession	24. ___ jump	42. ___ Chicago
7. ___ possess ___	25. ___ generous	43. ___ future
8. ___ vision	26. ___ Michigan	44. ___ sheer
9. ___ nation	27. ___ please	45. ___ certain
10. ___ large	28. ___ ocean	46. ___ cello
11. ___ beige	29. ___ Christian	47. ___ cheer
12. ___ soldier	30. ___ social	48. ___ congratulate
13. ___ sure	31. ___ chef	49. ___ chauffeur
14. ___ reason	32. ___ treasure	50. ___ easy
15. ___ project (v)	33. ___ tuition	
16. ___ kitchen	34. ___ menace	
17. ___ suggestion	35. ___ raise	
18. ___ sergeant	36. ___ extension	

Homework: Visit to an Exhibition

Check the local newspapers for current exhibitions at different museums. Select one museum and go to the exhibition. Prepare a five-minute talk on your visit using the following questions as a guide.

1. In which museum was the exhibition held? Had you visited the museum before?
2. Exactly where is the museum located? How does one get there?
3. On what days and at what hours is the museum open?
4. What type of exhibition did you attend? Painting? Sculpture?
5. Why did you select this exhibition?
6. Which painting, sculpture, etc. was your favorite? Describe it clearly but briefly or show a photograph of it.
7. What other exhibits were there at the museum? Mention them.
8. Would you visit this museum again? Why?

Appropriateness: Using the Telephone—Calling for Emergency Service

dialogues

1. **A:** Police Department. Sergeant Jason speaking.
   B: This is Miss Chapman calling from 711 Church Street. There's a stranger in my back yard, and she's carrying a gun. Please hurry!
   A: That was 711 Church Street.
   B: Right.
   A: Don't worry, Miss Chapman. A patrol car will be there in five minutes.

2. **A:** Fire Department.
   B: A fire just broke out on the top floor of my building!
   A: Your name and address, please.
   B: Joseph Jones, 1318 Yardley Place, Ocean Park.
   A: And what floor is the fire on?
   B: Tenth.
   A: We're on our way.

3. **A:** Speedy Ambulance Service.
   B: Would you please send an ambulance right away to 431 Chain Drive? My son is very ill. I'm afraid it's food poisoning. I have no car to take him to the hospital.
   A: Who's calling, please?
   B: This is Sarah Dodge speaking.
   A: And the address again, please?
   B: 431 Chain Drive.
   A: An ambulance will be there in ten to fifteen minutes.
   B: Please hurry! He's in very bad shape.

4. **A:** Coast Guard Rescue Operations. Petty Officer Wilson speaking.
   B: My name is Mrs. James. My husband left for a short fishing excursion this morning. It's already nine in the evening and he hasn't returned.
   A: Do you have any idea where he was headed?
   B: Green Island.
   A: What kind of boat does your husband own, Mrs. James?
   B: It's a 21 foot, blue and white Boston Whaler. It's registered under the name "Sea Urchin."

A: How many people are aboard?
B: Just my husband. He's all by himself.
A: Give me your phone number so we can reach you as soon as we have any news.
B: 751-3970.
A: We'll try to get some information for you.
B: Thank you very much.

useful information

It's a good idea to know where in your telephone directory the emergency numbers for your community are listed, and to mark them off in red ink. When you need a number in an emergency, you will know where to find it in a hurry.

The key to an effective communication in an emergency is to be brief and exact. In other words, give your name, your address, and explain your problem as briefly as possible. You do not want to waste precious time giving information that is unnecessary at the moment.

practice

In the following situations first determine the emergency service you should call and then make the call, keeping in mind the important information mentioned above.

With a classmate, work out a dialogue for one or more of the situations (according to your instructor's directions) and then present your dialogue to the rest of the class.

1. You are looking out the window and you see a man trying to jump off a balcony. You shout at him, but he screams back that he wants to die.

2. You hear screams coming from the next apartment followed by shots.

3. A fire breaks out in your kitchen and you cannot control it.

4. A member of your family suddenly collapses.

5. It has rained all night and when you wake up you realize your street is flooded and the water is continuing to rise.

6. A car turns over on the expressway and catches fire. Someone is trapped inside.

7. You arrive home with your family after having dinner at a restaurant. Suddenly everyone begins to vomit and complain of a stomachache and headache.

The Consonants: The Glides [j] and [w] and the Glottal Fricative [h]

The Sound [j]

description of the sound [j]

[j] is a voiced, postdental glide. For details as to the production of this sound, refer to Lesson 11. In the words below, watch your instructor's mouth as he or she pronounces them. Then, following your instructor's directions, pronounce the pairs of words yourself. Notice how the mouth changes shape depending on the vowel that follows.

| east | yeast | ale | Yale | am | yam | earn | yearn | oak | yolk |
| ear | year | L | yell | arm | yarn | ooze | use (v) | owl | yowl |

[j] appears initially as in *yeast* and medially as in *million*. [j] never appears before consonants, and it never appears finally.

important hints about the sound [j]

Listed below are clusters formed by a consonant + [j]. These clusters may be followed by [u] or [ə]. (See Lesson 11.)

[pju]	**pu**pil, dis**pu**te	[fju]	**few**, con**fu**se
[bju]	**beauty**, re**bu**ke	[vju]	**view**, re**view**
[kju]	**cu**be, pe**cu**liar	[mju]	**mu**sic, a**mu**se
[gjə]	re**gu**lar	[hju]	**hue**, in**hu**man
[kjə]	parti**cu**lar	[nju]	**annual**, ma**nual**

listening exercises and oral practice

Distinguishing [j] from [dʒ]

Your instructor will read one of the words from each of the following pairs. Circle the words that you hear. Then your instructor will read all of the words and ask you to repeat them. He or she will read the sentences next. Listen carefully and then read the sentences aloud, making a clear distinction between the sounds [j] and [dʒ] in the boldface words.

[j]	[dʒ]	[j]	[dʒ]	[j]	[dʒ]		[dʒ]
yet	jet	year	jeer	yellow	Jello	mayor	major
Yale	jail	yolk	joke	yes	Jess	[meʸɚ]	[meʸdʒɚ]

1. The **jet** hasn't landed **yet**.
2. He worked in a **jail** while attending **Yale**.
3. Lemon **Jello** is **yellow**.
4. He made a **joke** about the egg **yolk** on his tie.
5. **Jess** answered "**Yes**" to the question.
6. The **mayor** says she has **major** problems to solve.

Distinguishing [j] from Other Sounds

Your professor will read these sentences using one of the words in parentheses. Circle the word that you hear. Each sentence will be read twice.

1. I read an article about the (use, juice) of that tropical fruit.
2. They'll send us to (Yale, jail), won't they?
3. The children are very fond of (Jello, yellow).
4. The (major, mayor) received a phone call.
5. I've already used all the (jokes, yolks) I had.
6. This (jam, yam) tastes delicious.
7. Those (jeers, years) were very exasperating, weren't they?
8. The word (jet, yet) is often confused with the word (jet, yet).
9. The (owl, yowl) could be heard quite a distance away.
10. He had only one good (ear, year) left.

spelling hints

[j] is represented in writing by:

y: you, your, beyond
i: (before an unstressed vowel) million
u: [ju] union, usual, peculiar

frequently used and sometimes troublesome words

See Lesson 11 for additional vocabulary.

Initial [j]			*Medial* [j]		
yeast	use (n)	úniform	pure	cube	júnior
year	use (v)	uníted	púpil	cúrious	onion
yésterday	únion	univérsity	popular	pecúliar	million
young	unit	universal	reputátion	particular	annual
youth	usual	uníque	bureáucracy	régular	manual
youngster	universe	unánimous	fúrious	figure	January
			confúse	munícipal	contínue
			transfúsion	músic	réscue
			musícian		

oral practice: sentences with words containing the sounds [j] and [dʒ]

Read these sentences making a clear distinction between [j] and [dʒ]. Also, remember to use correct stress and intonation.

1. Yesterday the Youth Orchestra played some unusual music by modern European composers.
2. The mayor of New York City is elected every four years.
3. Mayor Jackson used to be a major general in the U.S. Army.
4. Yale University usually holds its graduation exercises in June.
5. The United States flag is known as the "Stars and Stripes", and the British flag is called the "Union Jack".
6. Jane Young joined the musicians' union last year.
7. These youngsters usually wear yellow uniforms to school.
8. The United Nations General Assembly meets annually in New York City.
9. The municipal workers voted unanimously to accept the union contract.
10. The New York Yankees played in Yankee Stadium yesterday afternoon.

mini-dialogues using words containing the sounds [j] and [dʒ]

Practice these dialogues with another student. Your instructor may ask you to memorize one or more of them.

1. **A:** Did Professor Young study in Europe or in the United States?
   B: She attended Yale, but she went to graduate school at a famous university in Germany.

2. **A:** Where did you buy that beautiful yellow jacket?
   B: I just bought it yesterday at the university bookstore.

3. **A:** Does your cousin Joe live in New York or in New Jersey?
   B: He used to live in New York, but last July he moved to Union City, New Jersey.

4. **A:** How many more units does Jim need to graduate from Yeshiva University?
   B: He just finished his junior year, so he still has a whole year to go.

5. **A:** Where can I find out how many million people there are in the universe?
   B: Millions? You mean billions, don't you? I think you can find the latest population figures in an almanac. Why don't you ask the librarian to help you?

Written Exercise: [j], [ju], [jʊ], [jə], or [dʒ]

Write the symbol for the sounds of the boldface letters. If the [j] is preceded by a consonant sound, write the symbol for that sound also.

example: **cu**te [kju]

1. ___ jet	18. ___ jacket	35. ___ volume
2. ___ yet	19. ___ yesterday	36. ___ register
3. ___ jail	20. ___ judge ___	37. ___ language
4. ___ Yale	21. ___ vacuum	38. ___ usual
5. ___ yellow	22. ___ January ___	39. ___ virgin
6. ___ joke	23. ___ humanity	40. ___ junior
7. ___ yolk	24. ___ bureau	41. ___ union
8. ___ peculiar ___	25. ___ jewelry	42. ___ young
9. ___ schedule	26. ___ yell	43. ___ job
10. ___ New York	27. ___ youth	44. ___ confuse
11. ___ yard	28. ___ giant	45. ___ pupil
12. ___ educate	29. ___ year	46. ___ jealous
13. ___ intelligent	30. ___ annual	47. ___ regular
14. ___ million	31. ___ union	48. ___ cube
15. ___ manufacture	32. ___ curious	49. ___ popular
16. ___ major	33. ___ gradual	50. ___ furious
17. ___ uniform	34. ___ project	

The Sound [w]

description of the sound

[w] is a **voiced**, bilabial velar glide. To produce [w], raise the back of the tongue up toward the soft palate (velum) as if you were going to produce [u]. Round your lips as you would to produce [u]. Push them forward as if you were blowing out a candle. You actually produce a very short [u] as you simultaneously move your lips and tongue to the position of whatever vowel is to follow [w]. Watch your instructor's mouth as he or she pronounces these words, and then, according to your instructor's directions, pronounce the words yourself.

E	we	ate	wait	ax	wax	oh	woe
ill	will	air	wear	[ɑ] on	wan	or	war
ear	we're	L	well	earn [n]	worm [m]		

[w] appears initially as in *women* and medially as in *frequent* and *persuade*. It never appears finally.

important hints about the sound [w]

1. [w] combines with other consonants to form the following clusters:

   [tw] : **twelve, twice, between**
   [sw] : **swim, sweep, persuade, swallow**
   [kw] : **queen, frequent**
   [gw]: **language, distinguish**

2. The letter *w* is silent in the following circumstances:
   a. In an initial position before *r*: write, wrote, wrong, wrap, wrinkle, wreck.
   b. Before the letter *h* in these words: who, whom, whose, whole
   c. In these words: two, answer, toward, sword, knowledge.

3. In some dialects the sound [hw] is used for the letters *wh* in words like the

following: wheat, whistle, whale, whether, where, what, while, white, why*

*To produce the [hw] sound, inhale and release a puff of air before making the [w] sound—as if to blow out a candle. In several texts [hw] is treated as a separate sound, but since [hw] is gradually disappearing from the language, and since failure to make a distinction between [hw] and [w] does not in any way interfere with communication, we do not feel that the sound warrants more extensive coverage in this text.

listening exercises and oral practice

Your instructor will read one of the words from each pair of words in the following sections. Circle the words that you hear. Then your instructor will read all the words in each group and ask you to repeat them. Next he or she will read the sentences. Listen carefully, and then read the sentences aloud, making a clear distinction between the sounds in the boldface words.

Distinguishing [w] from [v]

[w]	[v]	[w]	[v]	[w]	[v]
we	V	west	vest	wine	vine
we'll	veal	wet	vet	wow	vow
wail	veil	worse	verse	Y	vie

1. **We** drew a big letter **V** in the sand.
2. The second **verse** is **worse** than the first one.
3. The grapes from these **vines** produce fine **wines**.
4. I bought this **vest** on the **west** coast.
5. **We'll** roast the **veal** for dinner.

Distinguishing [w] from [r]

we'd	read	wan	Ron	war	roar
weird	reared	won	run	wide	ride
weighed	raid	we'll	real	wound (v.)	round
went	rent				

1. We **went** to collect the **rent** last Wednesday.
2. We promised Willie **we'd read** his new book.
3. We went for a **ride** on a **wide** new highway.
4. **Ron** looked very **wan** after his operation.
5. **We'll** buy Dad a **real** silk tie.

spelling hints

[w] is represented in spelling by:

w: weigh, away
u: persuade, suede, suave [swɑv]
o: one, once [wən] [wəns]

frequently used and sometimes troublesome words

Initial [w]				*Medial* [w]	
week	Wédnesday	world	wool	sweet	sándwich
weak	wax	worse	won't	twist	swallow
we'll	word	wórship	war	away	always
will	worry	work	warm	sway	awkward
wind (n)	won	wound (n)	warn	swell	forward
wómen	one	would	wind (v)	sweat	backward
waste	once	wood	wound (v)	swéater	outward
weather	were			swear	otherwise

oral practice

1. The purpose of this simple exercise is to practice making a distinction between the words *we'll* [wil] and *will* [wɪl]. In these sentences, since the pronouns are in contrast, they receive the stresses as marked. Add other verbs of your choice to substitute for *go*.

We'll go if yóu *will*. (Notice the stress mark.)

    run
    speak
    walk
    talk
    eat
    stand
    sit
    rest

2. This exercise is to practice the correct pronunciation of the word *wouldn't*: [wʊdn̩t]. Add other verbs of your choice. Student A will ask the question; Student B will answer.

A: Wouldn't you like to háve it?   B: No, I wouldn't.

    wear
    take
    save
    hear
    win

3. The purpose of this exercise is to practice the word *once*: [wəns]. Add other expressions of your choice to substitute for *an hour*. Student A will ask the question; Student B will answer.

A: How often does it happen?
B: It happens once an hour.

a day	in a while
a week	every so often
a month	in a lifetime
a year	a century

sentences containing words with the [w] and [v] sounds

As you read these sentences be sure to make a clear distinction between the [w] and [v] sounds.

1. This young woman is going to the village with us on Wednesday.
2. We wanted to invite Wilma to visit us last week, but she was away in Vermont.
3. Willy's vision was very good with glasses, but without them he couldn't see well at all.
4. When we visited Washington, we went to see my Aunt Vivian.
5. Wanda has a wonderful way of working with very young people.
6. I have to wind this alarm clock every day.
7. In Vermont, some people wear wool velvet clothes in the winter.
8. The wound will heal quickly if you wash it out with a disinfectant.
9. When the campers woke up they drove the van into the woods.
10. The weather bureau predicts strong winds and very high waves.

dialogues with the sound [w]

1. **A:** The weather is warmer today, isn't it?
   B: Yes, but the wind is from the west, and a west wind usually brings cold, wet weather.

2. **A:** Won't it be wonderful if we win some money at the racetrack on Wednesday?
   B: It sure will. My friend Wanda won $1200 once.
   A: Wow! Were you with her when she won?
   B: No, I wasn't. I was working. She went with some friends.

3. **A:** Excuse me, Madam. Is this sweater washable?
   B: All the sweaters on this table are wash-and-wear.
   A: What does "wash-and-wear" mean, anyway?
   B: It means you can wash the article and wear it without ironing it. It doesn't wrinkle.
   A: Oh, I see. Thank you.

3. **A:** Wilma, we're going to lunch with Vivian. You're welcome to join us if you'd like to.
   B: Ooo-oo. I'd love to. But I have to run an errand. Will you wait for me? I'll be back in one minute.
   A: Sure, we'll wait, or we'll walk along with you if you want us to.
   B: Don't bother. I won't be long. I just want to pick up my wristwatch from the repair shop down the street.
   A: Well, OK. We'll window-shop while we wait for you.

The Sound [h]

description of the sound [h]

[h] is a **voiceless**, glottal fricative. It is really only a puff of air. As the air passes through the glottis (the opening between the vocal cords) the vocal cords interfere with its passage, causing friction. This friction in turn causes the rushing [h] sound. [h] is also a glide because as you produce the sound, you place your lips and tongue in the position necessary to produce whatever vowel follows the [h] sound. Watch

how the shape of your instructor's mouth changes as he or she pronounces these words. Notice that the lips are unrounded for [h] plus a front or central vowel, and rounded for [h] plus a back vowel.

he's   his   haze   has   hollow   her   who   hole   haul   how   high

Now repeat these contrasts after your instructor.

ease	he's	N	hen	Earl	hurl	all	hall
is	his	at	hat	ooze	whose	owl	howl
ate	hate	arm	harm	owes	hose	eye	high

important hints about the sound [h]

1. [h] is strongly aspirated at the beginning of a phrase or before a stressed syllable:

Hénry will go.   Hé came, but shè didn't.

2. [h] is not pronounced in the following words:

hour, honor, honest, ghost, ghetto, shepherd, exhibit, exhibition, John, vehicle, heir, herb

[h] is often not pronounced in the word *forehead* [fɔrɪd] [farɪd].

3. [h] is not usually pronounced in a pronoun which follows a verb.

Give her a book.   Tell him to ask her.

4. When the pronoun *he* follows an auxiliary, the *h* is not usually pronounced. If you have trouble pronouncing the combination of sounds, use the full form. However, for communication purposes it is important that you be able to understand these combinations when you hear them. Listen as your instructor pronounces these sentences and then practice saying them.

[watəlɪ] What'll he do?   [hæzɪ] Has he gone?
[wɛrəlɪ] Where'll he go?   [hædɪ] Had he done it before?
[wɛnəlɪ] When'll he come?   [məstɪ] Must he go?
[hulɪ] Who'll he meet?   [kænɪ] Can he do it?
[haʊlɪ] How'll he know?   [ʃʊdɪ] Should he leave?

listening exercise and oral practice

1. Your instructor will read the following list of words. Circle those in which the letter *h* is silent. Each word will be read twice.

1. how	6. heavy	11. hurry	16. behave
2. hour	7. perhaps	12. hurricane	17. half
3. hollow	8. exhibit	13. vehicle	18. comprehend
4. honor	9. honest	14. heir	19. herb
5. he's	10. horrible	15. honorable	20. forehead

2. Repeat these sentences after your instructor. Be sure to make a clear distinction between the sounds in the boldface words.

1. **He's** swimming with **ease**.

2. This **is his** book.
3. The warm **air** dried her **hair**.
4. We **all** went out into the **hall**.
5. Sally **owes** me money for the **hose** I bought for her.

spelling hints

[h] appears initially as in *he's*, and medially as in *behave*. It does not appear finally.

[h] is represented in writing by: *h* :   heat, hill, ahead
wh: ẇho, ẇhose, ẇhom, ẇhole

frequently used and sometimes troublesome words

	Initial [h]				*Medial* [h]	
he's	health	hóliday	huge	ẇhole	aheád	mahógany
he'll	héavy	horrible	humánity	hóly	behind	prohibit
hill	heaven	hungry	humidity	hotél	behave	chíldhood
his	half	hurt	ẇho's	horízon	perhaps	anyhow
hear	hang	hurry	hook	how		
hate	hospital	hurricane	hole	height		

oral reading

Some of these sentences contain words in which the *h* is silent. Be aware of this fact as you read these sentences aloud. Make sure you use correct blending.

1. You look cold. I'll turn up the heat and make some hot chocolate.
2. Helen says her husband is in a hurry.
3. Hang your hat on that hook behind the door to the hallway.
4. Hilda's the heir to her father's huge estate in Hyde Park.
5. I hear they're having a sale on herbs at the health food store.
6. Henry was so hungry he ate a whole pizza by himself.
7. Both Harry and Sarah are known for their honesty.
8. Hal received an Honorable Mention award at the art exhibition.
9. Half of the furniture in the hotel is made of mahogany.
10. If you need help during the holidays, don't hesitate to ask us.

dialogues

1. **A:** What's the height of that mountain just ahead? It appears to be very high.
   B: That's Mt. Helen. It's about 4,800 feet high, the highest in this area.

2. **A:** Officer, may I park here? I have to visit my husband in the hospital. I'll only be about half an hour.
   B: Parking is prohibited until half-past seven. You'll have to park behind that building next to the hospital.

3. **A:** How many hundreds make a hundred thousand?
   B: Huh! How should I know? I don't have a head for higher mathematics. You'll have to ask Hannah. She'll figure it out in her head in half a minute.

    4. **A:** I'm so hungry I could eat a horse.
       B: Well, hurry up. There's a place called Hamburger Heaven right across from the hotel.

    5. **A:** What's your brother Herman's height?
       B: He's six feet, and my brother Henry is a whole head taller than Herman.
       A: No wonder I feel as if I'm standing in a hole when I stand next to either of them.

    6. **A:** This humidity has given me a horrible headache.
       B: Hot, humid weather like we've been having always makes me feel horrible.

    7. **A:** What's that ahead of us on the highway? It's raining so hard I can hardly see.
       B: It's a child! It looks as if he's been hurt! Be careful! Don't hit him!

    8. **A:** Did you know my brother John was hurt in a highway accident?
       B: Yes, I heard what happened. Was he badly hurt?
       A: Well, he had a huge cut in his forehead. He had to stay in the hospital a whole week.
       B: He'd better make sure he fastens his seat belt from now on. He wouldn't have hit his head if he'd had his belt fastened.

Homework

Prepare a two- to five-minute talk about your home town (or another city). Include information about some of the following: location, meaning of the name (if known), how to get there, when the city was founded, population, important historical information, principal industries (if any), famous people born there, important places to visit: museums, monuments, buildings, parks, etc., or other information you think would be interesting to your classmates. Please do not read or memorize your report. However, you may refer to notes if you need to.

Appropriateness: Using the Telephone — Making Long Distance Telephone Calls

Most long distance telephone calls can now be made through DDD (direct distance dialing). However, there are some types of calls which do require the assistance of an operator. Your local telephone directory contains information on how to make person-to-person calls, collect calls, calls using your credit card, and so on. For example, in some areas, you would dial 0 for operator, while in others, you would use a special code number to dial a long distance operator. Consult your local directory to find out which procedure to use. The dialogues illustrate two types of operator-assisted long distance calls.

dialogues
___

Making a Person-to-Person Call

Caller: Operator, I'd like to make a person-to-person call to New York City.
Operator: Just dial 0, then the area code, and then the number.
      (Caller then dials the number.)
Operator: Operator.
Caller: Operator, I'd like to make a person-to-person call to Mr. Anthony Johnson.

Operator: Just one moment, please. (Telephone rings.)
Anthony: Hello.
Operator: I have a person-to-person call for Mr. Anthony Johnson.
Anthony: This is he speaking.
Operator: Go ahead, please.

Making a Collect Call from a Public Telephone

Deposit a dime, wait for the dial tone, dial 0, the area code, and the number you wish to call.

Operator: Operator.
Johanna: Operator, I'd like to make a collect call to New York City.
Operator: The number please.
Johanna: 212-647-6754.
Operator: Your name?
Johanna: Johanna López.
Mr. López: Hello.
Operator: I have a collect call from Johanna López. Will you accept the charges?
Mr. López: Yes, of course.

practice

According to your instructor's directions, select one of the situations below, and with two classmates, prepare a dialogue to act out for the class. Refer to the previous dialogues and to your telephone directory for help.

1. Make a person-to-person call to a relative in a distant city to ask for advice about a personal problem. This person will be at his or her place of business. (4 participants)

2. You have been shopping at a large shopping mall in another city from where you live. You have just accidentally locked your purse and your car keys in the car. Make a collect call to someone in your family, explain what happened and ask that person to bring you an extra set of keys. (You'll have to explain where the keys can be found, and also where you will meet that person when he or she arrives at the shopping mall.)

3. You have just been notified that you have passed a very important examination (you decide which one). Make a person-to-person call to your father or mother at his or her office in another city. (This dialogue will require 4 participants because when the operator in the other city calls the office, the secretary answers the phone.)

4. Think up a situation of your own which would require you to make a person-to-person or a collect call. Work out the dialogue with two or three students and present it to the class according to your instructor's directions.

The Consonants: The Liquid Sound [r]

Description of the Sound [r]

[r] and [l] are called variously glides, liquids, approximants, or continuants. The truth is that these sounds have characteristics of both vowels and consonants. That is, they have the resonance of vowels along with the obstruction inside the mouth needed for the production of consonants. For this reason, [r] and [l] are also called semi-vowels or semi-consonants.

[r] is a **voiced** sound. To produce the sound, raise the tongue so that the sides contact the upper side teeth. The tongue tip does not touch anything. To produce an initial [r], round your lips, not as much as for the vowel [u], but moreso than to produce the vowel [ɔ]. To produce medial and final [r], move the tongue back. The production of [ɚ] is similar to that of [r], but [ɚ] forms a syllable while [r] does not. The diagram shows the correct tongue position.

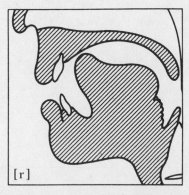

[r]

213   [r] appears initially as in *rain*, medially as in *morning*, and finally as in *store*. (In

some areas known as "r-less areas," speakers of English eliminate [r] at the end of words and before a consonant: *for*, *near*, and *park*.

Repeat the words *rain*, *morning*, and *store* after your instructor. Notice that in the word *rain*, the tongue is back but almost immediately moves forward to produce the front vowel [eʸ]. However, in the words *morning* and *store*, the tongue moves back and stays there because [ɔ] in both words is a back vowel.

Important Hints about the Sound [r]

1. [r] combines with other consonants to form initial clusters.

[kr]	cry, cream, Christmas	[fr]	free, fry, fresh
[pr]	pray, price, pretty	[θr]	three, through, throw
[tr]	try, true, train	[ʃr]	shrink, shrimp
[br]	bread, brown, brother	[spr]	spread, spray
[dr]	drink, dry, dress	[str]	strike, strong
[gr]	gray, green, grow	[skr]	scream, scratch

2. [r] combines with other consonants to form final clusters, many of which are formed with the addition of the *s* and *ed* endings. These have been discussed in Lessons 5 and 6, respectively.

[rt]	heart, part	[rp]	harp	[rdz]	cards
[rk]	park, lark	[rv]	carve	[rmz]	arms
[rθ]	forth, hearth	[rm]	harm, form	[rvz]	carves
[rn]	born, warn	[rtʃ]	march	[rts]	hearts
[rs]	force, nurse	[rdʒ]	charge	[rpt]	warped
[rl]	Karl	[rmθ]	warmth	[rkt]	parked
[rd]	lard, hard	[rz]	cars	[rtʃt]	marched
		[rbz]	curbs	[rdʒd]	charged
		[rlz]	curls	[rvd]	carved
		[rnz]	turns		

Frequently Used and Sometimes Troublesome Words with the Sound [r]

Initial [r]			*Medial* [r]		*Final* [r]	
read	rent	road	maríne	nárrow	beer	your
reach	wreck	robe	míracle	heart	year	poor
rich	wrap	wrong	mirror	foreign	bear	láwyer
ríver	rock	raw	eráse	horrible	wear	war
rain	rough	ride	arrest	heard	their	hour
raise	rúbber	right	véry	prove	there	fire
radio	rude	rice	bury	jury	they're	foyer
rare	room	round	dairy	quarrel		
		róyal	character	arríve		

Oral Practice

sentences containing the sound [r]

As you read these sentences be sure to use the correct lip and tongue position for the [r].

1. The rains caused by that terrible hurricane made the river rise.
2. We ruined a tire when we hit a rock on the road.
3. The storm wrecked my friend's dairy barn.
4. When I looked at myself in the mirror this morning, I saw the scar.
5. The jury arrived at a decision half an hour ago.
6. The date for next year's foreign car race was announced over the radio.
7. Please pour me some prune juice right here, in this red cup.
8. Right after the quarrel, the officers arrested someone near the bar.
9. The rent listed for this apartment is very high.
10. Who are the characters in that short story?

sentences containing words with [r] clusters

As you read these sentences be sure to pronounce the [r] clusters clearly.

1. Last Christmas my brother made some delicious cream puffs.
2. She served a new kind of drink made with champagne.
3. We parked our car on a side street and walked to the fair in the park.
4. I need some dark bread and some brown sugar from the supermarket.
5. We bought some fresh bean sprouts at the farmers' market.
6. Did you notice how fast that pitcher throws the ball?
7. I'll bet most of the batters will strike out.
8. Please give me three dozen red roses.
9. Are you sure this material won't shrink?
10. The kittens were scratching on the tree trunk.

questions with the sound [r]

Practice reading these questions aloud using correct phrasing, intonation, and blending. Be prepared to answer all of them in complete sentences. Your instructor may choose some of the questions as a basis for class discussion.

1. Do you ever read books or magazines in English for pleasure? What kinds?
2. How often do you ride on public transportation?
3. About how many letters do you write in an average month?
4. What do you prefer to drink when you are very thirsty?
5. How often do you borrow books from the library?
6. Do you always get up as soon as your alarm clock rings, or do you lie in bed for a while?
7. Do you ever bring your lunch from home, or do you always buy it?
8. Do you have any desire to run for a political office? If so, which one?
9. How many children did your grandparents raise?
10. Have you ever received an award for anything, or have you ever entered a contest and won a prize?
11. Which are you more likely to remember — a person's name? face? occupation?
12. How do you react when someone to whom you were introduced recently fails to remember you or when you fail to remember that person?
13. What kind of things are you afraid of — water? the dark? wild animals? Do you remember when you were first conscious of any of your fears? Have you ever tried to conquer any of your fears?

14. What kind of animals do you prefer as pets? If you don't have a pet, what kind would you like to have?

dialogues

1. **A:** What time did you arrive from the airport this morning, Richard?
   B: Around 3 a.m. Unless my watch was wrong.
   A: 3 a.m.! How horrible! You'd better get some rest right away or you'll collapse.
   B: You're right! I'm going to read awhile to relax; then I'll be ready to sleep until tomorrow morning.

2. **A:** I'm sorry to bother you, Randy. Could I borrow five dollars until Friday?
   B: Of course. Are you sure you don't need any more?
   A: Positive. I'll return the money next Friday.

3. **A:** Would you please gift-wrap this robe for me?
   B: What kind of paper would you prefer—this gray and pink, or that one with the green stripes?
   A: That green-striped one will be fine. Please use green ribbon. Oh, may I have a gift card?
   B: Certainly. Here you are.
   A: Thank you.

4. **A:** How far away is the road to the airport?
   B: Not very far. Just go straight for four blocks, turn right, and then go straight ahead on the narrow road.
   A: Thank you very much.

5. **A:** That razor blade is really sharp! Be careful not to cut your fingers on it.
   B: Don't worry, I won't. I just want to scrape this chewing gum off the floor.

Homework

Some people enjoy doing particular things on rainy days. Tell the class what you like to do when it rains, or tell about a positive or negative experience you had on a recent rainy day.

Appropriateness: Using the Telephone—Calling for Service

dialogues

1. **A:** Fast Service Plumber. Good morning.
   B: This is Mr. Ronald from 1340 River Avenue. My bathroom is all flooded, and I don't know what the problem is.
   A: Your address again, please, and telephone number.
   B: 1340 River Avenue; that's just in back of the Treasury Department building. My phone number is 731-5628.
   A: Our serviceman will be there in fifteen minutes.
   B: Thank you very much. Please hurry!

2. **A:** International Electric Corporation. Good morning.
   B: Service department, please.
   C: Service Department. May I help you?
   B: This is Mr. Ross. I have a problem with my refrigerator. The icemaker doesn't seem to be working properly.
   C: How old is your refrigerator?

B: It's still under warranty. I just bought it a month ago.

C: What model do you have?

B: CT-9357.

C: Name and address, please.

B: Ross. R-o-s-s. I'm at 3651 Ray Street, River View.

C: Very well, Mr. Ross. Will there be someone at home this afternoon?

B: Yes, there will.

C: Our technician will be there sometime this afternoon. What's your phone number?

B: My number's 837-1050. Please make sure your technician comes this afternoon.

C: Don't you worry. She'll be there.

B: Thank you.

3. A: Mr. Solve-It-All at your service.

B: This is Ms. Ramsey speaking. I have a terrible problem. My TV set shuts off when I turn on the bathroom light, and if I want to turn on the radio, I have to turn on the oven first.

A: You do have a big problem, miss. Please give me your address and phone number. A technician will be there some time this morning.

B: The address is 907 Reed Avenue, Apartment 9B, in Riverside. I'm sorry, I have no telephone. I'm calling from a neighbor's home.

A: OK, Ms. Ramsey. We'll take care of the problem for you.

B: Thanks a lot. I'll be waiting for you.

useful information

If you follow the tips below you should have no problem getting service over the telephone.

1. Ask for the service department when you are calling a big company.

2. Identify yourself.

3. Explain the problem as briefly as you can without going into too much detail. The person in the service department will ask any necessary questions.

4. Give your complete name, address, and phone number (if you have one).

5. Be prepared to provide information concerning model number or serial number of your appliance.

6. Make it clear that you will be waiting for the technician at the time he or she is supposed to arrive.

practice

1. Your air conditioner is making a terrible noise. Call for service at the main office of the company.

2. There's no electricity on one side of your house. Call an electrician.

3. Your car will not start. Call your mechanic.

4. The electricity went off and two people are trapped in the elevator of your apartment building. Call the elevator repair service.

5. You arrive home and find the whole house flooded. Call the plumber. If you have carpets, also call a carpet cleaner.

6. Work with another student and prepare a dialogue using the dialogues presented here as a guide. Follow the tips given. Be prepared to act out the dialogue in class, without using any notes.

The Consonants: The Liquid Sound [l]

Description of the Sound [l]

[l] is a **voiced**, alveolar liquid sound. To produce it, raise the tip of the tongue slightly so that it touches the upper alveolar ridge. The middle of the tongue is low in the mouth. The sides of the tongue are free; they do not touch the side teeth. The air escapes over the sides of the tongue. The diagram shows the position of the speech organs in the production of [l].

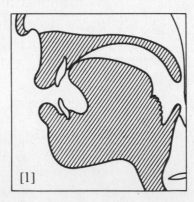

[l]

[l] appears initially as in *leave*, medially as in *lily*, and finally as in *bill*.

Important Hints about the Sound [l]

Sometimes [l] does not need a vowel to produce a syllable. In the word *little* some speakers of English go directly from [t] to [l] with no vowel sound in between. This is why [l] in this word is known as a syllabic [l].

1. [l] is a syllabic consonant whenever it appears in an unstressed syllable preceded by [t], [d], or [n]. The phonetic symbol for it is [l̩]. Listen and repeat.

little	saddle	tunnel	petal	final
bottle	ladle	funnel	pedal	

2. [l̩] also occurs after [p], [b], [k], [g], [s], [z], [m], [v], and [f].

simple	jungle	sizzle	possible	scuffle
able	muscle	animal	terrible	raffle
miracle	pretzel	devil	probable	ruffle

3. In the following words the letter *l* is silent.

half	almond	chalk	psalm	Lincoln
calf	could	walk	palm	salmon
	would	talk	calm	
	should	yolk		
		folk		

consonant clusters with [l]

[l] combines with other consonants to form clusters. Below you will find some frequently used clusters.

[pl]	play	[fl]	fly	[lθ]	health
[bl]	blow	[sl]	sleep	[rl]	girl
[kl]	cloud	[spl]	splice	[lv]	involve
[gl]	glide	[skl]	sclerosis	[lz]	calls
				[ld]	held, polled

| Listening Exercises and Oral Practice

Your instructor will read one of the words from each pair. Circle the word read. Then read all the words after your instructor. Next, practice reading the sentences. Be sure you make a distinction between the sounds of the boldface words.

distinguishing [r] from [l]

[r]	[l]	[r]	[l]	[r]	[l]
rate	late	read	lead	right	light
red	led	rock	lock		
here	hill	poor	pull	fire	file
fair	fell	pour	Paul		

1. The new postage **rate** began **late** in March.
2. The **red** car **led** the parade.
3. I **read** an article about **lead** poisoning.
4. He broke the **lock** by hitting it with a **rock**.
5. Turn to the **right** at the next traffic **light**.
6. My friend is buried right **here** on this **hill**.

7. I **fell** at the **fair** and broke my ankle.
8. That **poor** old horse had to **pull** the heavy cart.
9. I asked **Paul** to **pour** me a glass of milk.
10. Was the **file** cabinet destroyed by the **fire**?

distinguishing [l] from [r] in consonant clusters

plays	praise	blouse [s]	browse [z]	glass	grass
pleasant	present	clown	crown	flute	fruit
Blake	break	clue	crew	flank	frank
				flight	fright

1. The new **plays** received a lot of **praise** from the critics.
2. It was a **pleasant** surprise to receive a **present** from Glenn.
3. Did **Blake break** his leg?
4. **Browse** in the bookstore while I shop for a **blouse** at the boutique.
5. The circus ringmaster put a **crown** on the **clown's** head.
6. The flight **crew** gave us no **clue** about the problem.
7. Did you find pieces of **glass** in the **grass**?
8. I'll have some **fruit** after I practice the **flute**.
9. **Frank** bought some **flank** steak for dinner.
10. Larry suffered from **fright** during the whole **flight**.

Your instructor will read the sentences using one of the words in parentheses. Circle the word read. Each sentence will be read twice.

1. The papers were lost in the (fire, file).
2. Please get me a big (rock, lock).
3. That (towel, tower) is very old.
4. The (race, lace) lasted a long time.
5. She walked the (wrong, long) way to school.
6. She loves to read books about (pirates, pilots).
7. I'm sure I saw the (clown, crown).
8. The (bloom, broom) was yellow.
9. How much (grass, glass) was there?
10. Linda's cleaning the (fruit, flute).

Frequently Used and Sometimes Troublesome Words Containing the Sounds [l] and [ḷ]

Initial [l]		*Medial* [l]		*Final* [l]	
leave	learn	féeling	rúler	feel	pool
live	lose	filling	pullover	fill	pull
late	look	sailor	holy	fail	whole
létter	loan	yellow	belóng	fell	small
láboratory	law	family	ísland	doll	I'll
ladder	líbrary	dollar	oily	dull	owl
lot	loud	color	alóud	curl	boil
love	loyal	early			

Syllabic [l]

péople	táble	líttle	míddle	ánkle	chánnel
simple	trouble	total	pedal	uncle	colonel [kɚnļ]
sample	double	bottle	saddle	polítical	national
purple	possible	hospital	model	lócal	tunnel
pupil	probable	it'll	puddle		
	pebble	gentleman			

rúffle	péncil	sízzle
evil	muscle	animal
	pretzel	jungle

Oral Practice

Read the sentences in the following sections. Be sure to use correct stress, intonation, and blending.

sentences containing the sound [l]

1. All the students were still in the laboratory filling out registration cards.
2. Paula came late to school today, at least five minutes after the bell had rung.
3. The Lowell family home overlooks the smaller islands.
4. Life on land is very dull for sailors whose only love is the sea.
5. I broke my leg last week when I suddenly stepped in a hole while carrying a ladder.

sentences containing syllabic [ļ]

1. The people on strike at the local hospital were asking for a raise.
2. My uncle lost a little money backing a friend's political campaign.
3. Bill Logan had a very simple recipe for apple pie, but I didn't copy it because I couldn't find a pencil.
4. Can you give me a sample of that purple linen?
5. I found the bottle of pills in the middle of the table.

sentences with sounds [r] and [l]

1. The price of food will rise if there's a crop failure.
2. The old actor will be buried in the family plot in the local cemetery.
3. The toll road has bright lights on all the bridges.
4. Phil's regular breakfast consists of plain toast and a cup of black coffee.
5. Did you erase the whole last paragraph of the report?

contractions with the auxiliary verb *will*

Dialogues

These dialogues are extremely short and simple. Their purpose is to demonstrate the form and use of various contractions made with the auxiliary verb *will*. As you read them with you classmates, concentrate on the correct pronunciation of the contractions and pay close attention to how they are used in a sentence. These contractions are very frequent in everyday conversation.

1. **A:** Will Philip be early or late?
   B: He'll probably be late.

2. **A: When'll** Alice arrive?
   B: She'll arrive late tonight.

3. **A:** Do you think **this'll** be all right?
   B: It'll have to do. There's no time to make anything else.

4. **A:** Do you think **we'll** get there in time for the flight?
   B: I hope so, but **we'll** have to hurry.

5. **A:** Do you think **everything'll** be all right?
   B: No. I think **there'll** be a problem.

6. **A: Where'll** they go next week?
   B: They'll go to London.

7. **A: What'll** be the next activity?
   B: There'll be a dance next Saturday.

8. **A: Who'll** type this letter for me?
   B: I'll type it for you.

9. **A: How'll** we get to the city?
   B: We'll have to take a bus.

10. **A:** Would you like anything else?
    B: No. **That'll** be all, thanks.

Questions

Student A will ask Student B one of the following questions and Student B will answer with a sentence containing a contraction made with the verb *will*. Don't always use the same contraction. Use a variety. Some of the questions can be answered in several different ways.

1. Do you think this'll be a useful exercise?
2. What'll you do if it rains tonight?
3. Where'll you be this afternoon?
4. Who'll be the first person you see when you arrive home?
5. How'll you get home today?
6. When'll you get home today?
7. How much'll a trip to _____ cost?
8. How many people will there be for dinner at your home tonight?

dialogues

1. **A:** How are you feeling after last night's party?
   B: I feel terrible. I have a splitting headache.

2. **A:** Would you care for some olive oil on your salad?
   B: No, thanks. Salt and a little lemon juice'll be fine.

3. **A:** Did you file an application form at the personnel office?
   B: No, I didn't. I thought I had to wait for a letter from the director before filling it out.

4. **A:** Could I please borrow a salad bowl, Lenny?
   B: What size do you want — large or small?

> **A:** A small one will do.
> **B:** Let me get it for you right away.
> **A:** Thanks.
>
> 5. **A:** I lost my wallet somewhere on the way home and I can't imagine where I could've left it.
>   **B:** Now, calm down and try to remember all the places you went. Did you stop to buy anything?
>   **A:** Now that you mention it, I did stop at the drugstore to get some razor blades . . . That's it! I must've left my wallet on the counter.
>   **B:** You'd better hurry or you'll never see your wallet again.

Homework

Describe and/or demonstrate in class how to make or do something (no recipe or sewing instructions, please). Select a topic and then list, in order, all the steps involved in the process. Remember you are not going to read. You must explain the process in your own words. You may use any props or materials or audio-visual aids you wish to help you in your presentation.

Appropriateness: Using the Telephone — Calling for Telephone Repair Service

dialogues

1. **A:** Repair Service, Lane speaking.
   B: This is Joe Hall. I'd like to report that my phone is out of order, please.
   A: Your phone number, please.
   B: 741-6859.
   A: What seems to be the problem with the telephone, sir?
   B: The phone has no dial tone. The line is dead.
   A: That's 741-6859?
   B: Yes. That's correct.
   A: We'll try to repair the line today.
   B: Thank you very much. I'd appreciate your fixing the phone as soon as possible.

2. **A:** Repair Service, Ms. Lawrence. May I help you?
   B: Good morning. This is Mrs. Lowell speaking. I'm having trouble receiving phone calls. Calls don't seem to get through.
   A: Your number, please.
   B: 801-9567.
   A: Can you make calls?
   B: Yes, I can, but the people who try to call me say they always get a busy signal when they dial my number.
   A: Very well, Ma'am. I'll report your case right away. We'll try to repair your line as soon as possible.
   B: Thank you.
   A: You're welcome, Ma'am.

useful expressions

Below you will find a number of expressions you need to know when you call the repair service operator. Go over them with your instructor and remember that you must identify yourself and give your telephone number when you call the operator.

"There's a lot of static on my line."
"The line is dead."
"There's no dial tone."
"When people dial my number, they get a busy signal."
"When I make a phone call, I can't get through to the other party."
"Whenever the phone rings, and I pick it up, the call is immediately interrupted."
"My phone has been disconnected."

practice

Following your instructor's directions, get together with one of your classmates and choose one of the situations listed below. Work out a dialogue similar to the dialogues presented on page 223. Use the expressions given on page 224. Practice the dialogue so you can act it out in class.

Call the repair service and complain about one of the following problems with your phone.

1. Your phone is making a strange noise.
2. The line is dead.
3. Your phone has no dial tone.
4. People call you and they get a busy signal.
5. Friends try to telephone you, but when you pick up the phone, the call is interrupted.
6. You paid your phone bill, but still your phone has been disconnected.
7. People try to call you, but their calls never get through to you.
8. All the calls you get and make are poor connections.
9. Your phone rings; you pick it up, but it keeps on ringing.
10. You can make phone calls but cannot receive them, or vice versa.

The Consonants: The Nasal Sounds [m], [n], and [ŋ]

Description of the Sounds [m], [n], and [ŋ]

The sounds [m], [n], and [ŋ] are called nasals because the sounds are released through the nose instead of through the mouth. [m] is a **voiced**, bilabial, nasal sound; the nasal correlative of [b]. To produce the sound, close the lips and release the sound through the nose. You can feel your lips vibrating as you produce the sound [mmm]. If you close your nose with your fingers, you will stop the sound from being produced. [m] appears initially as in *me*, medially as in *famous*, and finally as in *same*. The diagram shows the correct mouth position for this sound.

[n] is a **voiced**, postdental nasal sound. To produce it, raise the tip of the tongue so that it is in contact with the entire alveolar ridge. Hold back the air and force it to escape through the nose. [n] appears initially as in *near*, medially as in *dinner*, and finally as in *man*. See the diagram for the correct mouth position for this sound.

[ŋ] is a **voiced**, velar, nasal sound. To produce it, part the lips and teeth. Keep the tip of the tongue behind the lower front teeth and raise the back of the tongue against the soft palate so that you stop the air and force it to escape through the nose. [ŋ] **does not appear initially in English**. It does appear medially as in *single* and finally as in *ring*. The diagram shows the correct mouth position for this sound.

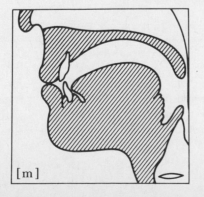

[m]

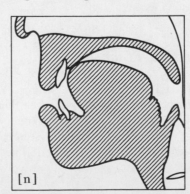

[n]

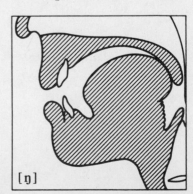

[ŋ]

Important Hints about [m], [n] and [ŋ]

1. Like [l], both [m] and [n] can be syllabic consonants whenever they are in an unstressed syllable preceded by a [t], [d] or [z]. Syllabic [m] and [n] are represented by the symbols [m̩] and [n̩]. Repeat the following words after your instructor.

[m̩] bottom, kingdom, communism
[n̩] button, sudden, reason

2. Special rules concerning [ŋ]:

   a.   Whenever *ng* is final in a word it is pronounced [ŋ] as in *sing*.
   b.   When the inflected endings *er, ed,* or *ing* are added to a *verb,* the pronunciation of the [ŋ] does not change:

hanger	hanged	hanging
[hǽŋɚ]	[hǽŋd]	[hǽŋɪŋ]

   c.   If the base of the word is not a verb, medial *ng* is pronounced [ŋg].

single	finger	stronger	younger	angry	English
[sɪ́ŋgl̩]	[fíŋgɚ]	[stróŋgɚ]	[jə́ŋgɚ]	[ǽŋgrɪ]	[íŋglɪʃ]

   d.   *n* before the sound [k] at the end of a word or at the end of a syllable is usually pronounced [ŋk]: thi**nk**, bla**nk**et

3. [m], [n] and [ŋ] all form clusters.

   a.   Initial clusters.

   [sm] **smell, small, smoke**   [sn] **snow, sneeze**
   [mj] **music**

   b.   Final clusters.

   [rn] **born, stubborn**   [ŋk] **think**
   [ns] **since, sentence**   [ŋkθ] **length, strength***
   [nt] **can't, paint**   [mz] **rooms**
   [nd] **wind, happened**   [md] **doomed**
   [ntʃ] **French**   [ŋd] **banged**
   [ndʒ] **change, arrange**   [ŋz] **sings**
   [nz] **burns**

   **also:* [leŋθ], [streŋθ]

All other final clusters have been discussed previously in other lessons on the consonants.

Listening Exercises and Oral Practice

In the following exercises, your instructor will read one word from each pair of words in each group. Circle the words that you hear. Your instructor will then pronounce each pair of words and ask you to repeat them. Next, he or she will read the sentences after each group of words. Listen carefully and then practice reading the sentences aloud, making a clear distinction between the boldface words.

distinguishing [m] from [n]

[m]	[n]		[m]	[n]		[m]	[n]		[m]	[n]
met	net		scream	screen		ram	ran		dimmer	dinner
mine	nine		Tim	tin		dumb	done			
			skim	skin		term	turn			
			came	cane		tomb	tune			
			them	then		warm	warn			

1. We **met** a fisherman with his **net**.
2. **Nine** of these are **mine**.
3. We heard a **scream** behind the **screen**.
4. **Tim** dropped a coin in the **tin** cup.
5. She was walking with a **cane** when she **came** to see us.
6. Give the music to me now, and **then** give it to **them**.
7. He caught the **ram** as it **ran** out of the pen.
8. I have to **turn** in my **term** paper at noon.
9. Please **warn** us if the water gets too **warm**.
10. The light grew **dimmer** while we were eating **dinner**.

distinguishing [n] from [ŋ]

[n]	[ŋ]		[n]	[ŋ]		[n]	[ŋ]		[n]	[ŋ]
been	Bing		thin	thing		ran	rang		lawn	long
sin	sing		wins	wings		sun	sung		gone	gong

1. **Bing** has **been** at work all day.
2. It's not a **sin** to **sing** in the shower.
3. That **thing** is too **thin** to last.
4. The children **ran** out when the bell **rang**.
5. Musicians have often **sung** about the **sun** and the moon.
6. The gardener took a **long** time to cut the **lawn**.
7. The guard had just **gone** when the fire **gong** sounded.
8. If Jim **wins** the race, he'll be awarded a pair of silver **wings**.

Spelling Hints

1. [m] is represented in writing by:

    m: may, come, something
    mm: swimming, summer

2. [n] is represented in writing by:

    n: no, nine, fan
    nn: funny

n is silent when it appears after *m* in the same syllable.

column   autumn   hymn

3. [ŋ] is represented in writing by:

> *ng:* tongue, sing, singing
> *n* before [k] bank, uncle
> *nx:* anxiety, anxious (unusual spellings) [æŋzɑɪətɪ], [æŋkʃəs]

Frequently Used and Sometimes Troublesome Words with the Sounds [m], [n], and [ŋ]

Initial [m]

médium	módern	móment
milk	money	morning
maintáin	murder	minor
médicine	movie	moisture
manual	munícipal	mountain

Medial [m]

immédiate	imágine	amúse
sýmbol	prómise	omit
famous	compromise	memorial
memorize	comfortable	admire
ambítious	thermos	amount

Final [m]

extréme	slam	tómb
swim	cóstume	comb
claim	thumb	storm
hem	firm	climb

Syllabic [m̩]

sýstem	cólumn
symptom	custom
kingdom	autumn
bottom	communism

Initial [n]

knee	néwspaper
knit	no one
nátive	north
nephew	knife
knock	noise
number	now
nurse	

Medial [n]

méaning	úniverse
Indian	tournament
danger	lonely
engine	annóunce
honor	nínety
honest	annóy

Final [n]

éven	learn
been	soon
brain	own
heaven	lawn
plan	nýlon
done	join
	clown

Syllabic [n̩]

eáten	cúrtain	súdden	isn't	hádn't
written	certain	lesson	wasn't	shouldn't
forgótten	fountain	reason	doesn't	wouldn't
cótton	mountain	prison	hasn't	couldn't
button	hidden	dozen	haven't	
		cousin		

Medial [ŋ]

sínger	evening
singing	being
anxíety	seeing
hánger	sing
hanging	ring
ringing	thing
bringing	bring
	saying
	anything
	everything

Final [ŋ]

hang	húrrying
bang	doing
cárrying	sewing
marrying	long
young	alóng
tongue	strong
amóng	enjóying
lung	exciting
nóthing	shóuting
studying	

Medial [ŋg]

fínger
single
English
angle
language
angry
hungry
younger
stronger
longer

Medial [ŋk]

wrínkle	léngthen	Thanksgíving
sprinkle	strengthen	ánxious
strength	blanket	ankle
length	thankful	punctual

Final [ŋk]

think
drink
thank
shrink
shrunk

Oral Practice

simple pronunciation exercises to practice difficult sound combinations

1. This is an exercise to practice the contraction *I'm*. Be sure to bring your lips together for the [m], and also remember to blend the [m] with the initial vowel of the next word.

   Student A will ask the question and Student B will answer, choosing one of the expressions on the list. Be sure to choose one that has not already been chosen.

   How do you feel? I'm _____ .

	astónished	excíted
ańgry	alarmed	exhausted
honored	amazed	all right
amúsed	ánxious	ill
impressed	offénded	uncómfortable
upset	up-tight	embarrassed

2. This exercise practices the contraction *I'm* and medial and final [ŋ]. Each person should answer with a different expression. Blend [m] and final [ŋ] with the intial vowel when this condition occurs.

   What are you bringing to the _____ party?
   (Add the name of whatever holiday is close.)

   I'm bringing some _____ .
   (Each person must bring something different.)

3. In this next exercise, blend the final [m] of *bottom* with the word *of* [bɑ́təməv].

   Where did he find it?   At the bottom of the stream.

page	cólumn
list	program
sea	mountain
bed	lake

4. These two exercises are intended to give you practice with the syllabic [n̩]. One student will make up a question by combining one of the verb-subject items on the left with an appropriate expression from the right-hand column. The student next to him will answer the question using the correct **negative** contraction which contains a syllabic [n̩]. Be sure to blend final consonants with initial vowels and pronounce final [t].

   examples: 1. Couldn't she ring it?   No, she couldn't.
                2. Didn't he win it?   No, he didn't.
                3. Wouldn't you climb it?   No, I wouldn't.

   1. Couldn't   (I, you, he, she, we, they) _____ it?
       Wouldn't   button
       Shouldn't   listen to
       Doesn't   drink
       Didn't   sing
                                               hang
                                               frame
                                               bring
                                               attend
                                               claim
                                               climb

2. Hasn't (he, she) _____ it?   No, (he, she) hasn't.
    Haven't (you, they) ridden   gotten
    Hadn't   chosen   forgotten
                         frozen   eaten
                         seen   written
                         drunk   hidden

oral reading

In reading these sentences aloud, concentrate on correct pronunciation of [m], [n], [ŋ], and, of course, on blending, intonation, and stress.

1. It's a custom among some immigrant families to wear native costumes in the annual Thanksgiving Day parade.
2. My grandmother remembers when you could buy an ice cream cone for a dime, and a pocket comb for only a nickel.
3. Jim was drinking lemonade from a thermos and eating a ham sandwich.
4. The automatic sprinkler system in the museum put out the flames immediately.
5. The physician said it was his honest opinion that the patient showed symptoms of having a brain tumor.
6. Even very tame jungle animals have been known to turn on their trainers if they are frightened by a loud noise.
7. Carmen banged her thumb with a hammer while she was hanging a painting.
8. Sam claimed that not a single sentence had been omitted from the training manual.

questions with words containing the sounds [m], [n], and [ŋ].

Each of these questions contains a verb or noun with the sounds [m], [n], or [ŋ]. One student will ask the question, and the next student will answer in a complete sentence. Listen to the person who is speaking and look at him or her when you answer. Do not write the answers in your book. Your instructor may ask everyone to answer some of the questions.

example: When did Jack climb the mountain?
              He climbed the mountain last week.
              He climbed it last month.

1. What are you thinking about at this moment?
2. What did you dream about last night?
3. How many of the states of the United States can you name?
4. Who is your favorite singer of popular music?
5. What are you accustomed to drinking in the morning—coffee, tea, juice, or milk?
6. How many glasses of water did you drink yesterday?
7. Do you ever daydream about becoming a famous person?
8. Have you ever known anyone before he or she became famous?
9. Do you know anyone who is more than ninety years old?
10. What are your favorite months?

dialogues

Remember to practice blending final [m], [n] and [ŋ] with initial vowels.

1. **A:** Are you sure you haven't forgotten anything?
   B: Nothing that I can think of. But then, I'm always forgetting something.
2. **A:** What's become of Jim? He hasn't come around for quite some time.
   B: I'm almost sure he joined the armed services. Someone said he's an aviation mechanic.
3. **A:** Have you ever tried to climb a palm tree?
   B: No, I haven't. But I once climbed up a pine tree, fell off a limb, and broke my ankle.
4. **A:** Do *immense* and *enormous* mean the same thing?
   B: Yes, they both mean "something very large."
5. **A:** Remember there's an important union meeting at the municipal auditorium next Monday afternoon at one.
   B: Wait a moment! I must've written down the wrong time. I thought it was announced for nine in the morning.

Written Exercise: [m], [n], [ŋ], [ŋg], [m̩], [n̩], or [ŋk]

Write the phonetic symbols for the sound of the boldface letters. Write *S* if a letter is silent.

1.	___ hanger	18.	___ English	35.	___ seeing			
2.	___ comb	19.	___ I'm	36.	___ seen			
3.	___ immediate	20.	___ finger	37.	___ stranger			
4.	___ drink	21.	___ climb	38.	___ drinking			
5.	___ been	22.	___ longer	39.	___ singer			
6.	___ being	23.	___ coming	40.	___ anger			
7.	___ ankle	24.	___ symptom	41.	___ sink			
8.	___ thinking	25.	___ ringing	42.	___ angel			
9.	___ belonging	26.	___ stronger	43.	___ strength			
10.	___ length	27.	___ single	44.	___ punctual			
11.	___ angle	28.	___ thankful	45.	___ knowledge			
12.	___ bringing	29.	___ evening	46.	___ dime			
13.	___ engine	30.	___ language	47.	___ Lincoln			
14.	___ bottom	31.	___ name	48.	___ tongue			
15.	___ anxious	32.	___ autumn	49.	___ uncle			
16.	___ column	33.	___ young	50.	___ handkerchief			
17.	___ rhythm	34.	___ younger					

Homework

Select one of the following topics and prepare a five-minute talk.

1. Describe the best or the worst day in your life and explain why you felt that way.
2. Choose a figurine or any other object which you like very much. (It could be a part of a collection—coins, shells, rocks.) Bring it to class, describe it in detail, and tell why you like this object.

3. Interview an older member of your family. Ask that person about the changes that have taken place in his or her lifetime (customs, environment, etc.). Ask how this person feels about the changes. Were they usually beneficial? Harmful? Tell whether you agree or disagree with your relative's opinion.

Appropriateness: Making and Accepting Complaints by Telephone

dialogues

1. **A:** Hello, Bob? This is Jack.
   B: Hi, Jack. How's it going?
   A: OK. But I've got a little bit of a problem.
   B: What's wrong?
   A: You know that video game you sold me? Well, it's incomplete. I put it on as soon as I got home, and I found that the first part was missing. What do you want to do about it?
   B: Sorry. I didn't know it wasn't complete. Bring it in and I'll give you your money back.
   A: OK. I'll bring it in first thing tomorrow morning. Sorry to have bothered you, but I thought you should know about it.
   B: That's OK. I'm very sorry to disappoint you.

2. **A:** Daily News, good morning.
   B: Home delivery service, please.
   A: One moment. The line is busy. Do you want to hold the line or do you want to call back later?
   B: I'll wait, thank you.
   (A few minutes later.)
   C: Home delivery service, good morning.
   B: This is Pauline Allen at 711 Penn Street. I'm calling because it's nine o'clock and I haven't received today's paper yet. It's usually here before seven.
   C: Sorry. We've been having problems with the delivery truck on that route. But you should be getting your paper in about an hour, Ms. Allen.
   B: Thank you.
   C: You're welcome.

3. **A:** Front desk, Travis speaking. May I help you?
   B: This is Jack Wilson speaking. I'm calling from room 1013. The TV set appears to be out of order, there is no hot water, the air conditioner is making an awful noise, and there's no light in the bathroom.
   A: I'm really sorry, sir. We'll get you another room immediately. Hold the line a minute, please . . . Sir, you can have room 1215. I'll send the bell boy up with the key in a few minutes. I'm very sorry for the inconvenience. But sometimes these things happen.
   B: I understand. Thank you very much.
   A: You're very welcome, sir. Enjoy your day.
   B: Thank you.

useful expressions

Making or Accepting a Complaint to a Friend or Acquaintance

When you are going to call a friend or an acquaintance to make a complaint about something, it is appropriate to start the conversation in an indirect way before you mention the problem.

"I'm very sorry to bother you with this, but . . . "
"I hate to bring this up, but . . . "
"I have a problem here; you see . . . "
"I'm sorry to have to say this, but . . . "
"I didn't want to trouble you, but . . . "
"It's rather difficult to tell you this, but . . . "

If you are the one to whom the complaint is made, you should assure the caller of the sincerity of your apology by saying

"Oh, I'm so sorry . . . "
"I didn't realize . . . "
"I just don't know what to say . . . "
"I'm awfully (terribly) sorry."

These expressions should be followed by ones which show your desire to remedy the situation as soon as possible.

"I'll be over in a few minutes."
"I'll send someone over right away."
"I'll try to take care of that right now."
"Don't worry. I'll make sure it doesn't happen again."
"I'm sorry you've been inconvenienced."

Making a Complaint to a Business

If you have to make a complaint to a business, you must identify yourself immediately. Then go directly to the point explaining the nature of your complaint. Notice that, as in dialogue 2, you do not make any apologies for complaining as in the case of a person you know or are friends with.

practice
_____

Working with another student, select one or more of these situations. Take turns making the necessary telephone calls, using expressions appropriate for a particular complaint. Present your dialogues to the rest of the class according to your instructor's directions.

1. Your neighbor has blocked the entrance to your garage or carport with his or her car. You must leave for work right away.

2. You did not receive the end-of-the-month statement from the bank. You call the manager to report this to him or her personally.

3. You lent your best friend ten dollars. He or she was supposed to pay you back yesterday but did not. Now you need that money urgently to buy a textbook for class tomorrow.

4. You are staying at a hotel and when you return to your room in the evening, you find that the heater is not working. The room is very cold. Call the front desk.

5. You go to bed, but you cannot sleep because your next-door neighbor's television set is too loud.

6. You placed an order from a catalog a few months ago and you still have not received anything. Call the company at the number that appears in the catalog and complain about the situation.

7. With another classmate, think up a situation of your own. Take turns making the necessary phone calls. Present your dialogues to the class.

Final Review Lesson

Silent Letters

In the various lessons in this book, you have learned that many words in English contain silent letters. You have become aware that certain spelling patterns indicate a silent letter, but that other words containing silent letters simply have to be memorized. Here then is a review of important words containing silent letters.

The following consonant letters are silent:

b   in final position after *m*: bomb, comb, climb, limb, tomb, dumb, thumb, lamb

b   before *t* in final position: debt, doubt

c   after *s*: scene, scissors, muscle, scent

d   in Wednesday (the first *d*) and in handkerchief

g   before *n* in final position: assign, design, campaign, foreign, sign

g   in initial position before *n*: gnat, gnaw, gnome

gh in final position: though, although, thorough, through, dough. **Exceptions:** rough, tough, cough, enough, trough *gh* = [f]

gh before *t*: sight, height, frighten, straight, caught, thought, and all the other past tense verbs ending in *ght*

h   in hour, heir, herb, honest, honor, ghost, rhyme, rhythm (the first *h*), exhibit, exhibition, ghetto, John, vehicle, forehead, Thomas, Esther, Utah, Thames River

k   in initial position before *n*: knee, knife, knight, knock, know, knowledge, knit

l   in could, would, should, salmon, Lincoln, half, calf, calm, palm, walk, talk, chalk, folk, yolk

n   in final position after *m*: hymn, autumn, column, solemn

p   in initial position before *n* or *s*: pneumonia, psalm, psychology, psychic, pseudo and many other less common words.

p   in receipt, cupboard, corps (the *s* is also silent)

s   in corps, aisle, isle, island, Illinois, Arkansas

t   in Christmas, christen, listen, fasten, soften, often, castle, whistle, ballet, crochet, bouquet, mortgage

w   in initial position before *r*: write, wrote, wrap, wreck, wrong, wring, wrung

w   in two, sword, answer, who, whose, whom, whole, toward

There are also some vowel letters that are silent under certain conditions:

i   in business, fruit, juice, suit

u   in aunt, laugh, buy, build, guard, guide, guess, guarantee, guilty, unique, circuit, biscuit, liquor

ue   in tongue, league, catalogue, dialogue

written exercise: recognizing silent letters

Draw a slash (/) through the silent letters in the following words. Do not mark the final silent *e*.

1. climb
2. muscle
3. Peace Corps
4. cupboard
5. sword
6. whole
7. castle
8. doubt
9. half
10. taught
11. design
12. suit
13. honor
14. could
15. receipt
16. fasten
17. ballet
18. guard
19. walk
20. though
21. debt
22. tomb

23. psalm
24. Arkansas
25. salmon
26. plumber
27. island
28. exhibit
29. heir
30. answer
31. often
32. guarantee
33. bouquet
34. build
35. tongue
36. scene
37. handkerchief
38. foreign
39. would
40. autumn
41. scissors
42. soften
43. mortgage
44. guilty

45. calm
46. doughnut
47. honest
48. knight
49. assign
50. whistle
51. wrong
52. pneumonia
53. comb
54. folk
55. guess
56. Thomas
57. liquor
58. aisle
59. juice
60. sign
61. rhyme
62. dialogue
63. rhythm
64. knowledge
65. biscuit
66. talk

Listening Exercise: Consonant Sounds

Your instructor will read these sentences using one of the words in parentheses. Circle the word you hear.

1. The politician responded to the (cheering, jeering) of the crowd.
2. Please bring me my (chair, share).
3. That child is not (choking, joking); he's (choking, joking).
4. The boy fell and cut his (chin, shin).
5. What a pretty (face, vase)!
6. Would you like a (cone, comb)?
7. (They've, Dave) found the money.

8. Did you see the (place, plays) Ann was talking about?
9. There's a long (robe, rope) in the closet.
10. The last word in the sentence is (very, berry).
11. I (send, sent) Ann a message every day.
12. The (thumb, sum) seems larger than usual.
13. That is one of my favorite (themes, teams).
14. The company will announce the (prices, prizes) next week.
15. I can't tell whether he's really (thinking, sinking) or not.
16. He said they'd leave a (guard, card) at the front gate.
17. Somebody put a (tack, tag) on this chair.
18. We haven't seen the (major, mayor) for several hours.
19. He'll have to get a bigger (boat, vote) if he expects to win.
20. He said he'd try to (cash, catch) it.

Written Exercise: Consonant Sounds

Write the correct phonetic symbol for the sound of the boldface consonants. These are the symbols you will need: [s], [z], [ɪz], [ʃ], [ʒ], [tʃ], [dʒ], [j], [θ], and [ð].

1. ___ lock**s**	21. ___ Charle**s's** ___	41. ___ pe**c**uliar
2. ___ fear**s**	22. ___ mon**th**s	42. ___ anxiou**s**
3. ___ laugh**s**	23. ___ carrie**s**	43. ___ confu**s**ion
4. ___ **y**ear	24. ___ boxe**s**	44. ___ con**sc**ious
5. ___ loo**s**e	25. ___ slice**s**	45. ___ bei**g**e
6. ___ lo**s**e	26. ___ refu**s**e	46. ___ sche**d**ule
7. ___ u**s**e (v)	27. ___ atten**t**ion	47. ___ **j**oke
8. ___ excu**s**e (n)	28. ___ vi**s**ion	48. ___ camou**fl**age
9. ___ advi**c**e	29. ___ physi**c**ian	49. ___ pa**g**e
10. ___ advi**s**e	30. ___ lun**ch**	50. ___ ti**ss**ue
11. ___ he'**s**	31. ___ ma**ch**ine	51. ___ tea**ch**er
12. ___ it'**s**	32. ___ ima**g**e	52. ___ pro**j**ect
13. ___ what'**s**	33. ___ congra**t**ulate	53. ___ you**th**
14. ___ who'**s**	34. ___ **ch**ampagne	54. ___ **g**eneral
15. ___ promi**s**e	35. ___ gra**d**uate	55. ___ **j**ump
16. ___ u**s**ually	36. ___ litera**t**ure	56. ___ sol**d**ier
17. ___ posse**ss** ___	37. ___ **s**ugar	57. ___ deli**c**ious
18. ___ bu**zz**es ___	38. ___ ca**s**ual	58. ___ confe**ss**ion
19. ___ chur**ch**es ___	39. ___ que**st**ion	59. ___ fa**sh**ion
20. ___ Ru**th's**	40. ___ brea**th**e	60. ___ reli**g**ion

Answer Key
for Written
Exercises

Page 46

1. ɪ
2. ɪ i
3. ɪ
4. ɪ ɪ/ə
5. ɪ ɪ
6. i
7. ɪ ɪ
8. i
9. ɪ i
10. ɪ i
11. ɪ
12. ɪ
13. ɪ i
14. ɪ
15. ɪ ɪ/i
16. ɪ
17. i
18. ɪ
19. i
20. ɪ ɪ/ə
21. ɪ
22. i
23. ɪ
24. ɪ
25. ɪ
26. ɪ
27. ɪ
28. ɪ
29. i

30. ɪ i
31. ɪ ɪ
32. ɪ
33. ɪ
34. ɪ
35. i
36. ɪ

Page 46

1. s
2. z
3. s
4. z
5. s
6. z
7. z
8. s
9. s
10. ɪz
11. s
12. ɪz
13. ɪz
14. s
15. ɪz
16. ɪz
17. ɪz
18. z
19. ɪz
20. s
21. z

22. z
23. ɪz
24. z
25. z
26. s
27. z
28. z
29. ɪz
30. ɪz
31. z
32. z
33. s
34. s
35. z
36. z
37. ɪz
38. ɪz
39. z
40. ɪz
41. z
42. ɪz
43. z
44. z
45. s
46. ɪz
47. z
48. ɪz

Page 58

1. i

2. eʸ
3. ɛ
4. ɛ ɪ
5. ɛ
6. ɛ ɪ
7. ɛ ɪ
8. ɪ
9. eʸ
10. i
11. ɛ
12. eʸ
13. ɛ
14. i
15. eʸ
16. ɛ ɪ
17. ɛ
18. i
19. eʸ
20. ɛ
21. ɛ
22. eʸ
23. ɛ eʸ
24. ɛ
25. eʸ
26. ɪ
27. ɛ
28. eʸ
29. ɛ
30. ɛ
31. eʸ
32. eʸ

33. eʸ
34. eʸ
35. eʸ
36. ɪ
37. ɛ
38. eʸ
39. ɛ

Page 59

1. ɪd
2. ɪd
3. d
4. ɪd
5. t
6. d
7. ɪd
8. t
9. ɪd
10. d
11. d
12. t
13. ɪd
14. ɪd
15. d
16. d
17. ɪd
18. t
19. t
20. t
21. d

22. t
23. t
24. d
25. d
26. d
27. ɪd
28. t
29. t
30. d

Page 67

1. ɛ
2. ɑ
3. æ
4. ɑ
5. ɛ/æ
6. ɛ
7. eʸ
8. æ
9. æ
10. ɛ
11. ɛ
    ɛ
12. eʸ
13. æ
14. eʸ
15. eʸ
16. eʸ
17. eʸ
18. ɑ

19. eʸ
20. æ
21. eʸ
22. eʸ
23. eʸ
24. æ
25. æ
26. æ
27. ɛ
28. eʸ
29. ɛ
30. ɛ
31. æ
32. æ
33. eʸ
34. ɑ
    eʸ
35. æ
36. æ/ɛ
37. ɑ
38. eʸ
39. ɛ
40. eʸ
41. æ
42. ɛ
43. ɛ
44. ɑ
45. ɑ
46. æ
47. æ
48. ɑ

49. ɑ
50. ɛ
51. ɑ
52. ɛ
53. ɛ
54. æ
55. æ
56. æ
57. æ
58. ɑ

Page 75

1. ɑ
2. ɛ
3. ɪ
4. eʸ
5. i
6. ɛ
7. ɛ
8. eʸ
9. æ ɪ
10. ɑ ɪ
11. æ
12. ɛ
13. eʸ
14. æ
15. æ
16. ɛ
17. ɛ
18. ɑ ɪ

19. ɪ ɪ
20. ɛ ɪ
21. i
22. eʸ
23. ɛ
24. ɛ ɛ
25. i ɪ
26. eʸ
27. i
28. ɪ
29. i
30. ɛ

Page 83

1. ə
2. ə
3. ɑ
4. ə
5. ɛ
6. ə
7. ə
8. ə
9. ə æ
10. ə
11. ə ɛ
12. ɑ
13. ɑ
14. ə
15. ɑ ə
16. ə
17. ɛ ə
18. ɑ ə
19. ə ɛ
20. ɑ
21. ə
22. ə ə
23. æ
24. ə ə
25. ə
26. ə
27. ə
28. ɑ
29. ə æ
30. æ ə
31. ə ɛ
32. æ
33. ə
34. ə
35. æ ə
36. æ/ɛ

Page 91

1. ɛ
2. eʸ
3. ɛ
4. ɛ
5. ɪ i
6. i
7. ɑ
8. ɪ
9. ɛ
10. ɚ
11. ɪ
12. ɑ ɚ
13. ə ɪ/i
14. ɑ
15. ə

16. ə ɪ
17. ə
18. ɑ ɚ
19. ə
20. ɑ
21. ə
22. eʸ
23. ɪ
24. æ
25. ɑ ɪ
26. ɚ
27. ɚ
28. ə
29. ɪ
30. eʸ
31. ɪ ɛ
32. eʸ
33. æ
34. ɪ ə
35. ɪ ɚ
36. i ə
37. ɛ ɪ/ə
38. ɪ i
39. i
40. ɪ
41. i
42. eʸ
43. eʸ
44. ɛ
45. ɪ
46. ɛ ə
47. ɛ ə
48. ɚ ə
49. ɛ ə
50. ɪ
51. i
52. æ
53. ə
54. æ ɚ
55. i
56. ɛ ɚ
57. ə ɛ
58. æ ɪ
59. ə ə
60. æ ɚ
61. ɛ/æ
62. ə i
63. eʸ
64. ɛ
65. ɛ
66. eʸ
67. æ ə
68. ə ɑ
69. ə
70. ɪ
71. eʸ
72. ɪ
    ə
73. ə
    ɚ
74. ɚ
75. ə æ

Page 102

1. u
2. u
3. u

4. ʊ
5. ju
6. u
7. ju
8. u
9. ʊ
10. u
11. u
12. ju
13. u
14. ʊ
15. ʊ
16. u
17. ʊ
18. ʊ
19. ʊ
20. u
21. ʊ
22. ju
23. ʊ
24. u
25. u
26. ju/u
27. u
28. ju
29. ju
30. u
31. u
32. ju
33. u
34. ju
35. ju
36. u
37. ʊ
38. ju
39. ju
40. ju
41. ʊ
42. u
43. ʊ
44. u
45. ʊ
46. ju
47. ju
48. u
49. ju
50. ju

Page 111

1. ɑ
2. oʷ
3. ɑ
4. oʷ
5. ɑ
6. ɑ oʷ
7. ɑ
8. oʷ
9. oʷ
10. ɑ
11. ɑ
12. ɑ
13. oʷ
14. oʷ
15. oʷ
16. ɑ
17. oʷ
18. ɑ

19. oʷ
20. oʷ
21. oʷ
22. ɑ
23. ɑ
24. oʷ
25. ɑ
26. oʷ
27. oʷ
28. ɑ
29. oʷ
30. ɑ
31. ɑ
32. oʷ
33. oʷ
34. oʷ
35. ɑ
36. oʷ
37. oʷ
38. oʷ
39. oʷ

Page 111

1. ɔ
2. ə
3. ə
4. ɔ
5. ə
6. ə
7. oʷ
8. ə
9. ɑ
10. ə
11. ɔ
12. ɔ/ɑ
13. oʷ
14. ə
15. oʷ
16. oʷ
17. ə
18. ɔ
19. oʷ
20. ɔ
21. ə
22. ɔ
23. ə
24. ɑ
25. oʷ
26. ɑ
27. oʷ
28. ə
29. oʷ
30. ə

Page 124

1. ɑɪ
2. aʊ
3. ɑɪ
4. aʊ
5. ɑɪ
6. ɑɪ
7. aʊ
8. ɑɪ
9. aʊ
10. ɑɪ
11. aʊ

12. aʊ
13. ɑɪ
14. ɔɪ
15. aʊ
16. aʊ
17. ɔɪ
18. aʊ
19. ɑɪ
20. aʊ
21. ɑɪ
22. aʊ
23. ɑɪ
24. aʊ
25. ɑɪ
26. aʊ
27. ɔɪ
28. ɑɪ
29. ɑɪ
30. aʊ
31. ɑɪ
32. ɔɪ
33. ɑɪ
34. ɑɪ aʊ
35. aʊ
36. ɔɪ
37. ɔɪ
38. aʊ
39. ɔɪ
40. aʊ
41. ɔɪ
42. aʊ

Page 129

1. i ɪ
2. æ ə
3. eʸ ɪ
4. æ ə
5. ɛ ɪ
6. æ ə
7. eʸ ɪ
8. eʸ ə
9. ɑɪ ɪ
10. ɛ ə
11. ɛ ə
12. æ ə
13. eʸ ɪ/ə
14. æ ə
15. ɛ ɪ
16. ɑɪ ɪ
17. ɛ ə
18. æ ə
19. æ ə
20. ɔɪ ɚ

Page 124

1. aʊ
2. oʷ
3. aʊ
4. aʊ
5. oʷ
6. ɔ
7. ɪ
8. ɑɪ
9. ɑɪ ə
10. ɑɪ ə

11. ɔ
12. aʊ
13. aʊ
14. wə
15. aʊ
16. u
17. aʊ
18. oʷ
19. aʊ
20. ɑɪ
21. ɪ
22. oʷ
23. ɑɪ
24. ɑɪ
25. eʸ
26. eʸ
27. æ
28. ə
29. oʷ
30. ə
31. ɔ
32. ə
33. oʷ
34. u
35. ɔ
36. ə
37. u
38. aʊ
39. ɑ
40. u
41. oʷ
42. ə
43. ʊ
44. ə
45. u
46. ʊ
47. ɑɪ
48. ɪ

Page 130

1. ɪr
2. ɛr
3. ɑɪr
4. ɚ
5. ɛr
6. ɛr
7. ɪr
8. ɚ
9. ʊr
    jʊr
    ɚ
10. ɔr
11. ɛr
12. ɚ
13. ɔ
    ɑ
14. ɑr
    ɚ
15. ɛr
16. ɚ
17. ɚ
18. ɑɪr
19. ʊr
20. ɔr
21. ɚ
22. aʊr
23. ɚ

24. jʊr
25. jʊr
26. ɚ
27. ɑɪr
28. ɑr
    ɔr
29. ɔr
30. ɔr
31. ɚ
32. ɑɪr
33. ɚ
34. ær
    ɛr
35. ɚ
36. ɑr
37. ɚ
38. ɛr
39. ɪr
40. ɪr
41. ɚ
42. ɑɪə
43. ɪr
44. ɪr
45. jʊr
46. ɚ
47. ɚ
48. ɪr
49. ɑr
50. ɚ

Page 146

1. d
2. d
3. t
4. ɪd
5. d
6. ɪd
7. t
8. t
9. d
10. ɪd
11. d
12. d
13. t
14. ɪd
15. t
16. ɪd
17. d
18. t
19. d
20. ɪd
21. ɪd
22. t
23. d
24. t
25. td
26. d
27. t
28. t
29. d
30. ɪd
31. ɪd
32. d
33. t
34. ɪd
35. ɪd
36. t

37. d
38. ɪd
39. ɪd
40. d
41. t
42. t
43. ɪd
44. ɪd
45. d
46. t
47. ɪd
48. ɪd

Page 155

1. k
2. k
3. s
4. s
5. s
6. k
7. kw
8. k
9. g
10. g
11. k
12. s
13. s
14. k
15. k
16. s
17. g
18. k
19. kw
20. s
21. g
22. s
23. kw
24. g

Page 155

1. ɪgz
2. ɛks
3. ɪks
4. ɛks
5. ɪgz
6. ɛks
    ɛgz
7. ɪks
8. ɛks
9. ɛks
10. ɪks
11. ɪks
12. ɪgz
13. ɛks
14. ɛks
15. ɛks
16. ɪks
17. ɛks
18. ɪks
19. ɪgz
20. ɛks
21. ɪgz
22. ɪks
23. ɪks
24. ɪgz

Page 165

1. v
2. k
3. s
4. s
5. f
6. v
7. s
8. p
9. f
10. b
11. s
12. s
13. f
14. v
15. s
16. k
17. s
18. f
19. g
20. s
21. f
22. s
23. s
24. k
25. k
26. b
27. s
28. g
29. s
30. f
31. s
32. k
33. k
34. g
35. s
36. s
37. k/k
38. s
39. s
40. k
41. s
42. b
43. s
44. p
45. b

Page 173

1. θ
2. ð
3. θ
4. ð
5. θ
6. θ
7. ð
8. θ
9. θ
10. θ

11. θ
12. θ
13. ð
14. θ
15. ð
16. ð
17. ð
18. θ
19. ð
20. ð
21. θ
22. θ
23. θ
24. θr
25. θ
26. ð
27. θ
28. θ
29. θ
30. ð
31. θ
32. θ
33. ð
34. ð
35. ð
36. θ
37. θ
38. ð
39. θ

Page 184

1. z
2. s
3. z
4. ɪz
5. s
6. ɪz
7. ɪz
8. ɪz
9. z
10. ɪz
11. s
12. ɪz
13. ɪz
14. z
15. ɪz
16. z
17. s
18. ɪz
19. z
20. ɪz
21. s
22. ɪz
23. s
24. s
25. ɪz
26. z
27. s
28. ɪz

29. s
30. z
31. ɪz
32. z
33. z
34. ɪz
35. z
36. z
37. ɪz
38. z
39. z
40. ɪz
41. ɪz
42. z
43. z
44. ɪz
45. ɪz
46. ɪz
47. s
48. s
49. s
50. z
51. z
52. z
53. z
54. ɪz

Page 191

1. kʃ
2. s
3. ʃ
4. z
5. ʃ
6. ʃ
7. s
8. ʃ
9. z
10. s
11. ʃ
12. ʒ
13. ʃ
14. z
15. ʒ
16. ʃ
17. ʃ
18. z
19. ʒ
20. ʃ
21. ʒ
22. ʃ
23. kʃ
24. ʃ
25. ʒ
26. ʒ
27. ʃ
28. ʃ
29. ʃ
30. s
31. z

32. ʃ
33. ʃ
34. ʃ
35. ʃ
36. ʃ
37. ʒ
38. ʃ
39. ʒ
40. s
41. ʒ
42. z

Page 199

1. tʃ/ʃ
2. tʃ
3. tʃ
4. ʃ
5. z
6. ʃ
7. z s
8. ʒ
9. ʃ
10. dʒ
11. ʒ
12. dʒ
13. ʃ
14. z
15. dʒ
16. tʃ
17. tʃ
18. dʒ
19. ʒ
20. s
21. tʃ
22. tʃ
23. ʃ
24. dʒ
25. dʒ
26. ʃ
27. z
28. ʒ
29. tʃ
30. ʃ
31. ʃ
32. ʒ
33. ʃ
34. s
35. z
36. ʃ
37. tʃ
38. dʒ
39. tʃ
40. dʒ
41. dʒ
42. ʃ
43. tʃ
44. ʃ
45. s
46. tʃ

47. tʃ
48. tʃ
49. ʃ
50. z

Page 205

1. dʒ
2. j
3. dʒ
4. j
5. j
6. dʒ
7. j
8. kjuj
9. dz
10. j
11. j
12. dʒ
13. dʒ
14. j
15. nj
16. dʒ
17. ju
18. dʒ
19. j
20. dʒ dʒ
21. kjɑ
22. dʒ ju
23. hju
24. bjʊ
25. dʒu
26. j
27. ju
28. dʒ
29. j
30. nju
31. ju
32. kjʊ
33. dʒʊ
34. dʒ
35. ju
36. dʒ
37. dʒ
38. ju
39. dʒ
40. dʒ
41. ju
42. jə
43. dʒ
44. fju
45. pju
46. dʒ
47. gjə
48. kju
49. pjə
50. fju

Page 231

1. ŋ

2. s
3. m
4. ŋk
5. n
6. ŋ
7. ŋk
8. ŋk
9. ŋ
10. ŋ/ŋk
11. ŋg
12. ŋ
13. n
14. m
15. ŋ
16. s
17. m
18. ŋg
19. m
20. ŋg
21. ms
22. ŋg
23. m
24. m
25. ŋ
26. ŋg
27. ŋg
28. ŋk
29. n
30. ŋg
31. m
32. ms
33. ŋ
34. ŋg
35. ŋ
36. n
37. n
38. ŋk
39. ŋ
40. ŋg
41. ŋk
42. n
43. ŋ/ŋk
44. ŋk
45. n
46. m
47. ŋk
48. ŋ
49. ŋk
50. ŋ

Page 235

1. b
2. c
3. ps
4. p
5. w
6. w
7. t
8. b
9. l

10. gh
11. g
12. i
13. h
14. l
15. p
16. t
17. t
18. u
19. l
20. gh
21. b
22. b
23. p,l
24. s
25. l
26. b
27. s
28. h
29. h
30. w
31. t
32. u
33. t
34. u
35. u
36. c
37. d
38. g
39. l
40. n
41. c
42. t
43. t
44. u
45. l
46. gh
47. h
48. k,gh
49. g
50. t
51. w
52. p
53. b
54. l
55. u
56. h
57. u
58. s
59. i
60. g
61. h
62. u
63. h (first)
64. k
65. u
66. l

Page 236

1. s

2. z
3. s
4. j
5. s
6. z
7. z
8. s
9. s
10. z
11. z
12. s
13. s
14. z
15. s
16. ʒ
17. z s
18. z ɪz
19. tʃ tʃɪz
20. θs
21. tʃ zɪz
22. θs
23. z
24. ɪz
25. ɪz
26. z
27. ʃ
28. ʒ
29. ʃ
30. tʃ
31. ʃ
32. dʒ
33. tʃ
34. ʃ
35. dʒ
36. tʃ
37. ʃ
38. ʒ
39. tʃ
40. ð
41. j
42. kʃ
43. ʒ
44. ʃ
45. ʒ
46. dʒ
47. dʒ
48. ʒ
49. dʒ
50. ʃ
51. tʃ
52. dʒ
53. j
54. dʒ
55. dʒ
56. dʒ
57. ʃ
58. ʃ
59. ʃ
60. dʒ